Praise for *On A Roll*

This book will help people look at disability, learn more, and feel more comfortable with it. It's wonderful how Greg has turned his own disability into an opportunity to inspire other people.

> — Larry Thompson, Hollywood film producer, author of
> *SHINE: A Powerful 4-Step Plan for Being a Star in Anything You Do!*

Sometimes we can't fix things and we just have to deal with them, like when we're born with a severe disability. Greg Smith has dealt a valuable lesson about inner strength to everyone who reads his story.

> — John Alston, Motivational Speaker, Author of
> *Stuff Happens and Then You Fix It*

From walking to *wheeling*, from being married to being divorced, from being a safe, secure corporate type to being America's *radio dude with attitude*. Let his extraordinary energy and optimism put you on a roll—right into your next great life.

> — Gail Blanke, Author of *Between Trapezes:*
> *Flying Into a New Life with the Greatest of Ease*

Seeing Greg rolling past goal after goal, inspires us. Reading about how he's done it teaches us. Read it and reap!

> — Willie Jolley, Award Winning Speaker and Best Selling Author!

ON A ROLL

SCUBA DIVING IN ST. THOMAS was a great thrill because I was so terrified of drowning, yet didn't let that stop me from experiencing the beauty of the underwater environment. Photo by Victoria Collins.

ON A ROLL

Reflections from America's
Wheelchair Dude with the Winning Attitude

A MEMOIR

GREG SMITH

On a Roll Communications
Ocean Springs, MS

Published in the United States by
On A Roll Communications
P.O. Box 1077
Ocean Springs, MS 39566
Phone: 877-331-7563

www.thestrengthcoach.com

Library of Congress Control Number: 2005926261

ISBN 0-9767111-0-9

Printed in the USA

First On a Roll Press edition published 2005

Cover and text design by Dotti Albertine

CONTENTS

CONTENTS

ACKNOWLEDGMENTS

Thanks to Adelia Smith, my mother, for blessing me with writer's genes and the skills to broadcast and communicate an all-too-often foreign message with effectiveness and clarity. You have also given me a sensitivity and compassion for my fellow man, which is a great part of my inner strength. Thanks to James Smith, my father, for showering me with tough love, which made me stronger and capable of breaking through the defenses of negativity, to emerge victorious much more often than in defeat. And Dad, thanks for taking me fishing and understanding when I didn't want to go. Thank you both for carrying that "damn radio equipment" around town in high school! You have made great sacrifices for me and my children, and we will always be grateful.

Thanks to Greg Jr., Donovan and Berkeley for giving me every reason to be a proud father, and for all the belly aching laughter we have shared already in your short lives. You all are smart, good-looking, athletic, and truly blessed by God. You will all go far in this world. May this book serve as a guide and steer you clear of the mistakes that you'll read about in the pages ahead.

Thanks Tonya Smith-Tetteh, my sister, my first friend, for all of your support all of my life. Your example gave me the realization that authorship was possible.

Thanks Terri Nealy for being my first love and the mother of our perfect children. Although our marriage did not live on, our unconditional love for the kids, and our respect for each other survived. God bless you.

Thanks to my friends and supporters who are no longer with us: My grandparents, "Johnny B" Barnes, Leona Barnes, Swinney Smith, Elease Smith. Disability rights leaders, Justin Dart, Ed Roberts, Evan Kemp, Heidi Van Arnem, Paul Hearne, and Christopher Reeve. Mentors, Chris Yaranoff, James Scott

Thanks to my current teammates, colleagues and associates that bring the joy to my work and my life: Mike Ervin, Kate Adamson,

ACKNOWLEDGMENTS

Murv Seymour, Bethany Broadwell, Michelle Carston, Candia Dye, Juliette Rizzo, Ed Butler, Ron Pope, Tarea Cammon, Dixon McDowell, Linda McDowell, Matt Nalker, Hope & Charity Drummond, Mike McDonald, Andi Peterson, Kim Dillon, Steve Davenport, Terri O'Hare, Carmen Jones, Simon Illa, Peter Trahan, Al Peterson, Brad Saul, Gail Blanke, Willey Jolley, John Alston. Aileen LeBlanc, Allyson Wynn, JR Harding, Marty Martinez, John Rubattino, Mark Johnson, Michael Ivey, Dr. George Kerford, Monica Moshenko, Alan Muir, Dan Carlson, and Ric Okoniewski.

Thanks to Joanne Caputo for making a great film.

Thanks to my personal assistants who have served as my arms, legs and sometimes brain: Bronwynne Bassier, "Mookie" Seals, Lori Juneau, Kayona Mack, Julie Daman, Dana Cullins, Carol Winters, and Gilda Dennis.

Thanks to everyone along the way who has said or done something to change my life for the better, including: Al Roslieb, Mike Lovins, Fritz Leigh, Sterling Bridges, Sandy Shipp, Jim Taszarek, Mike Hagans, Ron Cohen, Dave Howell, Susan Webb, Art Mobley, Les Brown, Anthony Robbins, Jerry Colangelo, Charles Barkley, John Mistler, Jude LaCava, Tom Dillon, Greg Schulte, Al McCoy, Mark Curtis, Tim and Denise Novoselski, Elaine Nesterick, Tory Roher, Robby and Rickey Heisner, Susan Elder, Hymie Pogir, Luanne LaLonde, Tari Susan Hartman, Steve Lucht, Dave Hansen, John Gaydash, Elliott Benson, Joni Eareckson Tada, Dave Szamanski, Chuck O'Neil, Gene Lindsey, John Frierson, Wendy McCaffrey, John Carlos, John Wooden.

There are so many other people who have helped me in many ways. I could go on and on. You know who you are. Thank you very much. If we could all get together, it would be a helluva party!

CHAPTER 1

Beating the Bottle Cap

I'VE BEEN THROUGH A SEVERE MUSCLE DISEASE, life threatening surgery, and dozens of hospitalizations to live a life beyond anyone's expectations. I've fathered three children, soared in a glider, touched the ocean floor with my hand, and changed people's lives with my words and insight.

Now, at age 40, I feel like it is only the beginning for me. I have lived a life inspired. But you may be surprised to hear about the moment in my life that gave me the most inspiration.

It was 1992. My then-wife, Terri and my infant son, Greg Jr., were in New Orleans, visiting her family. I was at home alone. It was late at night and I was watching a repeat broadcast of a college football game on Saturday evening.

I've always been inspired by the athletic drive. I think we can all learn a great deal about how to approach life by watching the determination of a champion and applying the same attitude exhibited on the field to the game of life. Life is a game. I decided to look at it that way a long time ago because like a game, I play for fun and I play to win.

So it was late on a Saturday evening and I was sitting in my power wheelchair in the living room of my house in Phoenix, watching football. As the game progressed, I found myself hollering at the television. During the break between the third and fourth quarters, I obeyed my rumbling stomach and as bachelors often do, I called for a pizza.

When the delivery boy arrived, I was intensely focused on the game. The doorbell rang just as the players were lining up for a game-winning field goal, so my mental focus was split between my television and the pizza formalities. I paid for it and gestured for the delivery boy to put the pizza and the accompanying two-liter bottle of Pepsi in my lap.

With half a mind, I tipped him and sent him on his way as I watched the football sail end-over-end through the uprights, sealing a victory for the team I had been rooting for. After one final yell in the empty house, it was time to enjoy my late night meal.

All my life, I've had muscular dystrophy, a severe muscle weakness, so I've always had to rely on leverage, balance and creativity to accomplish anything physical. Getting the medium pizza on the kitchen table required me to lift up my knees, slide the box across the corner of the rectangular table, past the balancing point where gravity would take over and bring the box to where I knew it would.

To open it, I didn't have the strength to use one hand, or one arm like most people. I grasped the cardboard with my right hand and placed my right wrist in my left hand. I then securely planted my left elbow on the table and leaned my whole body to the left. That complicated motion was natural and instinctual to me. I've always had to devise ways to compensate for my weakness. Like so much that I do in life, leverage and balance made the box top flip open without much effort.

Before acquiring a thirst, I scarfed down a few slices of my favorite: Hawaiian-style pizza with pineapple and ham. But in my enthusiasm for the game, I had made a critical mistake: I had never been able to open a two-liter bottle of soda. I do not have the physical strength in my fingers to grasp the white plastic cap and twist it with enough force to break the tabs that sealed the unopened two-liter. I was angry with myself because had I not been distracted, I would definitely have asked the pizza boy to open it for me before he left.

It was late, probably around midnight. My neighbors were friendly and always willing to help. But another thing you learn from disability is that you don't want to become a pest. I couldn't bring myself to roll to the next-door neighbor and ask him to open a soda for me that late at night.

I had a choice to make. I was thirsty. Did I want Arizona tap water? Or did I want a nice, cold Pepsi? It was a no-brainer. I decided I would soon be enjoying the sweet, refreshing taste of my favorite carbonated drink.

A two-liter of soda weighs more than I can lift. But somehow, using my mastery of leverage and balance, I was able to get it on top of the kitchen counter. I stood up from my wheelchair and leaned my elbows on the sink. I turned on the hot water and waited for the steam. My glasses fogged as I rolled the cap directly under the white-hot flow of water. I remembered from Jr. High physics class that heat expands the molecules and that the cap would easily twist off if I got it hot enough. Apparently, that does not apply to plastic.

I wasted about 15 minutes on the hot water experiment. Next, I got towels and tried to grasp the cap with enough grip to twist it off. No success.

I became even more determined. I studied the cap to the point where I had a firm mental grasp on the type of force I would need to solve the problem. I needed leverage. My solution was to use a pair of drumsticks and some duct tape. I carefully wrapped the tape around the cap and the drumstick, creating a surefire lever. I could then easily twist the cap with much more force! To peel the tape off its ring and apply it securely to the cap and the stick required focused energy and about 30 minutes of my time. But when I cut the tape from the roll and tested the strength of my invention, I was confident.

I laid the bottle down on it side and using all of my might, I pushed on the butt of the stick, applying pressure to the area where the tape, the stick and the Pepsi cap joined.

It had been a waste of time. The ridges on the cap were much stronger than the duct tape and when I turned my lever, the tape gave way. I had known this to be the weakness in my plan, but I thought it would hold!

I then became angry and emotionally involved in the effort. It was now 1 AM. The Pepsi was no longer ice-cold. I was extremely thirsty. I was ready to have a sip of soda, chill on the couch and watch some late night television. I was determined to have Pepsi, not water.

I rolled my wheelchair out to my garage, looking for tools! I dug through my toolbox until I found a pair of pliers! Confidently, I rolled back into the kitchen and laid the bottle on its side again. I squeezed the handles as firmly as I could and applied as much twist as my 65-pound, muscle-weakened body would allow. I thought I was making progress, but when I looked down at the cap, all I had done was put horizontal scratches across the vertical ridges.

My heart raced. My mind focused on the problem as I became emotionally involved. I had an unwavering determination for victory. Defeat was not an option. Giving up was not an option. Water would have made me nauseous at this point. I was having Pepsi, damn it!

Uncertain of the outcome, I rolled back out to the garage looking for better tools. Out of anger, I slammed the pliers in the general direction of my toolbox but missed. The pliers slid to the corner and were stopped by the presence of my dartboard. I smiled.

I knew at that moment that I had won this important battle. I rolled into the kitchen, laid the bottle back on its side again, raised my right hand into the air and stabbed the plastic with a dart!

I sealed the hole with scotch tape, rolled the bottle on its other side and stabbed it again, both times about two inches below the cap. I held a plastic cup under one of the holes, removed the tape from both sides, and squeezed! A thin stream of beverage slowly filled my cup.

Victory! I'll never forget how refreshing and sweet tasting that first swig of Pepsi was. It was by far the most enjoyable drink I've ever had in my life!

I know that opening a soda is not the most significant event in the history of mankind. But when I stepped up to that challenge with determination, when I lifted that weight, it was a huge victory that gave me an incredible confidence. I realized that night that with focused determination, there are no barriers, no obstacles, no limitations. I could do anything. Now, whenever I'm in a difficult situation in life, I'm reminded of the feeling of victory delivered by that lukewarm, refreshing, thirst-quenching Pepsi, and I press on. In any situation, there's always an opportunity for victory.

CHAPTER 2

"I've Never Felt Sorry for Myself a Day in My Life."

WATCHING MY CHILDREN DEVELOP constantly reminds me of my own childhood. I have tried to be an example of what happens when you combine hard work, determination, and optimism. It seems to be working. My oldest son, Greg Jr. is an honor student and a "Congressional Youth Leader." He's been to Costa Rica and Washington DC by himself and he's only 12. My 11-year old son, Donovan, is a standout athlete and one of the most popular kids in school. And my 7-year-old daughter, Berkeley is in the "gifted" program. She spends her after school hours in girl scouts and competitive cheerleading.

Recently, Berkeley sat with me at the kitchen table at my parents' home in Ocean Springs, Mississippi. She was presenting her "Tuesday Folder," showing me the grades she had earned in her 2nd grade class the previous week. For her, this has always been a pleasant experience. Berkeley was in control of this meeting, holding up the grades one by one and sheet by sheet, allowing the proper amount of time for me to praise each one before presenting the next.

"100! Excellent, Berkeley!"

She smiled.

"98. Great!"

She giggled, revealing her one missing tooth on the left side of her beautiful smile.

"Another 100! ANOTHER 100! 102! How do you get a 102?"

"Extra credit!" she exclaimed, beaming.

Then, she withheld a sheet by placing it under the table on a chair, and continued presenting her 100's and 98's.

"Hey! What about *that* one?" I demanded.

7

She refused to show it to me. She didn't realize that even if it had been a zero, I was proud of all of her other wonderful grades. When she was done with the presentation, I quickly snatched the sheet she had hidden on a chair under the table. It was her lowest grade of all... **a 90!**

Berkeley seems to have inherited a skill that has brought her father a lot of success in life: Accentuating the positive.

Because of a genetic muscle disease, my body is frail and my physical strength is severely limited. But instead of presenting my weaknesses to the world, I have always led with my strengths: creativity, determination, ambition, a competitive spirit; an unwavering desire to win at everything I do.

And there have been many victories, beginning with my very first steps. I remember them well. They came in Biloxi, Mississippi along a chain-linked fence surrounding a football practice field. My father, James Smith was the head coach at Nichols High School. In those days, the schools were segregated. The white schools played football on Fridays and the black schools played on Saturdays.

I sat with my babysitter on the grass, protected from giants in helmets and shoulder pads. I remember my father's booming voice, a trait I would one day inherit, shouting at his players on the practice field. I was four years old.

Less than a year earlier, my mother, Adelia Smith had driven me to the New Orleans Hospital for Crippled Children, where I was diagnosed with muscular dystrophy. The doctors urged my parents to stop having children. My little sister was an infant when they delivered the devastating news to my 20-year-old mom.

Of course, they were told the same thing that all parents of disabled kids were told at the time of diagnosis: "Don't expect too much from this child. He may never walk. He may only live ten years. He will probably develop respiratory problems and not be able to breathe on his own in a few years."

Despite the action taking place on the other side, the interesting thing for me was the fence itself. I remember the feel of the metal on my tiny young fingers. I remember pulling myself up using the fence for stability and balance. And I remember the outburst of encouragement I got from the football players, my father, his assistant coaches and my babysitter as I took those first steps, hanging tightly to that chain link fence for balance.

STEPPING OUT INTO THE NEW WORLD—onto the front porch of our home in Biloxi, Mississippi in 1967

"Yeah Greg! Way to go Greg!" This was my first round of applause. I have enjoyed the roar of the crowd ever since.

As a child, I knew early on that my mission on this planet would be a special one, although it took me a while to figure out exactly what it was going to be. I believe God works perfectly and for Him to create a skinny, black, physically weak, disabled man with a powerful voice and magnetic charisma was no mistake. To place him in a football family was no mistake. To make his experiences unique was a part of his game plan. I've never felt sorry for myself a day in my life. I've never questioned the reason why I am the one-in-a-million with the rare muscle disease.

I believe God spoke to me early and often in life about his plans to build my inner strength. I first heard him on a weekend afternoon in Corning, New York. The sun was setting on a spring day outside my parents' apartment complex. I was playing with the apartment kids, supervised by a neighbor's older child. Our family had recently moved north from Biloxi.

MY PARENTS AT ALCORN—My dad was the star quarterback and my mom was the home-coming queen... the perfect couple at Alcorn.

Mississippi in the late 60's was not a place for black people who had high aspirations. My parents were motivated, educated, and ready to elevate themselves toward the "dream" that Martin Luther King had recently talked about. After graduating from Alcorn A&M, teaching high school Chemistry and coaching football, my father took advantage of a new affirmative action program, which resulted in a job with Corning Glass Works. Our move was the first that anybody in either of my parents' families had made to get out of the racist, limiting environment of Mississippi at the time. Corning was welcoming to my parents and they quickly established life-long friendships with other new black employees at a company that embraced equal opportunities. It was an exciting new time, and my dad was on the cutting edge of opportunity.

My family settled in an apartment complex called "Mountain Brow," nestled in the foothills of Corning, overlooking the town below. Our pretty simple digs were much more sophisticated than those where the other black families in Corning lived. That was Jim and Adelia's style. My parents had decided to be one of the only black families living on the top of the hill. It was a two bedroom, split-level apartment, probably about 800 sq. ft. Upon entering through the front door, a staircase to the left led up to the bedrooms. Walk to the right past the tiny living room and you were in the family room. A sliding glass door led to the back patio. The kitchenette was off to the right. And that was it. No garage; just a parking lot. In an obvious afterthought, a swing set and a lone seesaw were situated on asphalt in front of the parking lot as the only playground equipment in that area of the complex.

God has a sense of humor. A seesaw is a balance—a scale, really. A balance is a symbol of justice and fairness. This was the setting of God's first commanding words to me. His message was loud and clear: "Your life will not be fair and it will not be just. But it will be. And you will be stronger because of it."

So there I was, playing with the other kids in a state of post-toddler-aged wondrous bliss. I saw one of my friends get on the see-saw and was mesmerized by the smile on his face, envious of the fun he was having, laughing, wide-eyed and fascinated; his face appeared as mine must have when my father would throw me up in the air and catch me before I hit the ground. I could hardly wait for my turn.

I got on the seesaw.

There is something very fundamental about the experience of your head hitting a rock hard surface. Time slows to allow the adrenaline to flow through your body as your heart races and your entire being prepares for impact. Then there is the sound of the initial crunch and

11

next, the immediate flam, the second impact from the bounce of your skull against the unforgiving floor of whatever cruel surface stopped its momentum. Pain waits until you know that you have survived.

The seesaw incident was the first message I got about the boundaries of my disability. Maybe that incident created a fixation on boundaries and on challenging them because I hopped right back onto other "see-saws" I would fall from in life to this very day. I've received plenty of lumps, but just as a broken bone recovers to be stronger than ever, so it has been my experience that every difficult, strenuous, agonizing and painful encounter has built my inner strength. I've had a lot of fun embracing life and stepping up to challenges. I've learned a great deal about the power of the human spirit to endure, persevere, and triumph.

Throughout my childhood, I was constantly falling and getting knocked over. Without the physical strength or the balance to prepare for a fall, I would consistently end up banging my head against the floor. The seesaw stunt was only the first of my many cranial/cement connections. Looking back at old home movies, my walk was a side-to-side balancing act, hurling my legs outward and forward due to the lack of strength necessary to pull one leg in front of the other. It is a wonder I survived.

My parents had to go through a lot of hassle just to get me in a regular school. But their tenacity landed me in an integrated kindergarten class. The greatest part of being in school with all the other kids was the social development. With my awkward walk, I drew a lot of stares and strange looks on the first day of school. Some kids were curious and would ask me, "Why do you walk like that?" The way my spine curved forward and my abdomen protruded made kids ask, "Why is your stomach so fat and the rest of you is so skinny?"

I don't really remember being sensitive to any of that. I just knew who I was and never really worried about the stares or the questions very much. I guess I became accustomed to looks of wonder and amazement and became numb to sensitivity about it at an early age.

One day, when I was about seven years old, my parents loaded my little sister, Tonya and me into the car. Along the way, I was asking questions, not really understanding what was going on.

"Were are we going, mom?"

"To the telethon."

"What's a telethon?"

"It's a TV program that is gonna find a cure to muscular dystrophy."

I didn't know anything about how a TV program was going to find a cure for me. All I knew was I was going to a TV station and was quite curious about this concept. Would I see Will Robinson and the *Lost in Space* family there? Maybe I would bump into the characters from *HR Puffinstuff*! To me, a TV was something you watched. The concept of a place where broadcasts originated never crossed my mind.

When we arrived, the place looked like any other building in Elmira, New York. But entering the studio to me was like Dorothy entering the Land of Oz. The lights! Bright, warm and inviting. The cameras. The director, calling the shots.

After a short wait, it was my turn. A man came, took my hand, walked with me around the camera, and squatted down to my level. The light was blindingly bright. I was just looking around checking the whole scene out, probably looking pretty stupid with my mouth hanging open.

"And we have here a young man named Greg Smith. How old are you Greg?"

"Seven."

"And when are you going to be eight?"

"March 25th." I wasn't paying any attention to him. I was looking at all these cables and wires and lights and cameras, and that microphone he kept putting in my face.

"Well Christmas will be here before your birthday. What do you want Santa to bring you this year?"

"A bicycle."

"A bicycle," he repeated.

He put his arm around me and started talking into the camera. He wasn't talking to me anymore so I started to walk away. But he grabbed my shoulder to hold me in place. He was talking kind of sad. He sounded like he was going to cry.

13

Then suddenly, he stopped talking. The lights went dim. He stood up and all of a sudden, he wasn't so sad anymore. He told me I did a great job, walked with me back to my mom and dad and then we drove home.

Those appearances on the *Jerry Lewis Labor Day Telethon* in my early years created a fascination with the concept of broadcasting. It also gave me a sense of delight in being the center of attention. I loved it when people would say, "I saw you on TV!" I did the telethon throughout my childhood, up until high school.

As a grade schooler, I was socially integrated and well liked. Every year, I had to endure the first day of school, when new classmates who didn't know me would ask the same questions, and some would attempt to ostracize me. Yet my popularity, built with strong bonds from other years made those attempts very feeble. I was popular, respected, confident and smart. I was a great student.

One problem I had was that because of my awkward walk, I didn't have the strength to react to changes in my body posture and I would fall down very easily. If any kid touched me while I was walking, I would end up tumbling to the hard tile floor. This happened just about daily. At first, teachers would scold students who "pushed" me, but I would quickly tell the teacher it was ok. I remember kids saying, "I barely touched him!"

We soon learned that I couldn't walk in those single-file lines or the double-file lines with the boys to the left and the girls to the right. They walked too fast for me and I would end up getting pushed to the ground. Each time the class would go to another room, I would leave five minutes early with another student who was my designated "walker."

Sometimes when I was lucky, it was cute girl. I remember in third grade, my helper was a girl named Theresa. She, like all the other kids in the school aside from me, was white. She had long brown hair and I remember seeing her with a soft focus and hearing harps play when she looked my way! After walking me to music class and recess during the first month or so of school, we became good friends. As a youngster, my vocal cords seemed to match those of a young Michael

Jackson perfectly, and I would serenade her in the halls with my best rendition of Jackson 5 hits like *I'll Be There*. I could sing these songs exactly like Michael Jackson; she and lots of other girls in my class were impressed. I would bring my little 45-RPM record player to school with a stack of songs and sing along with them at recess. And then one day, it happened. Under the shade of the school building, somehow out of sight of anybody else, she kissed me! On the mouth! Soon our classmates started a rumor about "Greg and Theresa" and that was the end of her brief career as my "walker."

My new "walker" was Richard, the class clown. Richard liked to laugh and was very inventive when it came to finding reasons to crack up. He would check out books from the library featuring naked black people from underdeveloped countries. His timing and silly mannerisms forced me to have outbursts of laughter when out of the clear blue, he would flash a photo of nakedness and cackle loudly. One day he did this to me while we were walking to the cafeteria for lunch before the rest of the class. We started laughing so uncontrollably that I couldn't walk. Nor could I stand. I collapsed against the wall, paralyzed in youthful giddiness. And then I discovered another boundary of my disability. Holding one's bladder is a muscular function, and I had muscular dystrophy. I guess standing up, laughing and holding my bladder was more than I could handle at one time. I realized what was happening and my laughter immediately turned into a serious look as I felt myself losing control.

I looked at Richard and he noticed the little yellow puddle expanding on the floor under my pants. Then he really lost it and cracked up even more. I didn't think it was very funny. I went to the nurse's office and my mother picked me up and took me home. That was the last time Richard was my "walker." Looking back, I remember every classmate from grade school through high school who helped me in the hallways.

As a child, my mindset was that my disability was temporary. I expected a cure for muscular dystrophy because Jerry Lewis promised it to me every year. So I held onto the dream of one day becoming an athlete, and in particular, a football player. Being the son of an ex-quarterback and former high school football coach, football has been a part of my life for as long as I can remember. Dad's athletic genes were unmistakably passed on to me. Despite my muscular dystrophy, I had a good throwing arm as a young child. I could throw perfect spirals and lead a crossing receiver, hitting him in perfect stride. My friends and I did this every day at recess and often after school. Because I couldn't run, and because I had the best arm, I would always play quarterback.

In third grade, I remember coordinating "official" games, drawing up flyers inviting classmates to come out and play. On one play, I threw an interception and the kid ran the ball back, straight toward me. I'll never forget how I hobbled over to try and tackle him and how effortlessly he plowed right through me! That was another defining moment in my realization that I was physically different. I didn't even slow him down. He wasn't any larger than I was or even very fast, but he handled me like a rag doll. It was starting to sink in that I was different from the other kids. While I realized this, I never stopped trying to test my limits. I was never able to tackle anybody, but that didn't stop me from stepping up to the challenge.

When I entered fourth grade, I had the option of pursuing the world of musical instruments. I always knew I wanted to be a drummer. It was just instinctive. I knew I couldn't lift a drum, or carry a drum case around. But I also knew that I wanted to play. It didn't take much convincing for my parents to make the investment. From the very first day of lessons, I caught on naturally. When it became obvious that I would excel as a drummer, my parents drove me to a music store in Elmira where they bought me a blue, transparent Ludwig snare drum! From the very beginning, I was "first chair" in the drum section. I learned my rudiments with no problems and began to sight-read music way better than the other students in the class did.

One day in 1973, when my dad came home from work, I found it odd that he and my mom sat down at the dining room table and talked. Usually, he'd at least take off his work clothes and go outside. I could tell that something major was happening. I learned that day we were moving to Chicago. My dad got a job as a sales representative for

Corning in the Midwest Region. I took it in stride and actually looked forward to this new future.

I would miss the friends who would come over and spend the night, or I have me over to their houses. We would play football, build model airplanes, make tents out of blankets and sleep on the floor, catch garter snakes and feed them toads that lived in the creek or in the basement window wells. All of that would be left behind.

We moved to Woodridge, Illinois, a suburb about 35 miles southwest of Chicago. I attended Meadowview Elementary School, which was located about a half-mile down the street from my house. We moved in the middle of the school year, so I had to go through the process of being introduced as the new kid. I was in the fifth grade. I had fears about it. The new kid that walked funny? The only black kid in the class? Surely I would have trouble fitting in. In New York, people had known me since kindergarten. But what about these strange faces in this strange place?

What was defining about this event in my life was how quickly the kids in this new school grew to accept and befriend me. It turned out to be a great experience from the very beginning. I was the only black student in my class, so I remember imitating the then-popular JJ on *Good Times* by shaking my rear end and saying "Dy-no-mite!" This would make the class erupt in laughter every time. I knew nothing about racial stereotypes associated with this behavior. I was just a kid having fun while getting to know the people in my new surroundings. I just fit in immediately, not only with my classmates, but with the teachers as well. I was a good, smart student and didn't make a lot of trouble. I was a good drummer and was respected for that as well. I was immediately elevated to the first chair and remained the top drummer through junior high school.

Meadowview School was NOT accessible for kids with disabilities. There was a huge staircase leading up to the main front entrance. I didn't have the physical strength to trot up the steps effortlessly like everybody else. Just getting to the front door of the school was a daily struggle! I had to lean most of my body weight on the railing and take it slowly, one step at a time. It wasn't easy to do, but I did it every day and thankfully, never fell. All of these grueling experiences continued to add up to a lifetime regimen of lifting the weights of life's challenges.

Living near Chicago added another new element to my life. In upstate New York, we didn't have any relatives nearby. Two of my father's sisters lived in Chicago with their families. So, about every other weekend, we would drive in to Chicago's South Side to visit Angie or Lena, or they would come out to Woodridge to visit us. My aunt Lena lived on 79th Street and Blackstone in a single family home. She lived there with my cousins, Ronald and Ouida. I loved seeing my cousins but I feared going there. I had heard a rumor that they had mice, and ever since the movie *Willard*, I had a phobia.

My aunt Angie lived on 77th and Carpenter on the second floor of an apartment building. They had a large, steep staircase that Angie made me climb when she would bring me over to visit, and I was always worried about falling down the stairs.

There was a marked contrast between the lifestyle that my parents lived compared with my aunts in Chicago. I love them all from the bottom of my heart, and I see them every year during the holidays and at family reunions. They are very proud of me. We have a great, close-knit family. But back then, to me the city was dirty. I was afraid of crime, and I didn't really understand black mentality. I grew up schooled and befriended by middle-class white people. Going into Chicago and fitting in was very tough for me because they spoke a different language than I did. They had a different way of thinking. It was hard for me to leave the lily-white mentality of Woodridge and fit in with the kids on the South Side. But I did it every other weekend, because when you're 10 or 11, you don't have much say in how you spend your time. I'm glad it happened that way. As a result of those South Side Chicago weekends, I am very close to my aunts and cousins to this day.

One thing I did like a lot about Chicago was Lake Michigan. My family had boats ever since I can remember, starting with a little 16" Wellcraft we owned in upstate New York. My dad would take it out on the lake on calm Saturday afternoons. My sister and I loved riding in the open bow, enjoying the slam of the waves and getting soaked by the splashes. We did a lot of fishing back then too. Shortly after we arrived in Chicago, we realized that the 16" Wellcraft was too small for Lake Michigan, so my dad bought a 19" Sea Ray with a cabin! It really wasn't much of a cabin. One step down and you could look out some windows. But to Tonya and me, it was huge! We loved being out on the lake, fishing and having a good time. We would go so far out onto Lake Michigan that even on clear days, we couldn't see the skyline! We caught tons of Coho and Chinook off that yellow boat, which my father named The TonGre.

MDA camp was a part of every summer, and departure from camp was a sad occurrence every year. I always instructed my parents to pick me up as late as possible on the last day. One year, Dad showed up a little bit earlier than I had hoped. After getting all my goodbye hugs and kisses, he lifted me up into the Dodge Ram Maxi Van. Its front tires crunched the gravel leading to the main road, and finally to the freeway. There were few words. Then after about five minutes of driving, Dad flicked the signal light and we exited the freeway.

"Where we goin'?"

"To look at a boat."

"Aww Dad."

I hated looking at boats because once Dad stepped into a boat dealership, he would never leave! So many times, I thought we were finally leaving and he'd remember one more question, which would lead to another 20-minute conversation! Even to this day, he loves hanging around boat dealerships! I was ready to go home and see what my neighborhood friends were doing. I didn't want to look at boats. But that day, Dad bought one—a 24-foot Sea Ray cabin cruiser. This one had a real cabin with a stove, kitchenette, sleeping quarters, a flying bridge, and a head. You could drive the boat either from the bridge or from the cabin. All through my high school years, that boat, named the "Lady Ruth"—after my mother's middle name—was the centerpiece of our weekends. We got a slip at Jackson Harbor, right across from the Museum of Science and Industry. Nicknamed "Chitlin Harbor" because all of the boat owners down there were black, it was perfectly located, close to family. With the museum within walking distance, there was plenty of room for us to play on its lawn. After coming back from early morning fishing trips, we would often barbecue right in front of the boat.

I'm blessed to have had a father who involved me in so many of his activities. I would sit on the padded ice chest on the stern of the Lady Ruth as we slowly moved through the harbor in the "no wake zone." Then after we cleared the breakers, Dad would open up the engine and the bow would rise. The white water behind the boat got larger and foamier as the engine hummed louder and louder. I would sing at the top of my lungs to an audience of one during those runs to the fishing holes. We'd cross the wake of a large tugboat or cruiser, and Dad would pull back on the throttle and look down the ladder at me.

"You alright?"

"Yeah."

"You wanna come up here on the bridge."

"Yeah, ok!"

He would stop the boat or have my cousin Ron take the wheel in the cabin while he bounded down the ladder and grabbed me under my arms. He'd then take me under his right arm like a football and climb up to the top of the ladder. Then he'd flip me over the rail, literally over the water, and land me in the passenger seat on the bridge! Dad was blessed with tremendous physical and inner strength, and it is the lasting kind. He is in tremendous shape today at age 65.

I loved my Chicago summers, which were structured by the Chicago Cubs schedule and watching or listening to the games on WGN. When I wasn't at summer camp or out on the boat, the Cubs were often the only thing to do. My love affair with Wrigley Field and those blue uniforms is just as strong today as it was when I was a child. The Cubs were so universally loved in Chicago, even though they never won. Every year we all had hope.

Going to camp appealed to me so much because it represented another opportunity to be the center of attention. What I remember most about camp was that it fulfilled my athletic needs. Even though I didn't use a wheelchair, they assigned me one to make it easy to get around the campsite. We played wheelchair hockey and I was always one of the best players. This wasn't because I was so good or so athletic, but because most of the other kids simply had more severe forms of muscular dystrophy than I did. But as a young child, I didn't understand that, and really didn't want to. I just wanted to be the most valuable player. There were other kids at about the same level as I, and I remember that we were very competitive.

Hockey was taken seriously. Each kid in a manual wheelchair and his attendant formed a unit. The attendant would push. The kid would hold the stick. I was lucky to have attendants who were every bit as competitive as I was, so we really did well. I remember wanting my attendant to literally run to catch the little plastic whiffle ball that served as the puck. I scored a lot of goals and loved hearing when they read my name in the mess hall during lunch.

Camp was also a time when we got a chance to get some winks and some kisses from the pretty female attendants! Every year, there was "Date Night" on the Friday of camp, and it was always my mission to make sure I got a sought after date before they all were "taken." It was a lot of fun. Camp was very crucial in my development, I might add, because a lot of the friends I met remained friends through the year. Every year, I developed a crush on some attendant, and we would write each other, and later in my camping days, go out together.

CHAPTER 3

The Walking Stops

AFTER THE SIXTH GRADE, I moved on to Jefferson Junior High School, where my mother was an eighth grade English teacher. I rode to school with her every day. This was my first experience with having to change classes every hour, having a locker and all that "big kid" stuff.

Jefferson was more accessible than my grade school. Everything was on one level for the most part. I got involved in the band and for the first time got a chance to get officially involved in sports. I volunteered to be a manager for the basketball team and was responsible for keeping the clock, the scorebook, and announcing on the public address system. For away games, I rode the bus with the team and the cheerleaders. The Wolverines of Jefferson Jr. High were exceptional during my seventh grade year. We never lost a game. It was great to be a part of the team. It was difficult for me to climb onto the bus, or up into the bleachers to get to the scorer's table, but I never let that stop me from getting involved.

In addition to being a part of the basketball team, I was in the band, and was selected to perform a solo for a seventh grade band competition. It was a song during which my band director played piano and I played snare drum. It involved a lot of "fancy" sticking and flipping my sticks around, hitting them together, as well as some pretty complicated rhythms for a seventh grader. My solo took third place in a community-wide contest.

One day, our band traveled to a nearby elementary school to perform. The kids sat Indian-style on the gymnasium floor and clapped their hands as the band played several selections. As a drummer, I stood behind the brass section playing my parts, but I began to get tired of standing up. I became very fatigued and my back started developing a dull ache.

But now it was time for my solo. The band instructor, Mr. Bartunek introduced me. The audience applauded. One of the other drummers carried my transparent blue snare drum to the front of the band next to Mr. Bartunek's piano. I started my painful, slow limp around the tubas, the trombones and the horns. The applause continued in length until it finally died down and an awkward silence gripped the gym. I could hear the squeak of my sneakers on the gymnasium floor.

I continued the grueling steps toward the snare in silence. Everyone looked concerned for me. I had to make it to the drum, play the solo and walk back to my place behind the band.

Was I too embarrassed to consider the possibility that I might not be able to play this solo? Was I afraid to yell aloud to the band instructor, "Mr. Bartunek, I don't have the strength to stand up and play any more"? Or was I just letting the adult inside me step up to the challenge and not give up, no matter what?

I probably had a frown on my face when I finally arrived at the snare and gripped the sticks. Mr. Bartunek looked concerned. I nodded. He started. I played.

It wasn't my best performance. I wouldn't have won any competitions that morning. I skipped some of the more difficult sticking intricacies. Finally, I made it through the solo. I started to walk back to the back of the band. The applause ended before I even rounded the flute section. The band started the next song as I reached the trombones. That's when I collapsed behind the bass drum onto a folding chair. Embarrassment or shame did not dominate my feelings at that moment. I remember immediately feeling very proud of myself for having chosen to fight through my pain and finish that solo. I would remember that in the difficult times that would soon follow.

A couple of weeks later, my mother and I went to the Loyola Medical Institute in Chicago where I listened as Dr. Wilbur Bunch explained the situation. I could always tell when my mother was upset or concerned, by looking at the wrinkles in her brow.

"What you have is called scoliosis," explained Dr. Bunch. "Your spine has a significant curve to the left. This is a result of the way you have walked all these years. You've been leaning from side to side, and because you've leaned to the left more, your spine has curved in that direction," he said pointing to an x-ray of my back.

"The pain you feel is your rib cage rubbing against your hip bone. And it is also a result of stress on your vertebrae," he said.

"So the solution must be some kind of a brace that he wears at night?" my mom asked. She had experience with braces because as a young child I wore them on my legs and feet.

"A brace is an option," answered the doctor. "But it is only delaying what is inevitable. My suggestion is that we surgically intervene and do a spinal fusion."

Dr. Bunch went through a detailed description of the procedure. I would be put under general anesthesia. He would make an incision along my spine from the base of my neck to my tailbone. Then he would break my backbone and attempt to make it as vertical as possible, and support my back with three long metal rods secured to my spine. After the surgery, I would have to wear a fiberglass body cast for six months. The lines on my mom's forehead became more defined with each word.

I was only 13 years old. Hearing this news brought back memories of surgeries I had earlier in my life. When I was only eight, I had muscle biopsies done so physicians could re-evaluate my diagnosis. My young body already had scars from incisions on my calves to get sample muscle tissue, and scars behind my ankles to loosen the tendons so I could walk with my feet flat instead of dragging my toes.

This spinal fusion was major surgery. It loomed just four weeks ahead. School had just started. I was running for Vice President of the student council. I was a manager of the basketball team. I was just trying to be a normal 13-year-old. My voice was changing. I had a garage band that played *Smoke on the Water*. I wasn't prepared for what this man was telling us, but I had to be.

It was reality. I just faced it. Dealt with it. When we got home from hearing this news, I remember sitting on the bottom step of our split-level home bouncing a tennis ball against the wall. I didn't feel like playing the drums. I didn't feel like watching TV. While my mom was cooking dinner upstairs, and before my dad came home from work, I bounced the tennis ball and cried quietly.

We pulled up in the parking lot at Loyola Medical Center on a Sunday afternoon, the day before the surgery. I walked with my family from the car to the base of the steps leading to the entrance. Dad grabbed me under the arms and thrust me up the steps with his knee, then released me as I took my final independent steps toward the admitting office and then to my room.

After going through the admittance process, we walked to the elevator that took us to the pediatric floor. I walked past kids in wheelchairs with I-Vs coming out of their arms. I noticed a playroom filled with toys and books. The walls were painted with colorful clowns and circus animals. It seemed like a fun place for kids. When we got to my room, there was a kid in the bed next to the far window with his leg in a sling. I was told to change into a gown, transferred into my hospital bed and told not to eat or drink anything after 5:00 PM. It was only 3:00, so I asked them if I could have a late lunch. They said I could have ice cream and juices.

The rest of this day was very irritating. Every hour or so, somebody was coming into my room to bother me in some way. First, a dietician came in and talked to me about what I ate, and how much food I would normally eat during a meal. An hour later, a female doctor whom I had never met came in to do a physical exam. She took all my vital signs, looked into my nose and throat. Pressed against my abdomen. I'll never forget the fact that she squeezed my penis and announced that she wanted to see if it would respond! I didn't mind. She tested the strength of my grip. She was very thorough. About another hour later, the anesthesiologist came and explained to me how they would put me to sleep for the surgery.

"In any surgical procedure where general anesthetics are used, there is a chance that the patient will not wake up," they warned, as they handed my father some paperwork to sign.

25

"We will put a little mask like this one over your face, and ask you to count backwards from 100. By the time you get to 90, you will be in deep sleep."

Finally, around 7:00 pm, Dr. Bunch made a visit to my room. He again summarized the procedure, and wanted to make sure that we had no questions before the surgery. At around 8:00, my parents and my sister gave me goodbye hugs and soon it was lights out.

A rude intruder who warned that he would be giving me a shot to make me drowsy awakened me from my deep sleep. It didn't make sense to me that he was waking me up to make me sleepy. The needle in my butt completed the waking up process.

Now fear sat at my bedside. My mom sat by my bed trying to hide her concern. Dr. Bunch's words resonated in my mind, explaining the mechanics of the spinal fusion. I was afraid of dying more than I was afraid of the pain. Mom gave me a goodbye kiss before they wheeled me down the cold corridor.

Moments later, I started to feel sleepy again. I was transferred from my hospital bed to a gurney. I remember the lights on the ceiling passing by in front of me as I lay horizontal, wheeling down toward the operating room. I was very cold and I remember asking for a blanket, but I didn't have the energy to raise my voice. Nobody heard me.

"Greg, we're going to set you right here outside the operating room and in a few minutes, we'll be rolling you in, ok?" someone said. I was very groggy and just nodded.

Seconds later, I felt myself being rolled again. I was fading in and out of sleep. I remember people wearing blue clothes and the bright lights of the operating room. I was transferred again, from the gurney to the operating table. I was lying on my back, and I remember wondering how they were going to work on my back from that position. Everyone was very polite, holding my hand, stroking my hair.

The anesthesiologist who had visited my room stepped up to me next.

"Hello Gregory. Here's the same mask I showed you yesterday. I'm going to put it over your nose and mouth, and we'll count backwards from 100, ok?"

I nodded.

"Here we go, Gregory."

He put the mask over my nose. I could feel even colder air blowing through it and it made a hissing noise. "100... 99..."

≈

I woke up to the sounds of moaning and crying all around me. I was alive. My body felt structured differently. How long had I been here? Was it day or night? My back was touching the bed. It must be straight.

≈

Incredible nightmares.

"Beep... beep... beep."

"What's that, Dad?"

"It monitors your heart."

≈

Weird dreams. And dreams within dreams. A fishing rod was implanted in my back, and the doctor left the hook attached to the line. Oh the pain! It must be hooked onto my heart! No, this whole surgery thing... it's only a dream. I didn't have surgery. I get up and play my drums.

"Greg. Greg! Gregory!!! I'm sorry to wake you up honey but we have to change your dressing."

She pulled my sheets back and retrieved packs of gauze, stained solidly with blood. The very wet parts were bright red. The older dried blood was darker. There was more of the red than there was maroon. I was losing a large quantity of blood. The incision extended from the back of my neck to my tailbone, and instead of stitches, Dr. Bunch used a new kind of tape to seal the wound so the scar would be less prominent. The blood transfusions were the most painful part of the whole ordeal.

By now, I wasn't on morphine continuously, only as needed. I became aware of some facts about my surgery. The operation lasted ten hours, six hours longer than predicted. There were complications. I was in the intensive care unit for seven days. There were times when I was in critical condition and I came very close to not surviving. One thing that I noticed immediately was that I could no longer extend my legs flat. My knees were pointed up toward the ceiling as I lay on my back. Dr. Bunch explained that before the surgery, the tendons at my hips were never stretched to their full range of motion. Now that my back was straight, those tendons would only allow my legs to extend down to a certain point. He scheduled me for surgery the next day to release those tendons.

The concern now became one of strength. The goal all along had been to get me quickly into physical therapy, so that I could maintain the ability to walk. The week in intensive care and the extra week in recovery from this unanticipated tendon release left me off my feet for two weeks. With muscular dystrophy, if you don't keep active and use your muscles, atrophy accelerates.

After being released from intensive care, I needed to get fitted for a fiberglass body cast. They rolled me down to the casting area in the basement. They wrapped some white, moist gauze-like material around my back, layer upon layer. It was very hot, but then cooled and hardened quickly. Then the doctor took out what looked like a circular saw, and held it against his hand to demonstrate that it didn't rotate and cut. It vibrated, separating sections of the now hardened fiberglass that surrounded my torso. He cut a hole around my abdomen area, allowing room for it to expand, which made breathing a lot easier. This cast became my shell for the next six months.

When I finally got back to my room, the same kid was still my roommate. He had some kind of major fracture in his leg. He was a big Elvis Presley fan. Paul had Elvis music going all the time. He had magazines featuring Elvis. He had a big Elvis poster hanging on the wall. And on October 19, 1977, there was an Elvis movie on WGN. This posed a problem. Game six of the World Series between the Yankees and the Dodgers also happened to be that night. I was a Reggie Jackson fan, and there was only one television. This was war. I volunteered to be rolled into another room to watch the game. Even though my back was aching and my hips were hurting badly, I wanted to watch the game, and declined the offer to take more morphine. Finally, they decided it would be easier to move Paul into another room than move me. So I lay there with the head of the bed raised

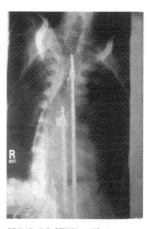

SPINE OF STEEL—These metal rods have supported my back since the age of 13.

slightly, my back seeping blood clots, my hips in stitches, and took in the game. I dosed off sometimes between innings, but there were three things I was fortunate enough to be awake for. Reggie's first, second and third homers of the night!

While I was hospitalized, the results from Jefferson Jr. High's student council elections came in. I had been elected President.

Physical therapy in the hospital was painful and grueling. My entire hospital stay lasted eight weeks. They didn't want to release me until the bleeding had stopped completely, and keeping me there meant they could be aggressive with my physical therapy. The therapy routine was agonizing. Stretching was the primary activity. I would lay on my back with my legs hanging over the side of the table. The therapist would push my knees down toward the ground, forcing the tendons in my hips to extend beyond their capacity. Then she would help me stand up. Using a walker, I would take a few steps. Every day, the distance of these walks increased from a couple steps, to a couple yards, and by the time I was released, all the way across the room. But that was about it. Making a 30-foot walk was my limit. They prescribed me a wheelchair upon my release from the hospital. I would never walk without a wheelchair close by again.

BODY CAST—After my back surgery, I had to wear a fiberglass body cast for six months. In this photo, you can see it rise behind my neck.

This surgery eliminated the pain in my back, but it forced me at the tender age of 13 to come to terms with a new identity—a kid in a wheelchair. This was an identity vastly different from that of a kid with muscular dystrophy who can walk. My voice was changing. I had started to shave. Hormones were raging through my body. My interest in girls and curiosity about sex was peaking. But I was the freak; the one who was propped up in front of the class in a standing frame to exercise my thigh muscles during school. From now on, I would move through the world navel high with my peers, but determined not to allow myself to feel below them. There was no time for self-pity. High school only happens once. My attitude was "bring it on."

To summarize my childhood, I would say that my disability gave me a familiarity with challenges at a very young age. Despite the fact that I hated my body and was ashamed of my appearance, I found comfort in my imagination and my dreams of a better future. I held onto the hope of a miracle. I always had faith and confidence that I was special and that my muscular dystrophy would one-day be cured. I would grow up to have a perfect body, a perfect wife, a perfect job, a perfect house and perfect kids.

Dreaming and fantasizing about these things, and escaping into those alternate realities is how I spent a lot of my "downtime" as a kid. You probably had that same optimistic outlook at some point when you were a kid. Can you remember that feeling?

CHAPTER 4

Rolling with the Band

ONE OF THE PATHS TO BUILDING INNER STRENGTH is reaching a confidence level that says you can achieve whatever you dream. In all our lives, we experience spurts of tremendous rapid growth in our confidence and development towards our potential. My freshman year of high school was my first inner strength growth spurt.

Jefferson Jr. High in Woodridge, Illinois, was a feeder school for the two high schools in Downers Grove. A majority of the students from Jefferson went to North High, including most of the kids from my neighborhood. But South High was the only school in the southwestern Chicago suburbs with a special education program for disabled students.

For me, this was no selling point. I wanted absolutely nothing to do with being grouped with a bunch of other cripples and segregated from my "normal" classmates. I had made it through school this far totally integrated and actually prided myself on being unlike other disabled kids. I was drummer in the band! I was getting good grades! I was involved in sports as the student manager, statistician, and public address announcer. I was president of my student council! I wasn't just your average unfortunate little handicapped child, and I was going to be damned if I would allow myself to even be seen as part of a herd of wheelchairs!

I put my parents through a lot of anguish surrounding where I would go to high school. I was quite certain that North was where I wanted to be. Despite my bias, logic dictated that South would be the better place for me. It was closer to home, more modern, and more wheelchair accessible. It offered support services perfect for me. I would not be a purple Trojan. I would be a blue Mustang. Once the decision was made, I was just looking forward to being in high school.

High school introduced me to an issue at the universal core of the disabled experience: the problem of transportation. When I was in elementary school, my mom or dad would drop me off at the front door and I'd walk into the school. Mom taught English at my junior high, so I would just ride to school with her every day.

Now I would have to take the bus to school for the first time. I couldn't just wait at the bus stop before school like all the other kids because the school buses had no wheelchair lifts. So I had to be picked up by the "short bus" with the wheelchair lift. These little buses had space for about five wheelchairs. Students were picked up one at a time in front of their homes. That meant somebody had to be picked up first and somebody had to be picked up fifth. I got the unfortunate #1 pick in my freshman year. I will never understand why my parents didn't raise more hell about this. You see, our house in Woodridge was about three minutes away from the school, but for some reason I had to be picked up at 6:00 AM—which meant that I had to get up at 5:00 every morning!

It was still dark outside. The bus pulled up at the end of the driveway and let the lift down; the grinding of the machinery in concert with the loud high-pitched rhythmic alarm beeping, seemingly announcing to the whole neighborhood, "Crippled kid getting carted off to school! Can't go to school like a normal person! Must leave two hours early!"

Each day, my mom and dad would take turns pushing me in my manual chair down the driveway and onto the wheelchair lift of the yellow short bus. The loud, slow ramp would raise me up in the air about four feet to the level of the bus floor. Then I would back in, face to face, and unfortunately, breath-to-breath with Eric, the elderly bus driver who would lean in way too close for comfort in order to guide me into the metal slots that would hold my wheels in place for the next hour-and-a-half.

The composition of characters on those buses was like many disability gatherings remain today, a random mixture of races, socioeconomic levels, educational levels, ages, physical and mental abilities. None of us was there because we wanted to be there. We were just doing what we had to do. From my perspective, I was on a bus with an old bus driver and a bunch of crippled kids. I would much rather have been on the regular bus with my classmates. To the bus driver, he was just doing his job. As a result, nobody had much to talk about, so Larry Lujack, the legendary disk jockey on WLS-AM in Chicago was our companion as we rode all around Chicagoland, picking up crip kids and adding them to the road trip to Downers South. Our only bond was his on-air shtick!

First stop: a kid named Chris Badtorf who lived about fifteen minutes in the opposite direction of the school from me. I had known him from summer MDA camp. He had a more severe form of muscular dystrophy than mine. Every now and then, old Eric would take a turn too sharp or hit a pothole and then he'd have to pull over to readjust Chris in his seat, obeying instructions to move an arm this way or an elbow that way until Chris regained his posture. If Eric hit a big pothole or turned way too sharp, Chris would fall over in his seat like the robot on *Lost in Space* would do when Dr. Smith would remove his battery pack. I felt sorry for Chris, but I sure did respect him for what he endured. Sometimes the severity of his disability struck me as comical, like a time a fly was pestering him and he would point his lips and make strange facial expressions while he blew at it because he couldn't move his hands to swat it away. It just looked funny to me and I'm glad that our relationship got to the point where I could share that perspective with him and he laughed at himself too.

(I can laugh at myself about this too because my disability has progressed, and I can no longer move my arms as well as I used to. I've puffed away flies and mosquitoes in my time as well. If you've ever had to blow away a fly or a mosquito, this Bud's for you!)

Next, we'd go pick up a little junior high school kid named Scott Gehrke, who lived in Naperville. This little dorky kid would roll out of his parents green house on a busy street, usually accompanied by one of his sisters. He'd slowly descend down a wheelchair lift attached to the front porch of his family's house. We never said much to each other back then. That little lucky kid would enjoy a short, direct 10-minute commute from his doorstep to the curbside of Lakeview Jr. High School, while I endured the daily 90-minute tour of Chicagoland on my way to school. I had no idea back then that Scott Gehrke would become one of my best friends.

Three down, two to go. From Scott's commute, we'd head northeast to Lisle to pick up Linda, a girl with CP who was so bad at driving her chair that she could never get the wheels to line up, so Eric started to master the art of pushing the joystick on her power chair. By the third week of school, I had become accustomed to this daily ritual and even grew fond of the crisp autumn Chicago air and the funny radio bits that Uncle 'Lar and Little Tommy would tell us every day on "Animal Stories," a part of their legendary talk show.

Last stop: Dave Walsh's house. It was broad daylight by now and I was usually about sick and tired of sitting on the bus by the time Dave was loaded. I had also met Dave at MDA summer camp. He was a loud boisterous Irish boy who could cuss like a sailor and had a great sense of humor. He was a little older than I, but we were in the same class. Dave was cool. He combed his hair. He cared about his appearance. He wasn't shy. He would crack jokes and laugh a funny giggle, forcing air into the back of his throat rhythmically to make that raspy scraping sound with his larynx. He was a sports fan. We soon learned that we had a lot in common and became great friends. Dave went on to marry Cathy, one of the assistants in the "crip room." Tragically, Dave fell forward in his chair one day in a position that suffocated him. When I learned of Dave's death in the late '80's or early '90's, it hit me very hard and I was angry with myself for not having stayed in touch with my friend.

When the bus arrived at South High School, it pulled right up to the front of the building. Sometimes we'd arrive at the exact same time as two or three other "short buses" so we'd jockey for position so we could unload under the covered shelter of the awning in front of the school. I was the first on, which meant I was seated in the back of the bus, so I was also the last off.

After getting off the bus, I'd propel the manual chair by putting my right foot over my left foot, using the traction from the heels of my tennis shoes on the tile floor and pulling my legs backwards. I'd then extend both legs and pull back again. After a few of these thrusts, I'd manage to gain some momentum if the floor was flat. You would be surprised to learn of the slight hills and valleys that exist in a supposedly flat hallway. During that year, I became an expert in hallway topography. Pulling the chair forward with my legs was a much more efficient engine than trying to push the chair with my weak arms. For some reason, muscular dystrophy didn't attack my legs as much as my arms. After about 20 repetitions of this motion on the slick tile floor inside Downers South's main lobby, I moved down the hall to the right and entered the starting point of my every day for the next four years, the crip room.

Actually, there were two crip rooms. The main room was about the size of three standard classrooms, nowhere near big enough for the 30 or so disabled kids. Many of us were in wheelchairs and many lacked speed or agility, or the ability to perceive depth and space enough to know that they were always causing traffic jams. I learned quickly that if I wanted to be on time for a class, I would plan my route so I wouldn't get stuck in the middle. The crip room featured a complete kitchen with oven, dishwasher sink and refrigerator to teach the kids independent living skills. Bill Muelhauser ran it, but I didn't learn his real last name until weeks after the start of school because he introduced himself to us at orientation as "Mr. M." Tall, with a big mustache and a friendly laugh, he was a comforting part of my accepting that I would be attending South.

In my freshman year, Mr. M was the captain of the crip ship. Looking back, I'd say it was quite impressive to consider that Mr. M and his staff took on the responsibility of receiving kids with disabilities from all over the western suburbs and giving them as integrated a school setting as possible. In addition to managing the Special Education department, he taught classes to special needs kids and supervised his staff. Mrs. Bretl, AKA "Mrs. B," and Miss Brown were the other two teachers in the special ed class. There were four paid staff assistants as well as several students who worked as volunteers.

One of them caught my eye the first day of school. Her name was Patty and I developed quite a crush on her.

The crip room was a place where those of us who were integrated in mainstream classrooms could get the physical help we needed, like removing jackets, gathering books for our next class, or getting some assistance with using the bathroom. We all had lockers for our coats, but unlike the non-disabled students, we kept our books in little plastic shelves with our names on them, for easy access. The crip room was like a headquarters for the disabled students. We could eat lunch there if we wanted to, but as a freshman, I would shudder to think of doing such a thing! I ate my lunches in the main cafeteria, determined to fit in and be as "normal" as possible.

Soon, the daily routine developed. Mr. M, Miss Brown, or Miss B —simple names for the kids with cognitive disabilities to learn and remember—or one of the staff or student assistants would help me remove my coat. I would then wheel myself over to my chest level, orange plastic shelf to get the books for my first class and place them next to me in my chair. Then I was out of there. I would leave for my classes five minutes early because propelling myself in my manual chair was a slow process. I could only manage a top speed of about two miles per hour.

Downers Grove South High School was enormous. It was three stories high and shaped like a square with a huge courtyard in the middle. The courtyard featured a pond where ducks, geese and even a peacock made their home. Every interior classroom had a window view of the courtyard. Many times, I would tune out from a boring lecture and watch the beauty of those birds. That year, there was one elevator, located on the opposite side of the building from the crip room. So sometimes five minutes wasn't enough time to make to the elevator and to class on time, but I did the best I could.

Being in high school was a liberating experience, but also a little intimidating as a freshman seated navel level with these giant, adult-looking peers. Here in mostly white suburbia in 1979, the fashion trend was blue jeans and a flannel shirt. The hairstyle was to part it down the middle and "feather" it back on the sides. So I did the same thing. There were not very many black students at South. All of my friends were white, and I guess at 14, I thought I was too. Genetically, the Native American and Italian in my bloodline must have been strong in the hair department, because my hair has always been much different from that of most black males. It is straighter and not as curly, so when I comb my hair, it lays flat. It is funny that black people refer to that as "good hair," or "pretty hair." So I could wear my hair in the same hairstyles as the white kids, and as strange as it probably looked, I thought I was cool back then. I remember one day after getting a new hairstyle, the part-down-the-middle, "feather" on the side standard issue, a couple of kids at school couldn't resist touching my hair and calling my feathering "fuzzy." I remember taking a little offense to that, but not too much. I wanted to fit in so much that I would give my parents a very hard time in the morning about the choice of each day's clothes.

Each morning I was awakened by a pair of hands grabbing me out of bed and "walking" me down the hall to the bathroom. "Walking" Greg means grabbing him under his arms from behind, letting his rear end rest against your thigh or waist, pulling back on his underarms to hold him upright and letting him support his own body weight with his legs while you walk in unison down the hall. My mom and dad mastered this skill, which had begun in physical therapy after my surgery. To this day, only they and my cousin Ron know how to do it properly. Anyway, I would be half-asleep, being "walked" to the bathroom, where I would be given two minutes to brush my teeth and wash my face. Then my dad would come in and lift me into the tub, wash me off and get me dressed.

We had to do everything in a rush. Remember, the bus would be there at 6:00 AM. More often than not, mom or dad would come into the bathroom with some dorky shirt my mom bought that she thought was stylish. There was no way I was wearing that to school and I would let them know. God knows we used to argue!

In retrospect, I think what was happening was my mom could afford to buy me nice shirts and she wanted her son to look nice. What she didn't understand was most of the kids' parents didn't make the kind of money that my parents made, so they wore the t-shirts and flannels and blue jeans that were popular, not colorful velour pullover sweaters with wing tipped collars!

"It's not about the clothes you wear," my dad would both preach and argue. "It's about what's in your mind and your heart."

"Dad, that shirt sucks. I just want to wear a different shirt."

Sometimes, if we weren't too pressed for time, he'd walk back to my bedroom and get me a plain old t-shirt, flannel or sweatshirt so I could be like everybody else, but there were times when we were rushing and he wasn't hearing me at all. So sometimes, I had to go to school looking like a nerd. After I was dressed, he'd carry me down the stairs to my wheelchair.

During that first week of high school, the thing I anticipated most was the auditions for band. Since the first day I picked up a pair of drumsticks in the fourth grade, I had been the best drummer at every level. Now, in high school, I'd be competing against much more talented performers. Al Roselieb was the band instructor at South, and thank God for that. As long as I live, I will find it hard to hold more respect and appreciation for anyone than I hold for "Big Al" (That's what we called him behind his back).

At first, I wasn't too thrilled with his decision to place me in the Intermediate Band instead of the Concert Band. It became clear early on that I wasn't challenged by the simple drum parts. Then I learned the real reason for that decision: the Intermediate Band gathered in a third floor room that was all one level. He figured that because I was in a wheelchair, it would be easier for me to simply roll my wheelchair up to my drum and rehearse. In the main band room, where they held the Concert Band and Symphonic Band classes, there were risers. Up one step were the flutes, clarinets and saxophones. Behind them and up a step were the trumpets, trombones and french horns. And up a third step were the tubas and percussion sections. These wooden risers had no wheelchair ramp and the third level was where I would have to be in order to be a drummer in the Concert Band.

Early in the first semester, I approached Big Al nervously.

"Mr. Roselieb, I would like to try another audition for the Concert

Band," I said quietly. "I think I can play much more challenging material than this."

"I know you're good enough, son," Mr. Roselieb replied. "I'm just a little concerned with how you're going to get up the risers to the drum section. I suppose we could put your drum down in front, huh."

"I can get up there," I replied. "I can climb out of my chair and if somebody can lift my chair up there, we can do it that way."

That was one of the first times in my life that I took the initiative to seek out an end result I desired. Big Al approved my transfer from Intermediate Band to Concert Band, a significant event in my life because it led to even greater things. In Concert Band, I was surrounded by musicians who took pride in their skills. We were mostly freshmen and sophomores, and we weren't as talented as the Symphonic Band members, the most skilled musicians in the school. But at least there was a passion for music in this group and a desire to improve. That wasn't the case in Intermediate Band.

Kindness and goodness in human nature begins at an early age. One example for me was my friend Kevin Toye. Kevin was the 5th chair drummer in the Concert Band, so he was delighted to have another drummer to relieve him as the lowest-ranked percussionist. But that wasn't the reason he took the initiative to welcome me to the group and lift my wheelchair up the risers every day. He was just a very nice guy. Still, I just can't see how Big Al ranked him over me as a drummer back then. He sucked! I'm only kidding. He is another one of those life-long friends I'm still in touch with today.

Shortly after my switch to Concert Band, Big Al started recruiting for Marching Band members. Around the band room, the Marching Band was respected. It was clear they had a strong bond and a lot of fun. I wanted to be a part of that. So, armed with confidence from my self-advocacy to get into the Concert Band, I went to Big Al in his office.

"Mr. Roselieb," I said, again very nervously. "If there is any way I could do it, I would like to be in the Marching Band. Can I play the drums from the sidelines and at least wear a uniform and be a part of the band?"

Reflecting back, this must have been an awkward situation for him. Here you have a kid who can't even walk and wants to be in a marching band. I couldn't play any of the standard Marching Band instruments because they were all too heavy. So it would require some ingenuity. Of course, Mr. Roselieb said yes before he figured out how.

The Marching Mustangs competed against bands from all over Chicagoland. We had a "show" featuring the same four songs we'd rehearse three nights a week and perform on Saturdays at football games. Big Al's solution for me was to place a set of concert tom-toms, some chimes, cymbals and other percussion instruments on the 50-yard line for me to play, and I would just sit there off to the side and play my parts.

Our program opener was *Pictures at an Exhibition*, followed by selections from *Porgy & Bess*, Chuck Mangione's *Feels So Good* and a tune called *Excitement*. In *Pictures at an Exhibition*, I stood at attention most of the song and banged on the chimes at the appropriate times. I enjoyed *Porgy & Bess* and *Feels So Good* because at least I got to play the concert toms and was part of a drum section solo. But I didn't really feel like I was a part of the band. I felt like a sideshow. While the rest of the band was marching behind me, I was sitting there facing the drum major and the bleachers in front of me. I couldn't even see the rest of the band. And as the band moved around the football field, the timing of their notes was delayed as they moved farther away, which made it difficult for me to play my parts in unison with the rest of the band. I had to play based on the drum major's movements rather than what I heard. I was proud to be doing this, but I wasn't really happy with my level of participation. I wanted more.

Sometimes, during band practice, I wondered why I was out there. We practiced in the school's parking lot for two hours at night. Big Al was serious about his bands doing well in competitions, and there were a lot of elements to work on. We had to be concerned with not only the way the music sounded, but also the movement of the group in unison, the spacing, and the sharpness of the band's motion as one entity. We would break up into sections and rehearse our music parts, or go off into corners of the parking lots as sections to master the steps. For me, this was a waste of time. I would be freezing there in my chair doing absolutely nothing while the rest of the drummers were trying to figure out where to step, how to turn or how to slide their feet in unison.

Early in the year, Marching Band practice was fun, but as autumn got older, it became a looming monster I knew I would have to face and overcome. Being cold to me is painful. I lose control of my muscles and cannot move. It is the most unpleasant sensation imaginable for me. I think it has a lot to do with the fact that I weigh only 65 pounds and that I have no insulation. My circulation shuts off and I experience numbing pain. But throughout that first band year, the thought of quitting never crossed my mind. I was too stubborn, and I was enjoying the socialization that being in band allowed.

Everyone knows that a marching band member must be in parades, so this posed the next challenge for Mr. Roselieb to figure out. His solution was to attach the same concert tom-toms to my manual wheelchair using rubber bungee cords. He assigned Lisa, one of the girls who flipped the wooden rifles to be my parade pusher. She also

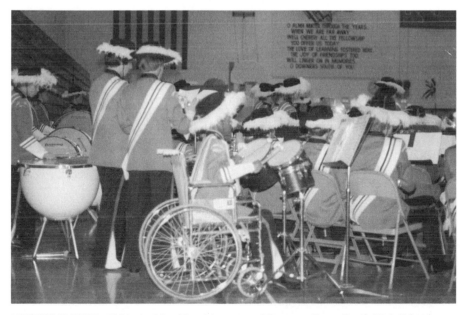

MARCHING BAND—With the Marching Mustangs of Downers Grove South High School

pushed me onto the field for our football game performances and competitions, and handed me the proper percussion instruments to play. I wonder what she thought of giving up her position as a rifle twirler to be a uniformed attendant for a disabled percussionist. I owe her a word of gratitude.

I remember feeling a unique sense of pride when I put on my Marching Mustangs uniform for the first time and looked in the mirror. We wore navy blue cowboy hats with white feather plumes. Our light blue jackets had golden ornamental buttons, and we wore white leather arm ornaments, like cufflinks, attached with Velcro. The Navy blue slacks had two light blue pinstripes up the side and a slit near the ankle, exposing a white flap underneath.

As a freshman, I split my free time between the band room, the radio station and the crip room, in that order. When I first learned that Downers Grove South had a radio station, the opportunity didn't really click in my mind immediately. My friend Robin had discovered the station and was friendly with some of the upperclassmen working there. She invited me to come in and visit.

WDGC FM was a community radio station broadcasting at 250 watts at 88.3 on the FM Dial. The station had two studios; one at North High School, where the transmitter was located, and one at South. North was the more "important" studio with the latest and greatest equipment.

I decided to sign up for orientation and training. Steve Stahl taught me how to "cue up records," placing LPs on the turntable and reversing their direction until the first sound scratched the needle (Steve is now VP of News Operations at CNN and keeps in touch). We had two turntables, two tape cart machines, two reel-to-reel tape decks and a 12-channel mixer with dial controls, or potentiometers. There was an announcing studio immediately across from the u-shaped on-air studio, separated by glass. Luckily, the on-air studio at South was a sit-down studio. At North, board operators had to stand up.

There were randomly placed posters of the musical icons of the time scattered on the walls: The Cars, Blondie, Rod Stewart, Devo, and Travolta and Olivia Newton-John's *Grease* poster. Some of them were hanging upside down. A Shaun Cassidy poster was ripped in half and carefully taped on the door showing the split between his eyes and the white paper tear down past his chin.

Soon, I was promoted from trainee to trainer. I quickly mastered production skills, which included using a razor blade to edit reel-to-reel tape, running the on-air audio feed from the UPI network that must have been delivered via some kind of phone connection.

That year, I continued a pattern I had developed early in life and still maintain today. I was involved in many activities at the same time. I was in band, in radio and taking classes. Back in the crip room, the only other mandate the group had was physical education. We were required to participate in Adaptive PE every day during the last period. This was a full gathering of all 30 of the disabled kids in the school, a combination of all the disabilities you could think of... amputees, stroke survivors, kids with cerebral palsy, muscular dystrophy, short stature, you name it. And many of the kids had cognitive disabilities as well as physical ones. Jenny Orr was the Adaptive PE teacher. The daughter of legendary Michigan basketball coach, Johnny Orr, Ms. Orr was also the swimming coach at Downers South. In retrospect, it had to be challenging to come up with ideas for physical education in which we all could participate. We played whiffle ball, bounced tennis balls to each other, wheeled laps around the gym, and studied the rules of various sports. Occasionally, we would go swimming in the school's pool. Those who could would dive off the high platform. I never did.

As the year progressed, I started to enjoy beginning my days in the crip room. As I would remove my coat and assemble my materials for class, I would engage in Monday-morning quarterbacking with kids who had severe cognitive disabilities but who knew sports statistics like computers. We would more often than not be discussing a bonehead decision by Bears Quarterback, Bob Avelini the day before, or a beautiful Walter Payton dash from scrimmage. This was a very opinionated group of sports fans!

For nine months, I rolled through the halls at Downers Grove South, a freshman wearing braces across my smile, inwardly mixed with raging hormones and cheerleader/drill team fantasies. My mission was to fit in, have fun and perhaps learn something, in that order. With this productive attitude, I struggled in Algebra and Biology. My Biology teacher was Mr. Mohns, the head football coach. As his team struggled to a 0-9 record that year, I struggled to understand chemical reactions, the molecular basis of heredity, and geochemical cycles, all the while wondering if my bewildered facial expressions would result in the same fate as some of Mohns' players—a slap upside the head or a yank on the facemask. I squeaked out a C, probably because I dared to engage him in some football discussion a few times after class.

My freshman year of high school was an incredible introduction to some of what would become defining elements of my life. The crip room was a new introduction to disability; a familiarity with the diversity and goodness of people regardless of disability, and an understanding that my cognitive abilities made me no better a human being than those who were both mentally and physically disabled. That year was also one of reward for initiative. I expressed a desire to become involved in Marching Band and radio, and both of those doors opened to me. Those three experiences, profound foundations of who I would become in life, share the same roots, 1979-1980, my freshman year at Downers Grove South High School.

CHAPTER 5

The Need for Speed

GRADUALLY, I WAS ACCEPTING THE FACT that a wheelchair would be my mode of transportation, but looking back, I guess I couldn't accept the slow speeds. When I was about fifteen years old, my cousin Ron, who had just received his driver's license, was visiting our house for the weekend. My parents had left us alone at home. It was a boring summer afternoon, and I was outside in the garage watching Ron as he drove my father's riding lawn mower across the lawn. My young mind searched for something to do to cut through the boredom of the day. I sat in my manual wheelchair, repeatedly bouncing a tennis ball against the wall. After one throw, the ball got away from me and bounded into a remote corner of the garage. As I bent over to get it, I noticed my father's water skiing rope at the moment Ron was completing the yard and riding the mower into the garage.

"Hey Ron, I have a great idea! Let's tie this ski rope to the front of my chair and to the back of the lawn mower and you can pull me around in the street."

"I guess we can do that. Gimmie that rope," Ron said, as he was thinking about tying it on right there and pulling me down the driveway.

"No, that wouldn't be safe," I said. "Let's get both the lawn mower and the wheelchair on the street first. If you pull me down the driveway and over the curb cut, it might be dangerous."

Ron drove the lawn mower back out to the street and pushed me in my manual chair down the curb, parking me just behind the mower. Ron strung the rope between the two armrests of the lightweight manual chair and round the seat of the lawnmower. I sat in the chair about ten feet behind Ron and he started to go. He looked back as he started out carefully.

"YOU OK???" He yelled at the top of his voice. I could barely hear him over the rumble of the mower.

"YEAH, LET'S GO!" I yelled back.

He pushed the throttle forward and we suddenly gained speed as we drove toward the end of the cul-de-sac. The wind blew through my hair as I laughed at the creativeness and spontaneity of our not-so-well-thought-out adventure.

"WOOO HOOO!" I yelled, smiling and laughing. This was great fun!

My smile quickly faded when Ron started making zigzagging motions with the steering wheel. He zigged! My chair zagged! He careened toward the rounded curb cut right in front of our house, capsizing my chair. As the world turned upside down, my head suddenly had a reunion with the asphalt, this time on Bannister Lane in Lisle, Illinois. Like the seesaw when I was four, this time, it was a lawn-mower facilitating the reunion. Suddenly I was once again kissing concrete. But the collision wasn't the worst part. Ron was unaware that the chair had tipped over! He continued to drive the lawn mower at full speed, dragging me down the street with the chair pinning my face to the road!

I remained conscious, believing that somehow I was going to survive. The stinging pain of my face being peeled off by the tiny rocks of the asphalt road was unbearable. I could see our house tilted sideways and panning downward when suddenly the front door burst open! It was Tonya.

"ROOOONNNNNNN!" she yelled at the top of her voice, and darted down the sidewalk to my rescue. Ron stopped the lawn mower and in seconds, his strong hands were suddenly lifting me up off the ground. My face was ruined. The skin on my forehead was completely gone, sagging over my right eye. Blood dripped from my face into my vision. He carried me into the bathroom to look in the mirror. When I saw how bad the damage was, I started to cry. Everything burned. Cold towels became bloody. Ice was painful. We couldn't find any bandages. Ron put me in the front seat of my father's car and drove me to the drug store to buy some. As I waited in the car and bled into a towel, I was most concerned with how my parents would react. Before Ron emerged from the drug store, my mother found our car in the parking lot. She was angrier than I ever remember.

"How could you let Ron do something so stupid?" she yelled. "You could have been killed!"

"It was my idea, Mom. Not Ron's." Man, she was hot!

"Well you both should have known better!" She was so mad she was crying. She pulled me out, put me in her car and drove me home. It was the only time I ever remember my mother speeding. In the side view mirror, I noticed Ron emerge from the drug store and seriously wondered if he would come back to the house or escape with the car to avoid the for-sure ass whoopin' that would accompany his arrival.

THE DAY AFTER THE LAWNMOWER INCIDENT One of the many adventures of Greg Smith and cousin, Ron Pope.

My dad was mild about it. He lectured about decisions as he bandaged me up and pulled the rocks from my face with tweezers. There wasn't a need to go to the doctor. There were no lacerations, just scratches and burns from layers of skin being pulled from my face.

Time would heal it mostly, although I still have barely noticeable scars today. The next day, we went boating, and my father took a now infamous picture of me and Ron sitting obediently, shamefully reflecting on our stupidity. We laugh about it at every family reunion now.

Not long after that, I followed a more traditional path toward accelerated transportation: a power wheelchair. The Muscular Dystrophy Association had earned tremendous brownie points in my book due to my wonderful childhood experiences with summer camp. The friendships that emerged from those weeklong escapes from the boundaries of family were refreshing and something I looked forward to every year. However, as a sophomore in high school, my attitude about MDA was balanced by my disdain for "clinic."

Each year, I would have to take a day away from school to go to the MDA Clinic in Hinsdale, IL. My mother and I gave these useless sessions a perfect nickname: the kangaroo court. Typically, we would arrive at around 9 AM. I would undress, get into a gown, and sit in a waiting room for 45 minutes preparing my mind to begin what would be an all-day slow parade. First, a physical therapist would instruct me to squeeze her fingers as tight as I could, raise my arms against her downward pressure, lower my arms against her upward lift, kick my leg forward at the knee against her downward pressure—you get the idea. Every possible muscle movement was evaluated and subjectively rated. Then she would leave us to another 45-minute wait for the occupational therapist, who had a similar routine. And then the dietician, the mental health counselor, and the respiratory therapist, who would make me blow into a tube and force water from one plastic column to another. It was a medical model torture chamber that loomed as a dreaded date on the calendar once per year.

It took awhile for me to get to the only thing that made me face this particular torture session with enthusiasm. While I waited, I did homework. My mom graded papers from her classroom. I drew pictures and wandered up and down the halls in my manual wheelchair, my feet pulling the chair forward slowly, and playing mental games like weaving between the intersections of tiles on the hospital floor. At the end of the day, Dr. Bunch—the guy who operated on my back—finally arrived. He was the only guy I wanted to see. All the other tests and evaluations were useless. Dr. Bunch raised my gown, looked at my back, and applied gentle pressure to gauge whether there was pain. He flipped on the x-ray light and placed my image against the white surface.

"Well it has been three years since the surgery and everything seems to be going quite well," he said. "The rods are connected firmly. Your muscle tissue has regenerated around the areas of trauma. Let me see you walk."

I climbed up against the examining table, using my elbows and chin to gain altitude and then turned around, resting my rear end on its padded surface. I then threw my head backwards and moved away from the table. Throwing the weight of my head backwards was the only way I could gain the balance necessary to stand upright. But once I was up, I paced the room three or four times before fatigue set in. I could still walk, but not very far, and I couldn't really see where I was going. At home, I walked from the kitchen to the family room. I had the ability to climb up on the arm of our Lazy Boy recliner and get enough height to drop down and take some steps. I could walk into the bathroom or into the kitchen. My range was probably 100 feet at a time. But I required the manual wheelchair to venture outside the house.

"How is school going?"

"It is going great. I'm in the band. I am working at the radio station. But it is a very large school and I get around so slowly in my chair. If I had an electric chair, I would be much more productive at school."

The issue was a battle of two philosophies: Electric wheelchair vs. manual wheelchair. If I got an electric wheelchair, getting around school would be much easier. I could go outside by myself at home and play in the neighborhood. I even had hopes that we could rig the wheelchair so that I could play drums in the marching band from the chair. But the danger was apparent. Muscular dystrophy is an unforgiving disease. Once you lose the ability to do something, you don't get it back. All of this struggling to pull myself around the halls at Downers South and all the strenuous effort I put into walking around the house was a good physical workout. If I suddenly stopped doing these things, would I lose strength quickly? Despite the setback from the surgery, I was doing much better than they expected. Would putting me in an electric chair confine me to a new level of disability?

"Greg, I'm going to go ahead and prescribe an electric wheelchair," said Dr. Bunch. "But I am going to caution you. You must remain as active as you can be. Use the chair for convenience around school. But I want you to park it at the house and continue to walk around and get all the exercise you can."

Yes! My first power wheelchair! I was so excited about the liberation this vehicle would provide me. Instead of inching at a snail's pace through the halls at school, I was motoring at four miles per hour, faster than people were walking. I was also seated higher off the ground and felt ten feet tall! After school, I would cruise the neighborhood and explore the trails around the house. It was indeed a new definition of freedom.

I motored into Al Roselieb's office. "Now, I'm ready to REALLY be a Marching Mustang," I smiled. He immediately started studying the chair. That first meeting revealed two challenges. First, how would we mount the drums to the chair so they would stay on solidly? And second, how would I maneuver the chair and be able to play the drums at the same time? We pondered these challenges for several days.

My parents' house was not wheelchair accessible. There were two steps to enter the front door. My bedroom was upstairs. So in the period before my dad built a ramp at the front door, we left the wheelchair at school. Mr. Roselieb would keep it in his office and probably spent many hours tinkering with it to come up with solutions.

After a couple of days, he had a solution. His first attempt was to use a foot petal from a drum set and weld a little circle on the toe of it. We strapped my right foot to the footplate. I was supposed to hook the circle around the joystick and move it in the direction I wanted to go. During the first try, I smashed into his desk! Then I started to get more skilled and was able to go straight for about 20 feet before smashing into the wooden risers in the band room. The concept of driving the wheelchair with my foot was a step in the right direction. But the footplate was heavy, and I didn't have direct control over the joystick. It was dangerous and I wasn't gaining any skills.

After a few more nights, Mr. Roselieb's came up with another design. He took the control box off the chair and mounted it onto the front of the footplate. Instead of using a foot pedal, I could reach the joystick with the bottom of my shoe! This worked just fine. It took me a little time to get comfortable with the concept of driving the chair with my foot.

One day, shortly thereafter, I was upstairs in Ms. Heiteen's journalism class. Someone called my name and I leaned over to see who it was. When I leaned, the weight of my foot on the joystick forced the chair to move suddenly to the right at top speed! To make matters worse, my balance shifted and I couldn't take my foot off of the control box! I spiraled around and around and around at top speed into a hopeless panic of blurred fear until I finally smashed solidly into a desk! Thank God, nobody got hurt. After that episode, I learned to respect the joystick. To this day, I have a cautious sixth sense about anything getting near it. Power wheelchair users know what I mean.

Soon my dream of being in the Marching Band full-scale came true. Big Al attached a set of blue concert tom-toms onto my chair with bungee cords. We needed to adjust the drums occasionally, but finally, I was able to get the feeling that I was just like everybody else. That sophomore season, our rendition of Chuck Mangione's *Feels So Good*, began with a drum solo! I had a prominent part. Not only did I have to learn the music; I was also responsible for learning the marching routine. And Big Al held no sympathy.

"Make that turn smoother, Greg!"

"Watch your spacing!"

"Do it again, from the top!" Big Al would yell from a loudspeaker while standing on a "Marching Mustangs" podium in the parking lot.

I enjoyed Marching Band practice tremendously. I was a teammate; a drummer. The friendships that emerged were genuine. They would load me up in the car and go to Burger King after practice. I got invited to parties. We would hang out together at school. It was probably the most important social development event of my childhood. I can clearly hear the pieces we played in my mind today, more than 20 years later, and I can still play all of my parts. This music is a trigger, which takes me to a place where I can hear the voices of my friends back then, see their faces and reflect on the laughs we shared, the triumphs and the tears we shed in defeat. We were competitive. We practiced just about every night, regardless of the unforgiving thermometer.

The marathon practices went on and on. Chicagoland at night on a frozen parking lot was not where I wanted to be. The sight of my every breath and the assumption that I still had fingers attached to my drumsticks were the only indication I was still alive, because I had no feeling in my frozen body. If I had asked to go inside, my request would probably have been granted, but to leave my fellow drummers in the misery that I couldn't stand wasn't within my ability. When my parents would finally pick me up, they would have to lift my stiff body into the car and turn the heater all the way up. Sometimes, when we got home, I still couldn't move. They would carry me upstairs and draw a hot bath. Then, finally snug in my warm covers, I would go to bed knowing that I did what everybody else did that day. And that's all I wanted... to be normal.

CHAPTER 6

"The Voice of the Mustangs"

LIKE SO MANY THINGS that were physically beyond my reach, sports beckoned at an early age, quickly becoming a fascination, an addiction, a fantasy. I was an eight-year-old limping sports encyclopedia, on top of all the latest statistics, trades, injuries and rumors. I collected cards, scrapbooks, pennants, autographed balls, jerseys, jackets, and anything I could get my hands on.

My favorite football team was the Washington Redskins, for no good reason. I just picked them. Maybe I liked the colors. I loved watching Larry Brown carry the football and cried when they lost the Super Bowl to the Miami Dolphins in January of 1973. Later that same year, on my birthday, my father took me to Madison Square Garden to watch Clyde Frazier, Willis Reed, Dave Debusschere, Bill Bradley and the rest of the New York Knicks play a game. It was my first live sports event. What an exhilarating feeling. We were in the "nosebleed" section, which made the enormity of it all burn in my memory forever. Later that season, I remember my father letting me stay up late to watch Wilt Chamberlain and the Lakers play my beloved Knicks in the NBA Finals.

Surely, I wouldn't always walk funny and be so weak. One day, I would be cured and take my rightful place as the quarterback for the Buffalo Bills, handing the ball off to the "Juice" of my time, or play-action faking and throwing the game-winning touchdown bomb. I could throw a Nerf football with a perfect spiral, right on the money, just not very far.

About every other Christmas, my family would drive to Mississippi to visit my grandparents. Often, the trips from my father's folks in Brookhaven to my mother's parents in Collins were on

Sundays and along the way, we listened to NFL playoff football. I was always the first to identify which game it was and who was playing. Listening to football on the radio was as good as watching it on television. We turned it up louder than my mom preferred, and when something favorable happened, we'd yell and scream. We paid attention to every word the announcer said, and we could argue strategic decisions because we were *informed* about down and distance, time left on the clock, injuries, momentum, and just about everything a coach needs to know.

"I would throw it," my dad would say.

"No, why risk a turnover?" I would argue.

The theatre of my young mind could see the action happening, the wide receiver diving in vain, unable to reach the spiraling ball as it sailed past his outstretched fingertips. I could imagine Fred Biletnikoff on the sideline with that aerosol can of "stick-um," just like they described it. I could see his wild hair, moustache and his dirty jersey.

The following week, as we climbed the country up Interstate 55 North, the signal was loud and clear as we drove within the coverage areas of stations in big cities: Jackson, Nashville, Louisville, Cincinnati, Indianapolis, Columbus, and Pittsburgh. One time the signal faded with 30 seconds left to go in the fourth quarter of a playoff game. We desperately scanned the AM dial in search of at least a final score, but had to wait for our next service station stop to learn who won.

When there were no games on the radio, I read books about heroes like Roberto Clemente, Jackie Robinson, O.J. Simpson, Wilt Chamberlain and Henry Aaron. The 20-hour drive from Brookhaven, Mississippi to Big Flats, New York was much more tolerable through the entertaining thrill of sports.

After our family moved to Chicago when I was 11, I quickly fell in love with the Cubs and the Bears. My father was able to get season tickets to the Bears games through his company, and he would take our family to many of the pre-season and early season games when the weather was still tolerable.

The buzz and excitement of a Sunday afternoon at Soldier Field was an incredible experience. From our suburban home, the drive into the city was quick and easy, but once we emerged from the Post Office Tunnel and reached the on-ramp to Lake Shore drive, the traffic would halt. It would take us longer to get to our parking space than the entire 30-mile freeway ride from Woodridge did. As we neared beautiful Soldier Field, that stoic edifice with its magnificent white columns, crowds of people who had parked nearly two miles away lined the street; people of all ages, most wearing the beloved blue and orange of the Bears. Of course, the radio was up LOUD as we inched toward the stadium parking lot.

"... *and hopes are high for the Bears this year as they welcome a man they believe to be a solution to the dismal running attack,*" said Brad Palmer on WBBM Newsradio 78. "*He's a rookie from Jackson State in Mississippi. He'll wear jersey number 34.*

"*Walter Payton!*" I yelled in unison with Palmer. I had already seen him play that summer at the College All-Star game against the Pittsburgh Steelers.

"Turn it down," my mom would yell. "You're gonna go deaf!"

Before my surgery, we didn't own a wheelchair, so when we went to sporting events, the quickest and easiest way to get from the parking lot to our seats in the Northwest end zone was for my parents to carry me. Piggyback" was the most convenient way, and we didn't care about the stares from the crowds of people walking in unison towards the gates of Soldier Field. Once, my father had dropped us off and gone to park the car and my mother was carrying me on her back. As we neared the entrance for our section, a man screamed loudly from behind us, obviously intoxicated from a tailgate party.

"Iss time to put that big nigga down!" he yelled. "He gettin' too <u>big</u> to be carried around on his momma's back."

He just wouldn't stop! He kept on talking about it and talking about it. "I can't believe you carryin' that big niggah around. I done seen you carry him *all the way from where we parked!*"

Finally, Mom had to put a stop to it.

"He's handicapped!" she turned around and yelled. Then the guy kept apologizing, all the way into the stadium. We would laugh about that for years afterwards.

Back in junior high school, it was starting to sink in that I would never be an athlete, but I still wanted to remain as close to sports as possible. In 7th and 8th grade, I was the "manager" of the basketball team, meaning I kept the scorebook and sometimes did the public address announcing for our home games. At home after the games, I would climb up the stairs into my bedroom and talk to friends on my home base CB radio.

"This is the scorekeeper. This is the scorekeeper. Any of my buddies out there?"

"We gotcha loud and clear scorekeeper, how ya doin' tonight?"

"Hey, scorekeeper! You done keeping score?"

In the second semester of my sophomore year, I had weekly disc jockey shift on WDGC. On Tuesday afternoons from 4-8 pm, I would play Pink Floyd, Led Zeppelin and other rock and roll, turning the music up loud during the songs, and clearing my throat with my headphones snug before flicking the switch that put my microphone on the air.

"Rockin' and rollin' on a Tuesday night, this is WDGC. 88.3 FM, Downers Grove. I'm Greg Smith, with ya til 8 pm. Here's some Beetles for ya. Gimmie a call on the request line, if I got it, ya got it."

Fred Moore was the faculty station manager. Students manned all the other management positions, including program director, news director, promotion director and sports director.

Sports director. That sounded good.

I had to stand up to read the job description posted on the bulletin board high above my wheelchair.

"Sports Director—coordinates all of the station's live sports programming including live play-by-play announcing of football and basketball games, recruits and selects additional on-air talent, secures underwriting to fund expenses such as telephone lines at remote locations."

I applied for the job. At the station meeting a few weeks later, Mr. Moore announced the position designees. As a sophomore, I was sure I would not be selected. I did have a chance because the former sports director had applied for the news director position, and I did have a lot of experience from being a statistician in junior high.

When Mr. Moore said my name, it was one of the greatest thrills of my young life to that point. Suddenly, I would *BE* somebody at Downers South. As a sophomore, I would be the voice of the Mustangs! I would be that clear, crisp voice painting those descriptive pictures for the mind's eye as residents of our town listened to high school football on the radio. All that summer, I paid close attention to radio broadcasts. I learned that a "spotting board" was a graphic representation of the football team on paper that announcers used to identify who made tackles or important plays. A "spotter" would sit between the play-by-play man and the "color" commentator.

South was the stepchild to North High as far as the radio station was concerned. The Downers Grove North Trojans played their games on Friday nights uptown and usually won. Downers Grove South's Mustangs played their games Saturday afternoons and usually lost. In fact, South lost all nine games my freshman year. On Friday night, I tuned in WDGC's scratchy signal and listened as North's announcers called the game. I remember thinking with confidence that I could do much better.

The morning of the first game, I arose energetically. Since North and South used the same equipment, it was my responsibility, I was told, to go over to North on Saturday morning and pick it up, then go all the way across town to South and set things up, leaving enough time to troubleshoot any audio problems.

"Dad, we gotta go. We're gonna be late!"

"Late? The game doesn't start until 2 o'clock, right?"

"Yeah, but we need to go over to North and get the equipment. Then we need to go to South and set it up, and we need to make sure it's working. We gotta go!"

Dad and mom would protest the morning before every game, but they'd do it out of love: "Why do I have to drive all over town to get the equipment? Shouldn't the school provide that? It isn't my responsibility to be the transportation for the damn radio equipment!"

On the morning of that first broadcast, we left the house at about

11:30. When we got to North, the studio doors were locked. It took about 15 minutes to get the disc jockey to come to the door and hand my father the suitcase holding a portable mixer and two headset microphones. By the time we got to South, it was around 1:00. The teams were on the field working out. My dad pushed me to the base of the bleachers in my wheelchair and made the first of two trips to the press box, lifting the equipment suitcase over the edge of the window. There was no door. You had to climb over the open window.

Then he returned to carry me up the bleachers under his arm and flung me over the window. I was able to land on my feet and lean on the window until he hurled himself into the press box and began to assemble equipment he had never seen before. No faculty from the radio station was there to help. I was panicking as I realized that we were either going to be able to get this stuff to work or we were not going to go on the air. In the full scope of the universe, it didn't really matter whether the Downers Grove South vs. Hinsdale South football game aired that day, but to me, it was urgent! I had my spotting board ready. I was focused on this as I had never been focused before.

Dad bumbled around with the suitcase. After about ten minutes he made an announcement, "I don't know how to do this," he said.

The public address announcer, the assistant coaches, my father and I all studied the plugs and cables and finally figured out how to assemble everything moments before kickoff. The Mustangs, wearing their blue pants and white jerseys burst through a paper barrier held by the cheerleaders. The band had already performed. The officials were at mid-field with the captains, tossing the coin, and I was on the phone.

"We got it! We got it! Punch us up on the board!"

"Can you hear me, testing one-two-three."

Moments later, the intro rolled. *"Live from Downers Grove South High School, it's Mustang Football on WDGC FM. Here's the voice of the Mustangs, Greg Smith."*

"Hello again everybody, this is Greg Smith at Downers South High School where the Mustangs will kick off the 1979 season hoping to improve on last year's dismal 0-9 performance."

Hello again? I'd never done a game on the radio in my life. I borrowed that phrase from Howard Cosell! I had never done play-by-play before and it showed. I bumbled through players' names and took too long to identify who carried the ball, who caught the ball and who made the tackle. I had a problem with identifying exactly where on the field the football was.

"And that will bring up a third down and, let's see... third down and about seven yards to go for the Mustangs, from the.... Ah 30.... Make that 42 yard line."

I sucked! But I didn't know that then. I was on cloud nine. Here I was, Greg Smith, on the radio for the very first time announcing a high school football game. The headphones hurt my ears by the fourth quarter. My voice was getting hoarse from all the constant talking. Our team was getting shut out and scored upon at will. But I was having a great time. I knew right then that my future would be in broadcasting. No other career option ever entered my mind since that autumn day in 1980.

The moment I arrived home after the game, I immediately went to my bedroom, closed the door, and inserted the cassette recording of the game into my stereo and listened. Over the next three years, I would follow the same routine for all 27 football games and all 78 basketball games. I would critique myself and make corrections the next game. I prepared by creating my spotting boards early in the week and memorizing the opponent's numerical roster. I selected my color commentators based on their knowledge of the team and their ability to communicate clearly.

I enjoyed doing football the best, although at times, it was very challenging for me to sit in frozen wooden press boxes. The unforgiving Chicago wind, known as "the hawk" would blow painfully in my face, to the point where my lips froze and I was unable to articulate my words. But as indecipherable as my words were, they continued. Quitting was not an option. I had been through worse at band practice. Yes, during those times, I looked forward to the thawing out bath that awaited me when I got home, but I was helpless to expedite the passing of the miserable time. The show must go on, and I was the show. I continued.

Though I loved football much more, I was much better at calling hoops. My collection of adjectives to describe the pace of the game, the location of the ball on the court, and the angle of a shot were things I consciously brainstormed as I daydreamed in class. I couldn't steal phrases from existing talents like Red Rush, who would say "tickles the twine" to describe a shot that sailed through the net without touching the iron rim. I had to develop my own style. By my senior year, I had crafted a suspenseful delivery, my voice getting louder as time progressed each time down the court, more frantic, more urgent, very much like what must have been going through the minds of the players as they worked the ball around to get off a good shot. By the fourth quarter in a close game, I was high energy, yelling and screaming, and not being ashamed to be a "homer" for the Mustangs. After a road game at East Leyden High School, where our radio phone line was installed under the bleachers, a parent of one of the Eagles approached me after I had signed off the air, as I gimped down from the bleachers to my awaiting wheelchair.

"How long have you been doing announcing?" he asked.

"About a year."

"I was sitting right behind you and I gotta tell you, I heard every word and you helped me follow the game tremendously. Keep it up!"

That encouragement from a total stranger meant so much to me. My broadcasting career was an unstoppable force. I would be a sportscaster. Nothing would be able to deny that.

CHAPTER 7

Rolling Into the Valley of the Sun

A S OUR FLIGHT APPROACHED SKY HARBOR AIRPORT, I got my first glimpse of an unmistakable landmark. "Look, Dad, there's the football stadium," I shouted while pointing at the bottom of the window on the airplane. My father leaned over across my body, while I sat back to allow him a peek. Our flight path had taken us directly over Sun Devil Stadium and the entire Arizona State University campus just before landing! It was August 10, 1982 and in less than a week, I would be a college freshman.

Ray Williams was to meet us at the airport. His wife, Pearl was a high school friend of my mom. The family, including their junior high school-aged daughter, Tracy now lived in Scottsdale. Not only had I never met them before, I had never even heard my parents speak of them. However, their existence didn't surprise me. I had learned long ago that my mom and dad knew people everywhere. When we went on vacations, we rarely stayed at hotels because every place we visited was home to a family with an inviting guest room for Jim and Adelia Smith. My choice of a college town was no exception. In the "Valley of the Sun," they would be my host family.

My luggage consisted of two suitcases and a large tan trunk stuffed with clothes, a simple stereo system including some albums and cassette tapes, an alarm clock, and bathroom items. That was about it except for my electric wheelchair, which caused a significant delay upon our arrival. For some reason, it was carted off to baggage claim instead of being available at the gate, and when we arrived downstairs to retrieve it, it was missing.

When my father and I finally hit curbside, Ray met us with his lime green, late 70's Chevy Impala. Like all who first immerse themselves in the Southwestern desert, what I remember most about my first breath of Arizona air was its temperature. There is no way to describe a cloudless August day in Phoenix if you have never experienced it, and there is no way to prepare for it. Since I had decided to attend ASU several months before, the temperature was a common topic of conversation. But I had no idea!

Dad grabbed me under the arms and flung me into the front seat of Ray's large vehicle. He folded my manual wheelchair, inserted it in the back seat and then walked behind the car to strategize with Ray about the best way to lift my heavy electric wheelchair into the trunk. I yelled suggestions, but either they didn't want to listen to me or couldn't hear. As expected, I next heard loud bumping noises to which the car moved and shook in response, and finally, felt the squatting of the vehicle due to the chair's enormous weight. I grimaced throughout the five-minute process, continuously shouting concerns. When my chair gets hurt, it hurts me!

Soon we were on our way to the Williams house to spend Saturday and Sunday evening before moving me into my dorm on Monday. Wow! What a different world. Different scenery: mountainous horizons, Saguaro cactus, Adobe designs. And the heat! God, the heat!

Ray and Pearl lived in Scottsdale, a 30-minute straight shot up Scottsdale Road from Arizona State. After our dinner the next evening, it didn't take much effort to persuade Ray to take me for a ride to ASU for a campus visit on Sunday evening. He was an ASU Alumnus and reveled at the opportunity to take a cruise down memory lane. When we finally arrived at the campus, it was nearing sundown. We drove past Sun Devil Stadium and the Activity Center, the sports hub of the campus. Ray pointed out all the changes to the stadium since his student days. Next we drove south on Rural Road and made a right towards the heart of campus.

"They have closed all the streets," yelled Ray. "You can't even drive onto the campus anymore." Roads that he used to drive were now permanent "malls or walkways for pedestrians only. We circled the campus on the four major streets surrounding it one more time. West on Apache, where Ray pointed out his old dorm. North on Mill, where our "tour guide" introduced me to Gammage Hall, a gorgeous circular building designed by the famous Frank Lloyd Wright. Then we headed east on University Drive.

"These are the new dorms," explained Ray. He slowed down as we passed Palo Verde East and Palo Verde West, twin five-story, red brick buildings with diagonal hallway extensions jutting out in about six different directions. PV East was the women's dorm and PV West was the men's dorm. "That's where I'm gonna be living," I announced.

Then, Ray revealed something to me that I didn't know. "That building over there is Manzanita." He slowed down even more. "That building had 14 floors of women, but I read that this year they are going to make it a co-ed dorm! A CO- ED Dorm!! And get this... 11 floors of women and only 3 floors of men!"

"Is that right?" said my dad, seemingly reading my mind and speaking the very words I wanted to say. Ray and Dad moved the conversation to their college experiences of sneaking into the women's dorms, getting caught, getting in trouble, and devising ways to lock the doors and buy time to escape out the windows. Pearl was quiet, smiling, but clearly a little uncomfortable with the topic. After a few minutes of reminiscing, Ray gunned the rhythmic engine on his Impala, turning north at the intersection of University and Scottsdale Road.

Monday morning came quickly. I climbed out of bed in the guest room. The bathroom was across the hall, adjacent to the kitchen. I didn't need my wheelchair to make that short haul. I rose from the bed, threw my head back to shift my center of gravity to a point of balance, and hobbled through the doors, holding on to the frame for stability. I leaned against the sink with my ribcage, brushed my teeth, washed my face and awaited my father's assistance to help me get into the inaccessible shower.

When we arrived at ASU, the sun was shining brightly. The parking lot at Palo Verde West was a bustling place, featuring a steady stream of people carrying many different versions of the same things —Lamps, stereos, milk crates full of books, suitcases and more. Some kids threw a Frisbee on the front lawn. In the distance, about 10 girls were lying out in bikinis in front of Palo Verde East. My roommate at

PV West was Don Thompson. He was also a wheelchair user. PV West was one of the few dorms on campus with provisions for disabled students, such as extra large bathrooms, lowered light switches and door handles. When my father and I read that I would have another wheelchair user for a roommate, we envisioned a rather large room.

Don had already arrived and had taken the left side of the room. The door was on the right. Two single beds were on opposite walls. Two desks, with shelving up to the ceiling were next to each other. The small bathroom was on my side of the room, but Don's shower chair took up most of the maneuvering space.. Don was a quadriplegic from Pennsylvania. Nice guy. We hit it off immediately. But I was a little disappointed with the size of the dorm room.

"Oh well," my dad shrugged. "That's freshman college life." For the rest of the afternoon, he and Ray unpacked all my stuff, assembled my stereo system, and went shopping to furnish me with basic necessities like a bed spread, shower curtain, desk lamp, and things like that. Finally, the process was over. I was officially living at college.

It was time for Dad to leave and time for me to begin to spread my wings. Until this point in my life, my parents helped me do everything, including showering, dressing, cooking, and laundry. I was 18 years old, alone and forced to make it on my own for the first time. I decided that I didn't want to hire an attendant to help me. I could dress myself. I could shower myself with the right kind of shower seat. It was time for me to step up and be independent. My parents weren't too sure that all this was possible and my mother especially wanted me to have an attendant. But I was firm in my decision.

"Alright boy," said Dad proudly before he left. "You're on your own. Good luck."

He waved, closed the door, and suddenly I was alone with the Top-40 sounds of KDKB on the radio of my stereo. I turned it up, elated at my newfound freedom! There was no fear or apprehension. This was what I had been waiting for. Where were the parties going to be tonight?

Two of my high school classmates, Kevin and Shannon were also attending ASU as freshmen, so I attempted to call them. Neither were answering their phones, so I turned the radio back up and started to browse through orientation pamphlets, ads for parties that evening, and dorm information. In a few minutes, I would venture out into this new exciting world and make some new friends!

The music bounced terribly off the tile floor and brick walls of this dorm room. But I cranked it anyway, the soundtrack to a blissful moment of satisfaction. I'll never forget this moment.

"Who can it be knocking at my door?
Go 'way, don't come 'round here no more.
Can't you see that it's late at night?
I'm very tired, and I'm not feeling right.
All I wish is to be alone,
Stay away, don't you invade my home.
Best off if you hang outside,
Don't come in—I'll only run and hide.
Who can it be now?
Who can it be now?" *

At some point during the saxophone solo, I thought I heard an actual knock at my door! I turned the music down and pointed the joy-stick to the long metal latch on the door where most rooms had door-knobs, and pulled the latch toward me. It was Dad, peering through the door, smiling. He had returned to shake my hand and tell me that he was proud of me.

The next morning, my alarm clock sounded. For the first time in my life there was nobody to come get me out of bed. Energetically, I rolled out of bed, into my wheelchair and began to get ready for the day.

After an awkward and lengthy process of showering, shaving and getting dressed, I left the room, went to enjoy my first college cafeteria meal and then darted out the electric doors of PV West toward the crosswalk on University Drive that, for the first time, led me to the campus of Arizona State University. I was a college student.

My roommate had spent another night at his hotel because we both had realized the room just was not going to be big enough for both of us. Just storing all of the wheelchairs consumed most of the space in that room. I had two wheelchairs and he had three. This left very little maneuvering room. It never would have worked. We agreed that we'd meet with the residence hall manager to determine a solution after orientation.

At the meeting, I was told that there was a room available at Manzanita (the co-ed dorm!). However, it was on the first floor where the residence hall staff resided. There were pros and cons to this situation. I would be in the co-ed dorm! That was the positive. The negative was that I wouldn't have peers as neighbors. The residence hall staff was mostly graduate students much older than I and with an authority over me. I would be getting my own room, much nicer than most dorm rooms, I might add. And it would be in the co-ed dorm. Still, I wouldn't have neighbor buddies. They suggested we walk over to look at the room.

I made my mind up before I even saw the room. Along the walkway leading from PV West to Manzanita, I probably could have counted 300 gorgeous women leaving Manzanita and heading toward the campus. They didn't make girls like these at my high school! These were *women* and most of them were very attractive.

We entered the front door and passed a lounge with couches and tables on the left and the cafeteria on the right. Straight ahead were the elevators the other Manzanita students used to gain access to their dorm rooms. I took a right and used a key to unlock a door leading to a single hallway. My room was at the end of that hallway to the left. Entering the room, I immediately knew I would love my new home. There was carpeting on the floor, my own bathroom, and a sliding glass door leading out to the parking lot for easy access to and from my room. What an upgrade! This was more like having a studio apartment than living in a dorm.

We discussed the issue of isolation from the "normal" dorm experience and agreed that my "adopted" floor would be the fourth floor. I would have membership in their "club." I would attend their floor meetings and be considered a resident even though I lived in the management wing.

As I write of my early college experiences and the adventures of my young adulthood, I have decided go into details about the good and the not so good, not from a place of pride over some of my habits and activities. Rather than hold back details about my life that I'm not proud of, I feel a responsibility to tell all. Hopefully, my story might save others from some of the pitfalls that delayed my growth toward my full human potential.

As an 18-year-old freshman, ASU was a dream world to me, a fantasyland. *Playboy* magazine had ranked ASU the #1 Party School in America that year, and *Sport* magazine picked ASU #1 in Football. These two distinctions competed for my top priority. I thank God for my passionate ambition to become a sportscaster, because without it I surely would have failed out of college from overindulging in the party scene.

After getting settled into my new place with the assistance of my high school friend Kevin Dail, we wandered that evening up to the various floors and a circus-like atmosphere of unchecked youthful exuberance! In high school, I was successful at immediately distancing myself from the typical "person in a wheelchair" stereotype. In college, I was determined to immediately do the same, and moreover create an edgier, more outrageous identity for myself. I had given this much thought prior to my arrival. No longer would I be known as Greg Smith, that boring, common name that I would be sharing with possibly a dozen other people on a campus of 50,000 students.

Music blared through hallways on the fourth floor of Manzanita Hall:

And the days go by
Let the water hose me down
Once in a lifetime
Water flowing under ground
Same as it ever was
Same as it ever was... *

Students screamed out their conversations.

"Hey, what's your name!!?"

"Smitty!"

"Where you from!!?"

"Chicago!!" (Not Downers Grove, or Lisle, or Woodridge!)

"Smitty from Chicago, I'm Mike from Boston. This is Bob from Wisconsin. That's Web from Chicago. Want a brewski?" He handed me a Molson Golden.

We wandered from room to room and floor to floor in search of a louder stereo, more intoxicated women, and import beers. In some of the wings, doors were closed and the smell of weed seeped into the hall. I stayed away from these corners, just wanting to meet as many people as possible and find some connection I could be comfortable with. By the elevator on every floor, crowds of students clamored to go up or down to find a better party. We didn't realize that there was no "better party." Every floor was a party and they were all the same. Lots of beer. Loud music. Lots more women than men. And corner dorm rooms with towels covering the door crack in an unsuccessful attempt to contain the smell of burning marijuana.

Before the night turned into dawn, I had toured all 14 floors, met dozens of people with whom I would feel comfortable sitting with at breakfast, and established a reputation as a party animal. I accomplished this with a device called a "beer bong." It was a plastic funnel connected to a clear plastic tube. The tube would be inserted in the back of your throat. The funnel would be held above your head. The entire beer would be dumped into the funnel and directly into your throat. The sight of little "Smitty" doing a beer bong inspired chants and cheers: "Smitty, Smitty, Smitty!" Friday had become Saturday. I didn't make it to breakfast that morning.

Before I got too wild that night, I did meet a girl that I liked. Her name was Loren. She was a very cute, light-skinned black girl from Las Vegas. We exchanged phone numbers and that accomplishment was the thrill of the evening. I also met Shari from New York, who was majoring in Journalism and wanted to be a sportswriter. Like so many people that I write about, I wonder what happened to her.

After an adventurous week of studying the campus map to make it from class to class, I found myself in the Tower Center, which housed the studios of KASR Radio. KASR was just beginning and not yet on the air. About 100 students crowded into the offices to hear Professor Fritz Leigh tell us that KASR was to be an AM carrier current station, broadcasting its signal through the dorms' electrical system. Professor Leigh was looking for people with experience to apply for station manager, program director, sales director, promotion director, production director and news director. Sadly, sports programming was not in the plan. Immediately after the meeting, I planted the seed by asking Professor Leigh if he had considered creating a sports department for KASR. I argued that ASU places a great deal of emphasis on athletics and it would make sense for students desiring a career in sports reporting to have a place where they could develop their skills. He said he would think about it, and urged me to submit my application for news director. I did so, knowing that my news background was far subservient to my experience as a sportscaster in high school.

Finally, two weeks passed and the same crowd gathered again at KASR. Professor Leigh announced all of the positions and there was applause and congratulations for each of the new directors. He interrupted the chatter with one more announcement.

"I've decided that we would add another level of management to the station based on the input of one of your peers," he announced, clearly and crisply as if doing a newscast. Fritz, as we would all soon be calling him behind his back, was very articulate. "We're adding the position of sports coordinator, to work under the news director and develop sports reporting opportunities for students who are interested in that. I'm happy to announce that the first sports coordinator at KASR is Greg Smith!"

My life as a freshman at ASU soon became pretty routine. I would get up at around 6AM, take a shower, dress myself, gather my books, roll out the front door, down the long ramp and assimilate with the crowd of other students waiting at the crosswalk for the traffic to stop on University Drive. The heat was burning, and people dressed appropriately. Everyone wore shorts, and many of the girls wore halter-tops or tube tops to class. Rolling to a lecture hall was often a pleasurable experience. Despite the fact that my chair could zoom ahead at three times the normal waking pace, I would often pass a cluster of guys and fall in pace behind one of ASU's thousands of leggy sun goddesses for the duration of a long trek across campus to my class.

On one of the first days of school, I pulled in behind a short girl with lioness-like blonde hair who just mesmerized me. She made a left onto Palm Walk, a long pathway lined by hundreds of enormous palm trees. Coincidentally, my journey required a left too. And then another left. I was sure she could hear me behind her, so I pulled up next to her and started a conversation. Her name was Dina, from Chicago. We were in the same Psychology class. After that lecture, we compared schedules and found we were in the same Math class *and* the same Literature class! Wow! Three out of five classes together! We had lunches together and became study partners. She would come to my dorm and hang out. Sometimes we would go to the movies, to the Drama department's performances and to concerts.

It didn't take long for me to become incredibly infatuated with her. She handled me gently, informing me that she was dating a rugby player from South Africa, but that she thought I was very nice and wanted me to be close to her and a part of her life. I had become

STUDYING BIOLOGY AT ASU—I had three classes with a girl named Dina my freshman year including biology.

accustomed to rejection, so this was nothing new. It was at this point in my life that the anchors of very limiting, damaging beliefs I had about myself began to emerge. It wasn't just Dina. It was every girl I approached. Everyone wanted to "just be friends." As my freshman year advanced, I had shed tears over Loren and Dina. I had rejected Shari because she didn't meet my immature perceptions of being attractive enough. So instead of enjoying her company, I was lonely. Next to the bed in my dorm, a tiled mirror covered the wall from floor to ceiling. It was obviously installed by someone who had more to look at than what I perceived to be a skinny, decrepit, misshapen skeleton covered with skin, sitting alone in a pitiful wheelchair or lying alone with a Playboy magazine in the bed. I started to hate myself inside about something over which I had no control.

Despite this lack of female response, I had other things going for me that kept me strong. As Sports Coordinator at KASR, I had managed to get the Athletic Department to allow us space to record the play-by-play of all the home football games from the press box at Sun Devil Stadium. I auditioned for both the play-by-play job and the color commentary role, expecting that I would clearly be the best play-by-play man available. I was right.

We formed a sports department with a small group of about 10 people. Bill was my first color man. He struck me as a big man in a little body who was a good athlete but didn't have the size to compete as a player at this level. He was a standout football player in Arizona as a high schooler, knew the game inside out, and had good relationships with the players. Paul was another character on our original team. His thick New York accent cost him points with me, but he had great knowledge and a lot of passion for sportscasting, more than I initially gave him credit for. There was Mike Lovins, a non-athletic, walking sports encyclopedia who really connected with me on a personal level. Mike became another one of those "best friends I've ever had in my life."

In 1982, The Sun Devils were led by Jeff Van Rapphorst at quarterback. Number 10 was a wise decision maker on the field and led a team that was expected to win the Pac 10. Darryl Clack was the

ASU SPORTSCASTING— ASU linebacker Stacy Harvey and I had much in common. We both loved football and we both loved to party in our college days. Here we are at Camp Tontozona.

tailback, and the ASU's sports information department was pushing him as a Heisman Trophy candidate. The Sun Devils coasted to victories in their first seven games, and with each win I became more and more immersed in the football family. I attended practices and got to know some of the players quite well. I continually rolled over to the Activity Center where the football offices were located and interviewed the coaching staff. Darryl Rogers was the head coach. His quarterbacks coach was Mike Martz, who would go on to win Super Bowls as head coach of the St. Louis Rams.

Our first home game was against Utah, and through hard work I was able to get the university to allow us room in the press box for three people. We would record the football game onto a cassette tape and then later that evening play the tape on the air. Sun Devil Stadium was due for a facelift the following year, so that first year, we would take the elevator up to the top of the West bleachers. From there, we would have to ascend a staircase to the roof of the press box, where we had our space. Bill would carry me up. Mike and Paul would carry the wheelchair. We would set up our equipment in time to have a hot dog and some nachos before kickoff. We treated the recording as if it was a live broadcast. We analyzed our tapes, and made critiques for improving the way we described and analyzed the action.

"Dan Saleamua on the stop for the Sun Devils," I'd say, thanks to my spotter, Mike, who would tap the number 98 on the cluttered chart. *"That will bring up another third-and long situation for the Utes, who obviously are not going to pose a threat to the Sun Devils in this game."* ASU won the game 23-10 and the winning continued from early September through mid-November, when the Washington Huskies finally put a scar on our perfect season, handing us a 17-13 loss in Tempe. We were not able to gain press credentials for the ASU-Arizona game in Tucson, so a few of us drove down as spectators and watched the Rose Bowl being snatched away by the Wildcats 28-18. In the parking lot after the game, some drunken Arizona fans were throwing beer cans at people who were wearing maroon & gold, like me.

From the chaos of that first night exploring the social scene at Manzanita, cliques emerged and groups of close friends formed. My buddies were Mike O'Toole, a tall, lanky Technology major from Boston, who drank constantly and loved to listen to Creedence Clearwater Revival. I hated that music, but enjoyed the humor of that drunken redhead playing his air guitar and lip-syncing to *The Midnight Special."* His roommate, Bob Ewing was older than the rest of us. This was not his first attempt at a college education. Bob had the best stereo system in the dorm (meaning the loudest), and we would crank the tunes in their room every night. Down the hall, Jim Webber resided. "Web" became one of my closest friends throughout college. He had unruly curly black hair, a weird looking pointy nose and a somewhat awkward, yet fit physique that he used in a comedic way. He was hilarious and constantly provided the laughter that bound our foursome.

After dinner, we would sit around Mike and Bob's room, the stereo cranked so loud that you couldn't hear. We could all agree on Led Zeppelin, The Doors, or The Who. We'd take turns leading the group on our own unique rock & roll tangents. Bob would force us to listen to Eddie Money. Mike would play a Creedence album. Web would put on something like Todd Rungren, and I would always choose Peter

Gabriel or Genesis. During Gabriel's *The Lamb Lies Down on Broadway,* O'Toole would yawn, and a second or two before the song ended, would rip the needle off my record and put on some more damn Creedence! I averaged three beers a night. But that wasn't the only poison I took into my body as an 18-year-old freshman at ASU.

In the desert, Manzanita was an oasis if you were physically fit. You could go outside and throw a Frisbee, play golf, play volleyball, go running, play Intramural sports, go swimming or diving or do any of a number of activities. These opportunities were all around us every day as chances to meet people, network and grow. For me, they represented more evidence that I was different and that there was something wrong with me. I couldn't do any of those things. My broadcasting was the only thing holding up my self-esteem. Thanks to my fourth floor buddies, I wasn't lonely, but I wasn't really enjoying the kind of lifestyle I somehow thought would magically happen for me when I got to college. I concluded that part of the problem was that I didn't have a vehicle. Without one, I couldn't drive to go out on dates or to experience anything in the Valley of the Sun outside of the ASU campus. In addition, for a combination of reasons, I didn't feel like I was connecting to my peers on a level I aspired to. I was looking for a place to fit in.

Sometime early that freshman year, when a joint was passed around the room, I extended my hand and took on a bad habit. No, I couldn't throw the Frisbee or go swimming, but I could get high and do that just as well as everybody else. So that became a way for me to connect. It hurt my schooling and my ability to concentrate on my studies. It had to have a negative impact on my health. I was already unhappy, so the weed gave me artificial joy and laughter. I often wonder how much farther along I would be in life had I not made that mistake. How crazy was I to have taken on this habit? Muscular Dystrophy usually kills as a result of respiratory ailments, and here I was smoking every day! It drained me of daytime energy. I would come home from classes and take a nap because I was physically spent. But at night, I embraced it, enjoyed it, and my friends enjoyed being around me when I was high.

I finished my freshman year of college without a great deal of self-esteem, and without a single girlfriend the whole year. I had a strange combination of "assets"—a strong foundation for my broadcasting career, a 2.5 GPA, my virginity reluctantly intact, a group of close friends, and a daily marijuana habit.

No one who has ever met me would ever question my work ethic, and by my sophomore year of college, it was fully engaged. In addition to my schoolwork, I spent a great deal of time sharpening my craft as a sportscaster. I would record every broadcast and listen to it multiple times the week leading up to the next game, searching for phrases that worked well and word choices that "popped." I'd also attend football practices and press conferences. I would spend time hanging out with area sportswriters and felt totally immersed in the Sun Devil beat. Like lots of students, I wore Walkman headsets on campus. While they enjoyed their music, I listened to myself do play-by-play, even on Saturdays, as I rolled my power chair across campus towards an empty, sunlit Sun Devil Stadium nestled between the mountains.

One Saturday afternoon my power wheelchair ascended the steep winding ramps leading to the press box elevator, as I rewound a phrase I noticed I continually used on the air: *The Sun Devils are on a roll now! First and 10 on the Huskies 13 yard line. Van Rapphorst breaks the huddle. Aaron Cox is wide right. Glen Dennard split left. Darryl Clack the lone setback… zzzzzzpppp! Devils are on a roll! Zzzzp on a roll now! Zzzzzzp on a roll… First and 10! ZZZZp "On A Roll!"*

"Cool" I muttered to myself as the elevator took me up to the press box.

As football season turned into basketball season and then baseball season led to summer vacation, Mike Lovins and I grew to become great friends. He was a Phoenix Suns fanatic and would take me to games at "The Madhouse on McDowell," Veterans Memorial Coliseum. Mike and I both believed that having as much sportscasting experience as possible would pave the way to careers in the industry, so we liberally spread our talents out across the city and the nation. For the Suns, I was a stringer (free-lance reporter) for Kansas City's KCMO radio. Back then, the Kings had not yet moved to Sacramento, so I would call in quarterly reports for each Phoenix Suns game, which they would record and air on their network in Kansas City. So I had press passes and passes to the locker rooms, where I would interview all of the basketball greats of the time. I met everybody—Jordan, Magic, Bird, Kareem Abdul-Jabbar.

Kareem embarrassed me once during my senior year. I was in the Lakers locker room interviewing players and noticed Kareem sitting by himself reading a book. Nobody was bothering him, and I saw it as an opportunity to get a one-on-one. Mike knew better and warned me, "You'd better have a good question." I should have heeded this advice, but approached him with the bonehead "Kareem, how do you feel about the win tonight?"

He glared at me. I had disturbed him from his reading and ignored his obvious 'don't bother me' body language the other reporters respected.

"We won," he said simply and returned his gaze back between the pages of his book! I rolled away, totally embarrassed but wiser. The incident left me with no less respect for him. It was a stupid question, poorly timed. He treated me as he would have treated any other reporter. He didn't have any pity for me because I was in a wheelchair. He dealt with me straight up.

A few days later, I found myself waist high among a crowd of reporters milling outside of Arizona State's basketball pressroom, located just outside the team locker room at the ASU Activity Center. After a longer wait than usual, we were finally let in. ASU had just upset Pac-10 conference champion UCLA.

When the doors opened, competitive reporters stormed into the media room like a herd of cattle. I forced my wheelchair into the jam-packed room, just barely managing to get my wheels through the door. Newspaper reporter Bob Moran from the Mesa Tribune politely moved aside, and several other guys followed his lead to allow me space to enter the room completely. But the television camera crews did not budge, and I could not get my microphone anywhere near the front of the room where the interviews would originate.

Suddenly, ASU point guard, Bobby Thompson, emerged from the locker room, still in uniform, and bright lights illuminated the scene. I was still forced in the back of the room. The TV guys knew they were blocking me from getting sound for my radio station, but probably felt they could do nothing about it. I grew frustrated.

Thompson answered a couple of questions about the big victory. I was missing this sound! In a press conference setting, getting your question answered requires perfect timing and a loud voice. My question was unique: "Bobby, can you come over *here*?"

He grinned, hopped down the stairs and sat on a bench right in front of me! Forward, Steve Beck followed, forcing a dozen TV cameramen and radio guys to scurry after them, reset their cameras, lights and microphones! The rest of *this* press conference was *wheelchair accessible!*

22 YEARS LATER—I revisited the ASU campus radio station in 2004 and found this article from the "State Press" hanging on the "Wall of Fame."

~

CHAPTER 8

Sweetness

WHILE AN ASU STUDENT, I spent most of my summers and Christmas vacations with my parents in Chicagoland. As a child growing up there, my moods on Mondays strictly depended on whether the Bears won or lost. No wonder I identified so strongly with that song, I Don't Like Mondays, by the Boomtown Rats. But I knew every week that the Bears had a chance to win, no matter whom they played, because of one ingredient that nobody else could match: Walter Payton.

I identified with "Sweetness." In his Bears uniform, he was greatness on a miserable team. In my wheelchair, I felt like I was greatness in a miserable body and a cold, physical world. Yet we both held onto our dreams. I grew up, went on to Arizona State and became the sports director of the campus radio station. His team grew up, became good and in 1985 hosted an NFC Divisional Playoff game against the New York Giants. I was home for the holiday break. I called the Bears office and was able to obtain a single locker room pass that would permit me entrance into the Bears locker room after the game. It would not permit me into Soldier Field or into the press box.

My parents and their friends had tickets and rented an RV for the game. The plan was for my cousin Ronald and me to watch the game from the parking lot and go directly to the Bears locker room afterwards to interview the players. Shortly after my parents left, Ron and I looked at each other with devilish grins and didn't have to say a word. We bundled up on this subzero Chicago December afternoon. He pushed me in my manual wheelchair to one of the entrances and to our amazement, the locker room pass gained us entry into the stadium!

We found a temporary resting-place in the wheelchair section just above the field at about the 40-yard line, but on this painfully frigid day, I could only endure it for 30 minutes. It was just too cold. We decided to try the press box as a last ditch attempt to remain in the stadium before surrendering back to the RV. And whaddaya know? The security guard allowed us on the elevator. Before we knew it, we were being served hors d'oeuvres in a heated press box, receiving detailed statistics, and enjoying the Bears thrashing of the Giants. In all the excitement, I had to continue to remind my cousin that this was the press box. Cheering was not allowed, even when the Bears pressured Giants punter Sean Landetta so much that he took his eyes off the ball as he dropped it in the general direction of his foot, resulting in one of the NFL's all-time funniest follies!

As time ticked off the fourth quarter clock, my greatest concern became how I would get from the press box to the Bears locker room after the game. The only wheelchair accessible path would have taken us completely outside Soldier Field and against the grain of the departing crowd. The Bears' public relations director said not to worry. He instructed ushers to meet me at the bottom of the elevator and carry me on their shoulders in my wheelchair, down the bleachers to the locker room level. I felt like royalty.

They set me down gently. Right in front of me was *The NFL Today's* Irv Cross and his camera crew about to enter the locker room in front of me! We wheeled through the door. Clusters of aggressive reporters so surrounded the most celebrated Bears that in some circles, I couldn't even see the players. I felt intimidated, sheepishly scanning the room for the slightest possibility that I could get an interview with just one big-time player. From my wheelchair, I could read the names of the players above their lockers. Huge crowds surrounded Mike Singletary, Willie Gault, and Jim McMahon. I must have looked pretty dejected at the realization that I would have to wait for "seconds" instead of getting those first, passionate statements from players after a victory that moved them to within one game of the Super Bowl. I was able to conduct a short interview with Bears offensive lineman Tom Thayer since he was sitting alone and neglected by the media.

Ever the optimist, I continued to seek an interview opportunity, and through a crack in the crowd, his eyes met mine. Slowly and softly, he extended his arm forward and moved it to his right, brushing it up against the abdomen of a reporter, who took one step aside. He nodded his head, looking me dead in the eye. He didn't pause from answering the question he was asked. He just moved his arm and created a space for me. I rolled forward and extended my microphone. I was so excited by the moment and so intimidated by my surroundings that I didn't even ask a question. But my tape recorder captured the voice of Sweetness.

CHAPTER 9

The Misunderstood Brother

I TURNED BLACK IN 1985, the summer before my senior year of college. I say that because although I'm African American and proud of that fact, I am also severely disabled and grew up in a predominately white environment. As a result of those factors, finding connection and acceptance in the black community had not come naturally for me. It was something I spent a lot of time analyzing and striving for.

A major element of my personal disconnection from other blacks stems from the "Oreo Syndrome," a term used to describe black people who "think they're white,"—"black on the outside, white on the inside," it is said. Throughout my childhood, I had been surrounded

ASU GRADUATION—I didn't care that I had to sit in an area for wheelchair users at my graduation from ASU. I was just glad to get out of school!

by and absorbed in white culture. In suburban Downers Grove, 30 miles southwest of Chicago, while most black kids my age were listening to Funkadelic, I was engrossed in Led Zeppelin. Genes from the touch of Italian and Native American in my blood are visible in my head of straight stringy hair, very unlike most blacks. As a teen, I parted it straight down the middle and "feathered" it back on the sides like all the white kids were doing at the time. I dressed "preppy" in blue jeans, pink and green oxford shirts and sweaters and "boat shoes," wearing no socks in the warmer months. Later, as I grew more rebellious, I traded the goody two shoes look for the "burnout" look at times, wearing Journey, Genesis or Pink Floyd concert T-shirts, blue jeans and tennis shoes. I actually had the Farrah Fawcett poster in my locker! Throughout my education, even through college, I never had one black teacher. Contrast that with my father, who grew up in Brookhaven, Mississippi and never had one white teacher until graduate school at Pratt Institute and the University of Rochester.

My parents were raised in entirely black environments in Mississippi. They met at an all-black college, Alcorn A&M. After they graduated, they taught at an all-black high school in Biloxi until my father left teaching, earned his MBA and entered corporate America. When we moved from Mississippi and an all-black environment to upstate New York, we moved to an all-white surrounding. My father's career quickly progressed from product engineer to sales and marketing, which put him squarely in the white man's business world, where he excelled.- It put my sister and me in schools where often we were the only black faces.

As a child, I never gave much thought to being black. I was fitting in as just another kid, molded and becoming what my environment projected upon me. When my father was transferred from upstate New York to the Chicago market as a sales representative in the Midwest Region, he chose a home in suburban Woodridge, in an all-white neighborhood southwest of Chicago. Several years later when we upgraded homes, we moved to an upscale subdivision in Lisle called "Green Trails," and built a home on a small lake, adjacent to a golf course. We didn't have any black neighbors, but the fact that I was black and different in that way from everybody around me was never something I consciously thought about. The fact that I was disabled, to me, was the extreme difference I tried to normalize as much as possible.

As I got older and started seeing the diversity that exists in the world, I began to question myself. In college, I started to sense a separation from other blacks. I started to try to hang out with the athletes that I interviewed and covered on the radio. I tried going to the parties on campus where the only kids present were black. I quickly learned that I had nothing in common with these people. You can't go through your life very much unaware of your history and your culture, and expect to blend in. These people didn't like the same music I liked. They didn't speak the way I spoke. The difference between black and white social cultures seemed like a giant chasm to me back then. But slowly I began to carve out some good friendships with blacks at ASU.

Dave Carruth was a political science major who lived in my dorm and who was always friendly. Dave was different from most black people at ASU in that he was always smiling. It seemed to me at the time that blacks didn't smile! We had some good conversations that developed into a friendship. There was also a guy named Herman Walker. Herm, also a political science major, was a smooth ladies man. Both Dave and Herm were a few years older than I, and they started to "school" me on black issues and culture.

In getting to know each other, Herm and I discovered that both of our fathers, and Dave's uncle were members of Omega Psi Phi Fraternity, one of the four black Greek organizations. We kept running into this guy on campus that everybody knew named Archie Gettis. He was also an Omega. For about a year, we'd see Archie and start talking about Omega. The more I thought about it, the more I realized that there would be no better way for me to totally immerse myself in the black community than to become a member of this most respected black fraternity.

Two more guys came forth to pledge, a freshman named Cornelius Simpson and a sophomore wrestler named Dennis Roberts. The five of us started spending all our leisure time together. We hung out at a bar called the "Devil House," carving a group identity, connecting and preparing to pledge in the summer of 1985. But when the line started, Dave and Herman—my closest friends—didn't meet the GPA requirements and were dropped. I was disappointed but went on with it with Dennis and Cornelius. After about a week, Dennis quit, leaving just Cornelius and me.

Over the course of the next eight weeks, I was put through the most challenging test of my young life. I was hazed physically and mentally to the point of torture in ways that my discretion will not allow me to divulge. I gained a new understanding of manhood. They taught us black history, which was, in an amazing sense, our fraternity's history, and I developed a new attitude about scholarship. There were periods of hopelessness and despair, but through it I learned about perseverance. The brotherhood I established with my line brother, Cornelius, a man I grew to both despise and love at the same time, taught me how to encourage and to be uplifted, often quite literally. He would have to carry me for miles when the "big brothers" made me go without my wheelchair! And suddenly, one hot Phoenix afternoon, we were initiated into Omega Psi Phi, shaking the very hands that had caused us pain and agony for two months.

My environment had shifted from an all-black nucleus to an all-white nucleus with my parent's move to upstate New York when I was four. Now, at the age of 21, a shift of equal proportions happened. From the moment I entered Omega my social focus became all black. Due to all I endured in order to make it into the fraternity, I was very proud to be an Omega. The bond of brotherhood at first seemed magical to me, almost akin to a cure to muscular dystrophy. It was a nurturing home base, a connection indescribable in words; that only other brothers could truly understand. And being an Omega carried a lot of respect with it. Suddenly I was center stage in the black community at ASU. I was meeting lots of other brothers from other colleges near and far; meeting plenty of black women; finally, for the first time in my life, finding a real "girlfriend."

I had solved the social disconnection that stemmed from race. But with it, I discovered another, even more painful separation—the chasm between "Blackness" and disability.

Part of the pride and celebration of being an Omega is expressed in a ritual known as "stepping." Stepping is an energetic, synchronistic dance and chant that brothers do with enthusiasm and power. Stepping is something that brothers take pride in and is such a crucial part of the fraternal bonding process. Obviously, I couldn't step, but I would holler the chants and sit with the "bruhs" for hours, enjoying watching them having fun. But it just wasn't active participation and it was somewhat segregating. In the full scheme of things, the fact that I couldn't step shouldn't have mattered significantly, but it was a little painful to be segregated from such a passionate part of fraternal brotherhood. The natural social development that stemmed from stepping was missing for me.

Another part of the Que experience is barking. *We're the "nasty Que-Dogs." We bark. We wear dog collars. We're just down right nasty and lewd and proud of it.* Some of my brothers can scare you with their barks. Although I have a deep and masculine voice, I do not have the lung capacity to bark with the same boldness, volume and force as my brothers do. For that, my bark was often called "cat," the worst insult that could be given a brother. Painful.

Dancing was another part of the black social experience where I found myself set apart. It seemed that when whites partied, they would sit down, drink, listen to music, play games and joke around. It wasn't a physical experience. But when blacks partied, they would cram themselves into crowded rooms that had no furniture. The lights would be very low. The scratching of the DJ would be very loud. There would be no conversation. The guys would try their best to look "hard" and serious, and the girls, in their tight skirts would flaunt their curves. And the activity was dance.

Imagine me, seated in my wheelchair, ass level with everybody else in the room, just sitting there, and like the other guys trying to look "hard." I wasn't "hard." I was a 65-pound skinny guy in a wheelchair in the same room with 290-pound defensive linemen that I'm lucky didn't step on me. Deep within, I was just as tough, just as bad, just as much there. Unfortunately, that confidence and inner certainty had no way to exude itself, and I often found myself lonely in a room filled with dozens of people.

I'm "bilingual." Blacks and whites speak two different languages. I can speak in such a way that you would never imagine I didn't grow up in the inner city or the all-black rural South. I can also speak in such a way that if speaking on the phone, you would never be able to guess that my last name wasn't Wojachowski. Often, my fraternity brothers from Phoenix would go down to Tucson to hang with the "bruhs" there. I was very proud of my accomplishments as a play-by-play announcer. I took some tapes of the Arizona State vs. University of Arizona game so that my frat brothers who played for the UofA could hear their names being called by me. I popped the tape in.

"The Arizona Wildcats facing a 3rd and 7 on the Sun Devils 23 yard line. A first down here would just about seal it for the Cats and give them their sixth straight victory over Arizona State. They come to the line of scrimmage with a deuce backfield..."

"When you comin' on the radio?"

"That's ME!"

"Das YOU? You sound like a WHITE dude. Dat ain't you!"

"The give goes left to Greathouse! Trying to cut the outside corner, chased by Harvey. He cuts up field and dives! It's gonna be close! Gonna be very close as the chains come out."

"Dat is you. Why you frontin'?"

"Frontin'? What'chu mean 'FRONTIN'?"

"You actin' like you *white*. You ain't speaking like you yourself. You actin' like you somebody else. You actin' like a white dude."

I replaced my tape with some rap music and we moved on to talking about something else.

It was through the fraternity that I met Sterling, one of my closest friends to this day. Through him, I met Terri, the woman I eventually married. Through her, I have my three children. And it all originated with an innate desire to connect with my people.

What is physical about being black hasn't changed. There is an admiration and high regard for physical prowess in the black community. Being black is, in a large way, a physical experience that holds a great deal of respect for athleticism, dance, your size, the way you walk, and the way you move. Those characteristics do exist within me like all black men, but without outward signs. They are invisible to those who don't know me well. Therefore, I have always sensed a feeling of distance from my own race. To make a statement so bold, and

perhaps controversial requires me to be introspective and thorough—
Is it just me? Since I've interviewed and spent time with many black
disabled people across the country in this decade-old research project
known as *On A Roll*, I know that disability and blackness have common side effects when mixed. Others feel the same way I do about the
subject.

Add to that the fact that African-Americans are a nurturing, loving people who haven't really received or embraced the message of disability pride yet. Therefore, there is a paternalistic attitude towards
people with disabilities—we are the beloved "sick and shut in" they
pray for at church.

We need to spread the word to the black population that there is a
new definition of disability. They need to know that we can function
in society as equal participants and that full respect, acknowledgement, and inclusion of disabled blacks into the mainstream of black
culture would offer freedom and happiness for blacks with disabilities
and their families. Unfortunately, nobody has done much to seek support from black leadership and the black media with respect to promoting that acknowledgement. To black agenda-setters, the issues that
concern the civil rights and equal participation of African-Americans
are so in need of emphasis that their eyes are strictly "on the prize."
The focus on creating equal opportunities in all aspects of society for
"their" people is unwavering. The black community hasn't fully
embraced the disability empowerment revolution—yet. I hope to be
able to help that process along.

CHAPTER 10

Working for a Living

In 1986, when I hit the streets as one of the most promising graduates from the Walter Cronkite School of Journalism at Arizona State University, I was quite sure I'd land a job soon. My aspirations to be a sportscaster had faded, but not because I didn't think I had the raw talent. I truly believed I was a good play-by-play man, particularly in basketball, but my father's constant lectures about the real world seeped in.

"What are the odds of you making it big as a sportscaster?" he would say. "To make any money doing that, you gotta work for a pro team. There are only a limited number of those jobs available, so you're gonna have to go out to Rockford, Illinois to some single A baseball team, making $10,000 a year if you're lucky."

Then he would twist the dagger into the heart of my play-by-play dreams. "How are you going to afford to buy a vehicle while making $20,000 a year? Business, my son. You need to start thinking about a career in business."

These lectures came more frequently and with more passion the summer before my senior year at ASU. Dad and I were connecting on a deeper level and communicating more. I was now his frat brother and that drew us a little closer together. I still didn't respect his decision not to help me finance a vehicle while I was still in college. To this day, I feel that decision stunted my social and career growth. But after I graduated, the talks about the van had more substance.

"Dad, I need you to help me get a van. It's the most important thing you can do for my career."

"Look, boy (I was 22), you need to get your resume out in the streets and get a job with a company. If a company wants to hire you, they'll buy you a van."

"Dad, if I want to work in this industry, no radio station is going to buy a van for me to do anything; not sportscasting, not sales, not even if I were running the station."

"But see that's where you're thinking is fucked up, boy. Stop looking through the narrow tunnel of radio. You don't know what field you'll end up in. When I went to college, I majored in Chemistry. I had no idea I'd end up in sales and marketing. Broaden your horizon."

Some of his lecturing seeped through. I dropped some classes I had scheduled in advanced news reporting and in videography and took some classes in the business college. I took Entrepreneurship, Media Planning and Buying, Advanced Marketing Strategies, among others. I graduated from ASU in the summer of 1986 with a Bachelor of Arts degree in Broadcasting. My emphasis was in Management. My related field was Marketing.

I had a killer resume when I hit the streets. In addition to my college radio play-by-play experience, it had the logos of all the media-related companies I had either worked- or interned for. I listed Phoenix's NBC Channel 12, where I logged highlights for the Sunday night sportscasts; ASU's Sports Information Office, where I had a paid student intern position writing biographies for media guides, features about the athletes for game programs, and worked as a buffer between the media and Sports Information Director Gary Rausch; *The Mesa Tribune*, where I wrote summaries of local area sports events, edited the box scores and wrote a feature article or two; KCMO radio in Kansas City, Missouri, for whom I was an NBA stringer covering the Phoenix Suns games.

I graduated from Arizona State in December 1986 and lived around campus for about six months. The next summer, I moved into a huge apartment complex about three miles away from campus called Superstition Springs. I had a little studio apartment with a foldout bed that doubled as a couch. I was 23 years old and out on my own, a full adult with a college degree. I signed a short, six-month lease. My parents had made a generous offer to help me with a down payment on a new home that I could live in and get roommates to help pay the mortgage. Also—finally!—my parents helped me make a down payment on a new modified van. So living in Superstition Springs was like sitting in a waiting room. Waiting for my house, my job and my van.

Throughout that summer, I worked hard to land a job in radio sales. My resume was solid. I had purchased a new suit. I rehearsed my interview answers and felt pretty good about my chances, considering that several of my classmates had been successful in getting hired as radio sales reps in the Phoenix market. The only thing I felt a little uneasy about was my lack of independent transportation. I'd call Rainbow Transport to set up a ride to a radio station interview in Phoenix. Each ride cost $50, but the state's Vocational Rehabilitation Program reimbursed much of it. I'd get to the interview early, looking good in my suit. I'd do very well, answering the standard interview questions. I'd be treated politely, and like clockwork, a week later, I'd receive a letter in the mail informing me that "at this time there are no positions available" I could fill. Of course, they would "keep my resume on file for future reference." I collected about 30 of these letters, one from every radio station in the Valley of the Sun. I actually began to give up on radio.

While I was looking for a job and still living around ASU, my friend Mike Lovins and I discovered an opportunity in the 976-telephone business. I saw an ad in the paper from a company called Telecontractor of New York. They ran pay-telephone services and chat lines. They had a teen line, a "talk-dirty-to-me" line (actually several of them), and they were looking for ideas for other lines. Mike and I pitched them on the concept of having a "sports line." We caught the bus to downtown Phoenix and met with them. They liked the idea.

We called it *The Sports Rapp Line*. Callers were charged something like 15 cents per minute. Our job was to get them to call and keep them on the line as long as possible. We would be paid a commission on the revenue the line generated.

Our plan was to treat it like a radio show. We would get big-name sports guests on the line and people would pay for the ability to talk to these sports celebrities directly on the telephone. So we worked the phones and lined up interviews with then-ASU head football coach John Cooper, who had taken the Sun Devils to their first Rose Bowl victory the season before; legendary UCLA Basketball Coach John Wooden; Paul Westphal, who was about to retire from his playing days as a Phoenix Sun; and Philadelphia 76ers shooting guard Maurice Checks (because the Sixers failed to deliver Dr. J). We would print up flyers for the line and put them under windshield wipers at ASU baseball games. We ran ads in the *Arizona Republic* and the *New Times*. We were there on the line from about 5 PM until about 10 PM each night to facilitate the discussion. The big-name guests were on the prime time show, at 7 PM each night.

I remember hanging out in my apartment on weeknights, when my frat brothers, Sterling Bridges and James Scott would be over.

"So what's up man?" Sterling would ask with mock-attitude. "Where the women at? Here I come, all the way out here to see you and you ain't got no women over here. What kinda nigga are you?"

James would chime in with his deep-voiced, slow drawl from above. He was a giant. "He ain't got no women, 'cause he sittin' here every night holdin' the phone! Ain't talkin' to nobody, just sittin' there holdin' the phone!!"

They would laugh at me and I'd laugh right with them. Nobody called the *Sports Rapp Line*. We'd sit there and hold the phone for five hours on alternating nights, playing backgammon, watching TV, and sometimes drinking beer, waiting for a caller. Every now and then, we'd hear "boo-beep"—a signal for a caller.

"Hey this is the Sports Rapp Line. Thanks for calling, I'm Greg, we're talking about the Suns win last night over the Lakers. What did you think?" Notice the lie. " We" was just me. And I wasn't talking about anything through the phone. I was just talking with my frat brothers about who was going to make the beer run.

"Hey, its Irwin," a squeaky-voiced kid would reply. *"I thought the Suns played an excellent fourth quarter..."*

I would interrupt him. *"Irwin, do your parents know you are calling this pay telephone service?"* Irwin called the *Sports Rapp Line* every night. His bills had to be over $100 per month. Either his folks were filthy rich and didn't care, or he was doing this without his parents' knowledge. We asked him every day just to protect ourselves.

When we had the big name guests on, the "boo beeps" would fill the lines to capacity, but the revenue from one hour of full activity was not enough to offset the advertising costs. *The Sports Rapp Line* soon became history. The sex lines were much more lucrative for Telecontractor of New York. It was a fun little gig, and it was a rehearsal at doing exactly what I do now with my radio show—booking guests, promoting, and interviewing. Mike went on to have a successful career in the telephone business, working at AT&T.

I continued to interview at, and collect rejection letters from Phoenix-area radio stations. When pressed, some of them would tell me that they didn't believe somebody in a wheelchair could do an adequate job of hitting the streets.

"You've gotta be able to get in and out of your car 10 to 15 times every day in this heat. You've gotta work hard to get the business. I don't think you would have the energy for this line of work," said one sales manager. In the lobbies of the stations, I would run into people who had graduated with me whom I had supervised at the campus station. They were getting hired. I wasn't getting a serious chance. I started to look outside radio for a job that would at least get me some sales experience.

Finally, I accepted an inside sales representative position with Statcom Communications, selling pagers and earning $15,000 per year. After getting doors closed in my face from radio station sales managers, I was excited when Sandy Shipp offered me the job, right around the time I had moved to Superstition Springs.

My social life was active, with many of my friends from college still hanging around or not having graduated yet. Yet I was glad to be a few miles away from the campus, because getting into stuff that was no good was too easy living in "Sin City," as we called apartment neighborhood east of the ASU campus. Now it was time for me to get serious about making a career. I was still somewhat active in the fraternity, which was the focal point of my social life. I had no woman and no prospects, but with the new job, the new house and the van on the horizon, I wasn't too worried about that. I was eager to make some positive changes in my life.

At Statcom, we sold pagers and cellular phones. I would go through the phone book and make cold calls to the usual suspects who needed pagers—landscapers, tow services, locksmiths, construction people. Usually, it was a matter of finding out how much they were paying for their current pagers and seeing if I could convert them with price. Or sometimes, a customer would have had a bad experience with PageNet, our biggest competitor, and I'd talk them into coming over to us.

When I got an order, I'd fill out the paperwork, get a pager from the supply room, and activate the customer's account. I'd polish up the pager if it was a used one. I'd put on a new Statcom label and take the order up front when the customer arrived. I imagine I shook hands lots of drug dealers, prostitutes and gang bangers as well as doctors, landscapers, locksmiths and all kinds of other people. A pager was not something everybody carried back then.

I worked in a little pink room with no windows, sharing an office with a lady named Judy. She made working at Statcom tolerable for the nine months or so I was there because of her personality and her incredible sense of humor. I don't really remember what we laughed so hard about so often, but it usually involved sexual jokes. Judy had a great sense of humor and very funny laugh.

One of my friends at the time was a fraternity brother named Dennis Roberts. Dennis was a country boy from Oklahoma who was a wrestler at ASU until he got into a motorcycle accident, which ended his wrestling career. Dennis helped me out a lot at the time. He would pick me up in the morning, saving me money that I would have had to pay a wheelchair transportation service to get me to work. So I'd leave the power chair at the office Monday through Thursday nights, and use Dennis to get to work. On Fridays, I'd hire the van people to bring me home, so I could get around in my power chair over the weekend. It all worked out pretty well. On weekends, I'd get together with Dennis and Terrence Kennel and perhaps a few of our female friends, and we'd barbecue at my complex, go swimming in the pool, or hit the Jacuzzi.

As the extreme Phoenix heat started to show signs of fading in the Fall of 1987, the search began for a home to buy. We decided on a single-family home near the Foothills in the Pecos North subdivision. It was a gated community, featuring a swimming pool located directly across the street from the house. The layout of the house worked fine. It featured a two-car garage, a large living room/dining room area with vaulted ceilings, two full bathrooms, and three bedrooms. Pecos North was a new subdivision and there were only two streets of completed homes at the time. Since we believed that this area would grow fast, we anticipated making a huge profit off of this home. But I didn't care about that. I was just excited to be moving into a brand new house.

The deal was that my parents would put a sizeable amount down, and I would make the mortgage payment. We agreed that I would get a roommate, or roommates to offset the costs.

When I moved in, I didn't have anything; No furniture, no personal belongings other than a little stereo and a television. One evening in October, Dennis drove me to the house for the first time. I gave him the key and he went through the front door to get the garage door open before taking my manual chair out of his trunk and helping me get into it. My power chair was at work. He walked around the sidewalk leading up to the home and turned on some lights. Then he returned, shaking his head as he walked.

"*What*?"

"You ain't ready for this, Smitty."

"What you mean?"

"You just ain't READY for this house, dog! What you gon' do with all that house?"

I slept on the floor in a sleeping bag that night. The next afternoon, the builder sent some construction people over to lay cement ramps leading to the front door, the door leading from the garage, and the door leading out to the back patio. He also drilled a peephole into the front door at a height where I could see out. That weekend, I went to Sears and bought a cheap couch and loveseat combination that was also a foldout bed. I also bought a bedroom set, including a double bed, a dresser and chest of drawers. I also bought a refrigerator, a washer and dryer and some kitchen stuff like plates, pots and pans. Over the course of the next several weeks, I bought some artwork to hang on the walls. I had my little ceramic bulldog in the corner, offsetting the room nicely. This was home.

It was an exciting time, living in my own house. But there were two things missing: A vehicle and a woman.

~

CHAPTER 11

A Woman, A Vehicle, and a Break

I DON'T EXACTLY REMEMBER where I met Daina Devereaux, but I remember our first date. About two years before I moved into the house in Ahwatukee, I was living at Cortez apartments in "Sin City," on the outskirts of ASU off Rural Road. My frat brother Archie Gettis was a concert promoter who had landed a gig with Wynton Marsalis at an upscale jazz club in Phoenix. Since Archie was one of my best friends, I would have VIP access to this show.

Daina was the perfect girl to take to an event like this. She was sophisticated, articulate, and very attractive. She was a good conversationalist with a great sense of humor. She had style. She knew how to dress and what to say to make a great impression. And she had a level of sensitivity that seemed to connect to me; the way she held my hand and looked into my eyes seemed very sincere and real. We had a great time at the concert and on other dates. Once, we went to a Kenny G concert and at one point, Kenny took his saxophone into the crowd, spotted us together and positioned himself right behind us with the bell of his sax right next to both of our ears. He stayed for about a minute, wailing his sax loudly into our ears, serenading us as we stared at each other smiling. When he was done, he screamed, "yeah!" patting me on the back before moving on.

Daina and I remained close friends who occasionally kissed over the next couple of years. She by far controlled my emotions more than any woman ever had to this point. At times, I felt like I was in love, only to be disappointed by a word or a gesture from her, such as going on a date with my roommate Terrance, or refusing my effort at intimacy. Comparing notes with Terrence, we discovered that she treated us similarly, and we crowned her with a new nickname: "The Queen of Jive." For the culturally challenged, "jive" is a verb meaning, "to cajole or mislead."

When I moved into my home in Ahwatukee, it had been a while since I had heard from Daina. I don't exactly remember how we met up again. She just sort of appeared back in my life. She told me she was pregnant and not happy with her current living situation. I offered to let her stay with me for very low rent. It seemed like a wonderful idea. Here was a woman I had always admired. Granted, she was pregnant with another man's baby, but she was a friend in need. At least I wouldn't be alone. And who knows what would happen between us as far as a possible relationship?

When Daina moved in, she brought her style to the décor of the home. She lined the shelving along the vaulted ceilings with antique books, for example, and added many other inexpensive, yet aesthetic improvements to the home. We would lie on the couch and watch movies. She would do all the laundry and put my clothes away, cook the meals and engage me in great conversation. Daina and I were playing "house," albeit platonically. From my perspective, as her belly grew, sex with the Queen was not an important issue. I wondered what would happen after the baby was born and imagined scenarios in which I might become a father figure. But those thoughts were often offset by erratic behavior and moodiness that I attributed to a combination of her pregnancy and her "royalty."

The vehicle was on order and extremely delayed. Several months earlier, I had decided to go with a local modifier in Phoenix called Care Concepts. I had heard some good things about them and their relatively new design, taking a Dodge mini-van frame, cutting the entire floor out of the vehicle and lowering it about eight inches. Then they attach a ramp that folds out from the inside of the van to allow the wheelchair user to roll into the vehicle. I think this concept first appeared about 1986, so it hadn't been around very long.

I was so excited to be finally making this move in my life. I wanted to watch costs, so I didn't get a fully loaded Caravan. Instead, I chose a Dodge Ram mini-van, which saved me a few grand. It was a basic van, so everything extra was done "after market," including heating and air conditioning, stereo, power windows, and even the side panel windows. I had known how to drive since high school driver's ed classes, but the two things limiting me were my lack of physical strength to turn the steering wheel quickly and with force and my inability to hold my head up to look over my shoulder to check other traffic. Also, being able to drive a normal car would have done me no good because I wouldn't have been able to get my wheelchair in and out. So a modified van was the only alternative. The costs were high for a new modified van, and I couldn't have afforded to buy even a cheap used one when I was in college. I lobbied for it with my father throughout the four years I was in school, to no avail. He later revealed to me the reason for his foot dragging. He didn't want me to get killed in a car accident while out partying.

I chose a white van with a silver interior. I was told that the van was going to be made at their New Mexico plant, so I never actually saw the vehicle they chose. I ordered a six-way swivel seat, which is an electronic driver's seat that swivels to the right, moves up and down, as well as forward and backward. The process of getting in the van would be to back my chair up the ramp, transfer to the swivel seat and position myself behind the wheel. I also ordered "zero effort steering." This spin-off technology from the lunar land rover allows me and thousands of other disabled drivers to turn the steering wheel quickly and easily with very little force. In August, I made a $5,000 down payment and they told me the van would be ready in six-to-eight weeks.

In October, I started calling to find out what was going on, and kept getting promised that the van would be ready soon. It got to be quite frustrating. One day, I was in the office at Statcom, and Judy walked in.

"Greg, your van is here!"

"What? You're kidding! Where?" I turned around, excited about the possibility that they hadn't told me they would deliver it to me at work, but not surprised by their lack of communication.

"It's right here!" she said holding out a little Matchbox van.

"Not funny," I muttered, and put the Matchbox van on top of my computer.

October and November passed. December was getting old. I probably called them every week to find out what the hell was going on with my van. Finally, on December 24, 1987, the day arrived. After work, Sandy Shipp, my boss, volunteered to drive me over to Care Concepts. I was so excited about this life-changing event. She dropped me off and before long, I was alone behind the wheel for the very first time in my life.

Care Concepts offices were on 35th Avenue, on the complete opposite end of town from my home. By the time all of the paperwork was signed and I had been through my orientation with the vehicle, it was post-rush hour. I drove my wheelchair into the vehicle, climbed into the six-way swivel seat, and pressed the appropriate switches to get myself positioned properly in front of the steering wheel. It felt a little awkward. The back of the seat seemed too low to support my head comfortably. I could see out the front of the vehicle, but I was looking down at the road through the bottom of my glasses. We agreed that a pillow would serve as a temporary solution, and they would order a seat with a higher back. The van was parked inside the Care Concepts garage, so my first maneuver was to back it out, down a steep ramp. Soon, I was doing 65 miles per hour down Interstate 17, flying past construction barriers inches away.

Alone in my vehicle, I felt a strange combination of fear and triumph. I had never driven anywhere alone before. This was a significant moment of accomplishment and I didn't want to screw it up by having an accident. I immediately developed a sense of respect for the vehicle and its ability to end my life at any second. I carefully and proudly guided the van down I-17, connected to Interstate-10 East, and exited at Chandler Boulevard. I didn't turn the radio on the whole way. I didn't know how to reach it and didn't want to take my eyes off the road. Instead, I sang Christmas carols.

When I arrived home, Daina emerged from the garage door with a wide smile. I carefully guided the van into the garage, turned the engine off, and lowered the ramp. Finally, it was here. The next day was Christmas. When I rose, I didn't go immediately to the Christmas tree. I went to the garage, just to look at my shiny new van and

101

memorize every curve of its shape. I enhanced the beauty of the vehicle in my mind, and pretended not to notice the many signs of shoddy workmanship. There would be plenty of time for that later. For now, I just appreciated the fact that I had a way to go anywhere I wanted in the world—with my vehicle, my power chair, and my freedom.

The next night, we went to my office Christmas party. The following Monday at work, lots of questions were thrown my way about that incredible girl I brought to the party. Nobody asked if she was pregnant with my baby, so I volunteered that she was my roommate and I was not the father of her child. I think Daina started to pick up that people were making assumptions about us, and that bothered her. I confronted her with questions about the source of her frustration. If it were my child, would she be ashamed? She moved out before the friendship was damaged beyond repair, or so I thought, but since that day, I have never seen nor heard from her. I recently found her name and a phone number for her employer on an Internet search engine, but I haven't called.

I soon interviewed for roommates at the request of my father, who thought it only logical for me to get some help paying the $600 mortgage, not to mention the $500 monthly car payment. My $18,000 salary (I had received a raise) was not enough to meet my expenses, so I soon understood his sense of urgency. But after several weeks of searching, I couldn't find anybody I could see myself rooming with. Besides, I had higher aspirations for myself than my father had for me. I was going to get a job in radio that paid at least $30,000 per year, which would enable me to afford the mortgage payments, car payments and all the other bills necessary to live independently. So I focused more on the job search than the roommate search.

With the ability to get around independently, I had overcome the primary reason why every radio station in town had denied my desire for a sales representative position.. I scheduled interviews during lunch breaks or late in the afternoons after work. I updated my resume to include my sales experience and independent reliable transportation. I interviewed at KOOL-FM, the oldies station; KFYI and Power 92, the talk and contemporary stations; KZZP, the Top 40 station, KTAR, the news/talk station, and on and on and on. People were polite, professional, and persistent in the presentation of possibilities that someday they may have a position for me. They would keep my resume on file. They admired my courage and perseverance. They had a cousin, a nephew, or an uncle who uses a wheelchair. Did they mind if I showed them my van?

But no jobs.

Socially, Omega Psi Phi was still the center of my life. I was involved in the graduate chapter and attended meetings where I was able to remain in touch with guys like Sterling Bridges, James Scott, Melvin Patrick, Craig Swain and others. Melvin, whom we called "Muscle Dog" because of his size and physique, called me one day after work.

"Whas up Smitty ditty?"

You, Muscle Dog!"

"Hey I ran into yo' girl the other day on the bus. You want her number?"

Melvin was referring to Terri Nealy. I had met Terri in 1985. She was a lady that my fraternity brother, Sterling Bridges had introduced me to. She had been through some tough times, recently ending a relationship with a guy who had been taking care of her. She didn't have any place to live, and Sterling had given her all the time at his place that he could afford. He introduced us by first telling each of us a lot about the other.

"What does she look like, Sterling?"

"Well I'll tell you the truth, Greg. If you saw her, you would want her."

"So when are you bringing her by?"

So one Saturday, he came over to my studio apartment and she stepped through the door. He was right. She was tall and slim. She had a nice tight figure. She was dark and lovely and she had potential, although she didn't have on very much makeup, if any. I could tell that she would be very beautiful if she were dressed right and made up right. When she opened her mouth, I detected a strong southern accent and poor English. She was much different from the college girls I had been chasing around Arizona State. She only stayed for a short time and as she was leaving, I told her, "If there's anything I can do for you, just let me know."

Terri called me a day or so later and asked if she could stay with me for a while. A few days later, she was residing in my apartment. She was studying medical assisting at Apollo College in Phoenix, so we both attended classes during the day. Sometimes, I would come home from class and she'd be sitting on the ramp in front of my apartment waiting for me. She would try to fix something that resembled dinner, although she couldn't really cook. She helped me clean up my apartment, did my laundry and kept me company, all in exchange for free rent. Eventually, sex came into the picture.

We would get into little arguments and she would move out, only to come back a few weeks later. She was the kind of girl I couldn't take around my friends, because she said and did weird things, but she was fine for having around the apartment. Once, I took her to the movies. I went to get popcorn and left her in the theatre. The line was long and it took a little longer than I had expected. She came running out of the theater and found me in line. She said she was scared to sit in the theater by herself.

Another time, when my father was visiting, she came over to my apartment with a big, open bruise on her leg. She said she got it from jumping out of a car. It was a nasty cut and she walked with a severe limp. I didn't want to ask a lot of questions about what she was doing when she wasn't with me. I didn't really care either. I lost track of her. I graduated. Right around graduation time, she called and told me that she was home in New Orleans and wished me a happy graduation. Several months later, when I was living in a two-bedroom apartment with Terrence, she called me and informed me that she was incarcerated. I felt bad about that and spent some time on the phone with her a couple of times when she again called from jail. Then I heard nothing until Melvin's call at work.

Terri was delighted to hear from me, and accepted my invitation to come visit me in my new home. I had seriously moved up in the world since I last saw her. Instead of living in a roach-infested apartment, I was in a new $100,000 home, with a new car and a paying job. She was living with friends and had just moved out from a relationship with a guy who had hit her.

Shortly after she arrived at my home, we engaged in a sexual marathon that lasted the entire weekend. We discovered new ways of doing things; for me, literal "Ahaa" moments where I realized how wonderful sex can be. The following Monday, I drove her to North Phoenix to pick up all her stuff and move in with me.

Terri was much different than Daina. She spoke with a combination of New Orleans drawl and black dialect that was often difficult for me to understand. She often had strange reactions to situations I knew were red flags, but I was willing to compromise. Up to this point in my life, I had never had a real sex partner. I had never had a woman who loved me and wanted to be with me. Sure, she was much unpolished, but she was physically there. What had started as a short-term fling soon evolved into thoughts of a possible future with this woman. Several reasons led me to thinking this way. First, she had an incredible body. She looked much better than the college girls who had blown me off during my four years at ASU. My damaged self-esteem and limiting beliefs told me that this might be the only chance I would ever get to be able to have sex with a body like that in my entire life. Second, in this relationship, she had a lot of respect and admiration for me. She looked up to me and saw me as the man. This I found to be very rewarding.

I soon learned that it came with a cost. She had a sensitive side that if violated, would result in a violent reaction. If she felt disrespected or ignored, she would respond with rage and throw things across the room. She would smash and break things and cause destruction. Once, she found a stack of Playboy magazines in my bathroom. She responded by destroying the living room. But after these episodes, the make-up sex was a powerful force that kept me from ridding my life of her.

The next day brought an exciting new beginning. As I reversed my van out of the garage and headed to work, I was clearly aware that I'm en route to a job I am rapidly growing to despise. When I got to work, I began the tedious process of making phone calls to hospitals, doctor's offices, locksmiths, towing companies, and anybody else whose job required a pager. Between my outgoing calls, a call came in!

"Greg Smith."

"Greg Smith, it's Jim Taszarek at KTAR. Can you talk?"

"Yes Sir."

"Ok, knock of the "Sir" shit. I got your letter and talked to Kirk about you and I'm very impressed with your style. I think we might have something that you might be interested in. How do you get around town?"

"I drive."

"OK great. Can you come down here again, say Monday, January 11?"

"Sure."

"OK Kiddo."

I sold more pagers that afternoon than at any time in my short career at Stacom. Finally, something positive in radio became a real possibility. And it was with the top station in town!

Being with Terri was a slow immersion into a lonely world that consisted of just the two of us. Friendships seemed to fade. We created our home and the outside world seemed to darken around it. But we didn't care. Terri had replaced Daina as my couch lying, movie watching buddy, my cook, my companion—except Terri would shower with me. Terri would sleep with me. And she believed in me and urged me to move forward towards my goals.

I talked to Judy about her at work.

"Her name is Terri. She's a tall slender black chick with a really nice body. But she's kind of untamed. She doesn't really know how to carry herself. When you meet her, you'll know what I mean."

"Do you love her?"

"No way. I'm just in it for the sex. But I think that I can work with her and teach her some things and maybe, since Miss Right won't consider me as an option, I can create my own Miss Right. Maybe I can mold her into what I want her to be."

"Awww that's cute. Kinda like 'My Fair Lady.'"

"Whatever."

I pulled Sterling aside at a frat meeting.

"Dog, Terri is living at my crib now and I'm thinking about having her stay and live with me for a long time. Do you think I'm making a mistake digging in with a girl like that?"

"She's a very beautiful girl," he responded. "There'd be no shame in that. Enjoy it man."

With the new clothes and the makeup I had purchased for her, I began to feel very comfortable with her appearance. But as soon as she opened her mouth, she revealed how naïve and silly she was. Her grammar was atrocious. I really couldn't put my finger on it, but I suspected that she might have had a mental illness. Maybe, I thought, it was just a matter of a lack of education. I tried to help her early in the relationship. She had a book that she had purchased to prepare for her GED. She had not completed high school, but was taking college classes at a medical assisting school, using her twin brother's high school diploma to gain entry. Her brother's name is Terry. Close enough, I guess. I learned quite early on that Terri didn't know how to read properly. She read by remembering how words looked instead of understanding phonics. I thought if she learned phonics, it would really open up her ability to read and comprehend, so we sat at the kitchen table and we began.

YOUNG TERRI—My then wife, Terri, was the most beautiful woman I knew and I felt very priviledged to be with her early in our relationship. Here she is at "Granny's" house in Brookhaven, Mississippi.

"What's that letter?"

"*A.*"

"And the sounds it makes?"

"What 'chu mean?"

"The *A* makes the sound aaaah or ayyyy. Say aaaaah…"

"What you talkin' bout ' say aaaaah. You think I'm stupid or something? I know what *A* is mother fucker."

"Well, I'm just trying to help you understand the code of phonics. You'd have a much easier time if you understood this. Let's try *B*. The *B* makes the *buhh* sound. Say *buhh*."

"Greg, I don't wanna do this. I read like I read, ok? I don't need you talkin' *down* at me, treatin' me like I'm a buffoon or something."

"I'm not trying to talk down to you. I'm trying to help you understand something you don't understand. Don't you want to grow?"

She slammed the book down on the floor and started cursing and pointing her finger. "You think you so smart 'cause you went to college! Well look here. I went to college too. College in the streets! And I don't need no mother fucker like you talkin' down at me!"

"Well shit, you just wanna stay like you are? You don't want to grow? Learning is a life-long process. If you think you know everything already and don't want to take on new knowledge, you are pretty much stuck where you are. You'll never get ahead."

"How you gon' say I'll never get ahead? I'mo get mine! I got what I got without you and I'mo get what I get just like I been gett'n!!!" She knocked the kitchen chair over on the floor and proceeded to take everything off the table and throw it against the wall. A plate shattered. Silverware left marks in the sheet rock. A glass shattered. The phone rang. It was Sterling.

"Hello? Hey Sterling, whas up man? … This bitch goin' crazy over here, that's all."

"Who you callin' *bitch*?" She ripped the silverware drawer out of its track and it splintered on the floor with forks, knives and spoons everywhere. She broke a plant vase and then headed dangerously close to my old cheap stereo.

"DON'T FUCK WITH MY STEREO!!!"

She didn't. Thank God for my commanding voice. She disappeared into the back room for a minute, yelling and cursing at me while I talked to Sterling, loud enough for her to hear me.

"Man, this girl ain't gon' work out. I need somebody with more confidence in herself to accept a little guidance and education. This girl won't even let me teach her anything without getting all crazy."

"You think you SO FUCKIN SMART!!!" she screamed and stormed over to the microwave oven, grabbing it and holding it as if to slam it down.

"DON'T YOU THROW THAT MICROWAVE!!!!"

Again, she didn't. Sterling laughed on the phone about the microwave, and I had to smile at the situation. She stormed into the family room quicker than I could turn around and see where she was headed. Before I could flip my wheelchair around, I heard a shattering sound. My beautiful ceramic dog, the symbol of my fraternal brotherhood, the focal point of my family room was shattered on the carpet. That was it.

"Get your shit. You're out of here!"

"Fine."

She grabbed two bags of stuff. One had all the new clothes and things I had bought for her and the other had all her stuff, just crammed into a bag. Terri never folded anything. She just crammed things into drawers, suitcases, whatever. That's one thing that never changed about her. I got in the van and waited for her. I was polite enough to take her anywhere she wanted to go. I offered to take her back to her friend's house where she had been staying. I didn't really know where she wanted to go, but I just knew that this wasn't going to work. I was still very pissed about the ceramic dog. Her directions landed us on Van Buren Street, in an area where I wouldn't have wanted to be out of my car. She told me to turn down an alley behind a trashy bar. Then she violently opened the door of the van, took all the clothes I had bought her and one piece at a time hurled them up into a garbage dumpster.

"I'mo show you how much I need YOUR shit. I don't NEED your shit. Good BYE!!!" With that, she threw ALL her bags into the dumpster, slammed the door and walked down the alley. I followed her around the building and watched her walk into the bar. I drove down Van Buren and headed home, but something made me turn around and go back. I actually worried about her, and wondered why she had thrown all her stuff away. Was she going to commit suicide? I guess I cared. I turned around and circled the block a few times. On the third pass around the block, I saw her walking briskly out of the bar and down the street.

"Where you goin'?" She didn't respond. "Where you GOIN'?" I yelled louder. She stopped, walked to the van, opened the door and got in. We didn't speak at all. I drove to the alley where she had dumped her clothes but the dumpster was too high and she couldn't get them. We drove south towards Tucson for miles, just to cool down and take in the desert view. When we finally returned home, we went straight into the bedroom and took our sexuality to a new level. When I woke up the next morning, all the mess from her tirade the day before was cleaned up and it was just a new day. It was the beginning of a vicious cycle.

We were both in too much need for the other to let go of the situation. I had been mentally abused by women so much in my young adult life; told things like "I'm looking for Mr. Right, and he's not in a wheelchair... or "You mean you and ME? Ha ha ha!" Those were crushing blows to my self-confidence and I believed at the time that there would be no woman for me, particularly one as attractive as Terri. To let this woman leave my life would be stupid. I had tried so hard for so many years to meet someone and have a relationship. It never happened; not even close. I thought, "I should be grateful for what I have here and be patient with her." From her perspective, I think being in that bar on Van Buren may have reminded her of some things in her past that she didn't want to go back to. To compare that stench to the nice suburban environment of Ahwatukee and a smart, handsome and stable young man like me was a no-brainer. We were stuck together out of necessity, and drawn together out of attraction. We were welded together, like it or not.

At work, Sandy came to my desk with a brochure for a telemarketing conference in Long Beach, California. There were several workshops she wanted me to attend and asked if I would be interested in going. Without hesitation, I said "yes", looking forward to my first road trip in my new van.

It was on that trip that I first developed feelings of love for Terri. We parked on the beach and made love. We shared romantic moments despite some travel inconveniences, like my wheelchair breaking down. We went to Disneyland and rode Space Mountain, during which one of my contact lenses popped out and I had no replacement. Nearly blind in one eye, I maneuvered through Los Angeles freeway traffic safely en route to visit my aunt Jacque and her family on Sunday before heading back to Phoenix the same day.

I was tired and gave some thought to spending the night at Jacque's and leaving the next day. I had that second interview with KTAR set for Monday. To me— at that time, on that couch—it was no big deal. I had lots of interviews with lots of radio stations, so what would be different about this one? I made the decision to spend the night with Jacque, reschedule the interview, and get up the next day rested for the drive back to Phoenix.

"We need to get back," said Terri. "You don't want to miss out on this interview with KTAR. This is the first station that's called you back for another interview. Let's go." It was January 10, 1988.

AN EXCITING RIDE—Terri and I in 1995, after our first separation, enjoying a romantic reunion which included a helicopter ride in Sedona, Arizona.

111

CHAPTER 12

"I Got the Job!"

THERE WERE NO WHEELCHAIR ACCESSIBLE PARKING spaces at the KTAR building on the corner of Third Avenue and Osborn amidst the northern cluster of high-rises around Central Avenue in uptown Phoenix. St. Joseph's hospital, where I was supposed to have been going to MDA Clinic all these years, was a few blocks to the south. Park Central Mall was right across the street. Monday, January 11, 1988 was a bright yet brisk day in the metropolis. I was feeling nervous, yet confident as I climbed from the driver's seat into my wheelchair. I had parked diagonally, taking up two spaces to avoid being trapped out of my vehicle by another car that might park beside me. As I lowered the ramp, the city sounds of traffic blended with birds chirping under the morning sun. My slippery dress shoe glided awkwardly across the joystick of my power chair and caused me to pay close attention to my control of the chair. I normally wore more casual shoes to work, but for this interview, I wanted to look my best. I appeared formal and professional in my suit and conservative red tie.

As I neared the front door, I passed two white vans with sophisticated antennas and towers painted red and blue with the words "KTAR 620 AM—News Talk Radio."

I grabbed the vertical metal handle on the heavy glass door and pulled my joystick backwards. As I moved, my grip slipped. It was too heavy. People inside the ground floor lobby seemed to race to the door to open it for me, allowing me entrance into the dark and air conditioning-chilled building. I adjusted my tie in the mirror as I awaited the elevator along with several other people. When it arrived, I asked that somebody hit button 4.

As the elevator door opened and I rolled out, I was immediately greeted by a strikingly attractive young receptionist named Marianne, to whom I announced that I was here to see Paddy Ramsay, KTAR's Director of Sales. After a short wait, Paddy emerged from a narrow hallway leading to the offices and guided me through a security door, at which point she paused to punch in a code that allowed us access. Soon we were seated in the KTAR conference room.

In the conference room, Paddy pulled a chair away from the long wooden table and gestured for me to park. She began by handing me a couple of Arbitron Radio Market Reports from 1987 and a Media Audit Phoenix Radio Report. I had studied these books during my senior year of college in a grueling class called Media Planning and Buying. From that class, I knew that "cume" meant the total number of listeners a radio station reached in one week, and that "average quarter hour" meant the total number of people tuned to a given station for at least five minutes during a fifteen-minute period. But I had never seen or held an actual Arbitron report in my hand.

"We need somebody to help us out in a sales support position," said Paddy. "But I don't want you to think of it as a secretarial position. We need somebody to take these books and look for positive information about our radio audiences, and develop materials that our sales people can use when they are out selling our radio station to advertisers."

"You mean like a media kit?" I asked, demonstrating my limited knowledge of the lingo.

"Well, in a sense, yes. I want you to take these books home with you and study them, and in a week or so, come back to me with a presentation of some of the things you would stress to help us sell advertising."

As I pondered this, a giant figure stormed into the room.

"Hi Greg, I'm Taz. Have you ever seen one of these books before?" he asked, tapping his large index finger on the Arbitron.

"Well, I had a class at ASU called Media Planning and Buying, and we studied this," I replied, adding a layer or two of bullshit about how I led my group to develop a plan that included a national radio "buy," and that we evaluated Arbitron ratings to determine cost-per point.

"Well let's see what you can do with these. Why don't you come back here in, let's say, two weeks and show me what ya got?"

Great, I thought. I show up expecting them to offer me a job and instead I get homework.

Back in the van, I couldn't wait to start absorbing the Arbitron. I sat in the car right there and started to gain a familiarity with its structure. It was broken down into "dayparts." The first category was "Monday through Sunday 6AM to Midnight." This was the overall ratings area of the book that took into account all of the week's audience. Down the left side column was an alphabetical listing of the stations. Across the top were the demos, or age groups. On the first few pages were the "cumes" (cumulative audience) of each of the stations in that daypart. On the next few pages were the Average Quarter Hour (AQH) listeners. The book was a series of tables with numbers. Finding positive stories was a matter of looking at the numbers and ranking the station against the competition in the various categories. The Arbitron report consisted of over 150 pages of tables, each number representing a station's audience in a particular daypart. It was really quite simple.

Finding positive sales stories to tell about KTAR was easy. Finding categories where the station was ranked number one was more of a challenge. KTAR dominated every other station in the market except one: KNIX, the country station. KNIX kicked KTAR's ass in every single daypart; every single category, it seemed. But upon further careful review, I was able to highlight some areas that KTAR actually won. KTAR edged KNIX in Adults 35+ Middays and in all of the older demographics, such as 35-64 and 65+. Over the next week, I studied this book all the time—at the kitchen table, in the bathroom, in the car while waiting for Terri to get off her job as a housekeeper at a hotel. I even sneaked it to work and looked at it in my spare time at Statcom.

I also did one more resourceful thing. I visited a media buyer—the kind of person to whom I would present the material. They gave me some sample materials that radio stations had given to them. I noticed that much of it was just graphs, charts, and words printed on white paper. The information was good, but it wasn't presented in a manner that communicated value.

Finally, after about a week, I had gathered the material that most positively put KTAR in a good position to sell. How would I convey that information? How would I put together a presentation that looked good? I wanted to go back there with at least a mock sales brochure that would be presentable to clients! I didn't want to go to Kinko's and do Microsoft chart graphs on white paper. I wanted to "wow" them and make it a "no brainer" to hire me and pay me what I'm worth.

I went to the College of Art at ASU and asked for a student who would like to make some extra income. I visited her at her apartment and gave her all of the material, my deadline and my urgent appeal. I asked her how much she would charge me to design a good looking book with three-dimensional aspects, a different shape and size than 8-1/2 by 11, and used color effectively to communicate its message. I gave specific instructions for certain things, and left her imagination open for others.

One of the things I requested was to have my resume in a pocket in the back of the book, along with an illustration of a KTAR business card with the name "Greg Smith, Research and Sales Promotion Director," surrounded by a cloud to suggest imagining this as a reality. My finished project was a summary of dayparts, with graphs and charts that had texture, graphics that connected with the theme of each daypart, and carefully written copy about the various programs, hosts and talent. It included pictures of the talent as well. It was a truly smashing presentation, and it was obvious that I had spent a lot of time on it.

Two weeks after that second interview, I rolled into the KTAR offices, confident that I was about to be hired. In the conference room, I handed Paddy my book with a reserved smile. She was silent. She flipped through it carefully, slowly. I held my breath. I actually couldn't read her. She excused herself for about five minutes and returned empty-handed, but smiling.

"Greg, it is amazing. Outstanding! Wow."

As she was talking, Taz entered the room.

"*How* did you do this?" he demanded.

I chuckled and started to answer his question when he interrupted again in a much more friendly tone.

"How did you do the *graphics*?"

I was starting to learn how to deal with him. Short quick answers and then shut up.

"An ASU art student I hired," I said.

"Ahhhhhh?"

He slowly flipped through the pages and found the business card in the back. He held it up and chuckled.

"There's a *TYPO!*" he shouted suddenly.

My heart skipped and my jaw dropped.

"Just kiddin'! Get Kirk in here," he ordered Paddy.

Soon the tall, athletic Kirk Nelson entered the conference room. Kirk, the local sales manager, was the guy who had given me my first interview at KTAR. It was after this first interview two months earlier that I was inspired to write a letter to management, asking them to look at my experience and qualifications more closely. I had some hesitation about going over Kirk's head directly to Taz, but I felt like I would never get a chance if I played by the unwritten rules. Kirk had been very friendly and polite in that interview. He was much more encouraging than many of the other sales managers at other stations. But the song ended in the same tone: "Radio sales is a tough business to get into. You have to have experience to work here. Go get a job with another station for a year and I'll be here waiting for you." Now, I shook his hand and was excited that we were in a position where we were skipping that year, it seemed.

"You want $100,000!!???" Taz yelled and then paused to gauge my response.

Before I could rid my face of what must have been a stupid look, he said, "How 'bout 30?"

"That would be acceptable."

For the next half hour, I listened as Taz told me about his vision for KTAR and "the sleeping giant down the hall," K-Lite 98.7FM. There was energy and chemistry here, the likes of which I had never experienced. Everyone was focused, task-oriented and motivated to go beyond the minimum for the station. There was a pride about working at KTAR, which was an institution in the Valley of the Sun. It was, after all, the home of Arizona State sports and the Phoenix Suns. It was the trusted radio source of news and information. It was the station people in Phoenix turned to in order to be informed and to express themselves on the talk shows

I was given the "ten-cent" tour to the sales offices, into the newsroom and the on-air studios, through the lobby and over to the K-Lite side of the building, which was quite a contrast from the bustling, KTAR side. I signed the proper paperwork and left the building that day as research and sales promotion director at Pulitzer Broadcasting's Phoenix properties, KTAR and K-Lite. I would start in a week.

"I got the job!!!"
Terri was giddy with excitement. I couldn't get off the phone that night because I was calling everyone I knew with the news that I had finally landed a real job in radio. I called my parents. I called my sister. I called my fraternity brothers. It was truly a time for celebration. I was very proud, not only to have landed a job in radio, but of landing one at such a prestigious station. I knew I would learn so much about radio. The atmosphere there was truly incredible and I was immediately passionate about my new job.

The next day, I couldn't wait to tell Sandy the news. I knew she would be disappointed that I was quitting, but excited for me. Her reaction was pleasant. She started walking down the halls from room to room announcing, "Greg is leaving us to take a job at KTAR." I think, in a way, she was glad I was leaving, because my heart had left that job a long time ago. Symbolically, I turned in my pager, gave Judy a hug goodbye, and bid farewell.

The commute from Chandler Boulevard and 44th Street to the uptown studios of KTAR was about 90 minutes during the height of rush hour. On the way in, I listened, of course, to KTAR's Arizona's

Morning News with Bill Heywood. The backup on the freeway began early and didn't let up for any extended period until I exited the freeway at 7th Avenue. From there, the congestion was due to signal light backups. My commute became a time to think, strategize and deal with the frustrations of sudden lane changes, people slamming on their brakes, and other irritating characteristics of Phoenix drivers. When I finally arrived, I made a right turn from 3rd Avenue down the steep dark ramp to the basement parking and around the lot towards the exit side of the same entrance. Just before the incline exit, I made a sharp left turn into my designated parking space, a slot right in front of the elevator. After letting my ramp down, I had to roll around a large white support beam to the back of my van to hold a switch, which enabled the ramp to rise and the door to close. I was dressed in business slacks, a shirt and tie, and my formal dress shoes, which made it difficult to drive my chair.

When the elevator doors opened, I greeted Marianne and rolled to the door to punch in the secret password. The doorknob was difficult for me to grasp, and the narrow hallway left no room for me to align myself for maximum leverage. To enter the station through that door would require assistance. I learned that the best door for me to open was across from the elevators leading to the snack room and the K-Lite studios. From there I could go around the K-Lite sales department into my office. But most mornings, as I rolled off the elevator, Marianne would rise and open the door for me with a smile.

I would share an office with Annette, who worked in the promotion department and also handled KTAR's co-op advertising. She had been at KTAR for a couple of years and was very welcoming, in addition to being strikingly gorgeous. She offered to help me become accustomed to the office culture in any way I needed and quickly confided in me about her own career and aspirations. She was my new Judy, only much better looking. The sports guys joked with me that I needed to get a couple of mirrors to put on my desk so I could admire her without turning my chair all the way around. She had an amazingly positive aura and helped make the workplace a pleasant place to be. She was always offering an encouraging word, and was always there to help me by proofing my work or telling me what she thought about copy I wrote or a graph or chart I made.

One of the many laughs Annette and I would share came on my first day, when a Macintosh SE was placed on my desk. This would be the machine from which I would work to produce graphs, charts and one-sheets. Annette got down on the floor with her head under my desk to plug it in while I pretended not to admire her curvaceous ass. But she knew. "You're getting a good show up there aren't you?" she joked. When she rose to her feet, we both looked at this computer and neither one of us knew how to turn it on! We spent ten minutes searching for a button or a switch, moving the mouse around and wondering whether it was broken before we finally found a little switch on the back. I would grow a lot in the coming months and years, from a person who couldn't even turn a computer on into a desktop publishing and graphic design talent.

On that first day, Ruth, Taz's executive assistant, came in distributing a memo. It was from Taz to all employees of both stations and it was about me. "For a long time, I've felt that KTAR/K-Lite's sales presentation materials needed a punch. I'm excited to announce that the man who will provide that punch is Greg Smith. "

Then, a new paragraph...

"One more thing. Greg was born with Muscular Dystrophy and gets around in an electric wheelchair. While the sight of a wheelchair in our hallways might seem awkward, please look past that. Wait 'til you see this guy's work. It's fantastic. Please stop by and say hi to Greg and welcome him to the Pulitzer family—Taz."

One morning during that first week, I was nearing my office when someone called my name from behind. When I spun the chair around, I lost my balance slightly and my weight shifted to my right foot. I was wearing those slippery dress shoes and my foot slipped onto the joystick of the chair! Suddenly I was spinning around and around in the middle of the hallway, completely out of control. Gail, the business manager had to jump away to avoid being hit. After about five top speed rotations, the chair slammed into the drywall of the hallway, making a thunderous noise and leaving a sizeable hole in the wall.

During the accident, I feared I would get hurt, but afterwards, that quickly turned into embarrassment and a little anxiety that they might see this as a hazard and a safety risk.

"Are you alright?"

"I'm fine."

"Are you sure?"

"Yes. Is everybody ok? This has never happened to me before," I said, and immediately remembered the time in high school, although I didn't correct my statement. I was afraid for my job. I had no idea how people might respond to something like that. I'm lucky nobody was injured.

It was forgotten immediately. I bought some new shoes with textured bottoms to ensure complete control of my chair. My work started to have impact. I made one-sheets (promotional pages) for both stations that featured sharp graphs and charts, and included unique clip art, station logos and crisp, clear copy. "The book" coming out was an exciting quarterly event. Arbitron issued the first electronic release of the book in 1988. The modem connections were antiquated, so it took forever for one page to come through. Just the same, the whole station would huddle around and wait for the numbers to screech out on the dot-matrix printer. Taz had the best view. The sales managers next. Every sales rep huddled closely behind. Since I was the "research director," I felt a responsibility to wheel myself in there next to Taz and stare at the ink as it stained the page, line after line. Looking back now, it seems so stupid! Everybody would see the numbers within a half-hour anyway, because Ruthie would copy and distribute them to all the managers. Maybe we just wanted to appear so involved in our jobs that we had to be the first to know

For me, the 24-hour period after the book was an all-nighter. For each station, I would make an initial "batch" of about 20 charts that presented the station's audience with numbers from the Arbitron and the Media Audit. The sales people ate them up and asked for more. They made requests for specific charts and I obliged. I became quite skilled at making one-sheets. Soon, this led to presentations. I was quickly given the responsibility of handling all of the printing jobs for both stations, including media kits, business cards, and promotional materials. I got a crash course in the printing process. I took competitive bids for print jobs and managed projects through to completion.

In that first book, KTAR got a "10 Share" which meant that ten percent of the radio audience was listening to us, which is a very good amount in a highly competitive market. We designed a direct mail campaign called "How to Get a 10 Share in Phoenix" which consisted of a series of pieces promoting our programming and talent, so popular in the Valley of the Sun. I designed them, wrote the copy and managed the production.

Presenting a concept to Taz became a skill I quickly mastered: Roll in there and check your ego at the door. Show him the work and don't talk too much. Take notes and watch as he scribbles all over your copy with his green Sharpie. And be ready to discuss how you feel about certain phrasing. Usually, Taz knew exactly what he wanted. He was a straight shooter, and very polite to me. I had heard horror stories about his anger and his temper, but he never showed this side to me in the five years I worked for him. He took me under his wing early on and pointed me in the direction of learning about the radio business.

For example, one day I was in his office going over some drafts. His administrative assistant, Ruthie reminded him that he had to go in about ten minutes to work on some KTAR television commercials. He was going to ride over there with Bob, KTAR's operations manager, because his Lincoln was in the shop. As they were leaving, I asked if I could meet them over there. "I've never seen television commercials being produced," I said.

The spots featured our morning news anchor, Bill Heywood smiling into the camera, sipping coffee and welcoming viewers to Arizona's Morning News. I watched as Taz decisively selected certain takes and rejected others. Bob had to leave for a meeting before the session was over. When it finally ended, Taz called Ruth on his cell phone. It seemed nobody was available to pick him up and bring him back to the station.

"I'm going back to the office," I volunteered. I knew that if I were "normal," he would have assumed he would ride back to the office with me. He was afraid to ride with me, but there was no avoiding it. It made too much sense. He watched as I held the switch down at the back of the van, which slowly opened the door and lowered the ramp. He stood outside the van observing as I backed the chair up the ramp and spun my body from the wheelchair to the six-way swivel seat. Still standing outside the van, Taz watched me spin the driver's seat around to a comfortable driving position, then lean over and hold the switch that raised the ramp and closed the door. This process took about five minutes. Finally, he sat down in the passenger seat and put his seat belt on. I could tell he was a little nervous, and I milked it. We turned onto a busy street.

"So, how long you been driving?"

"Oh, a couple of weeks," I said with a straight face, eyes mostly on the road, but occasionally darting in his direction to take in the sight of this large man, face beet red, holding on for dear life! I laughed.

"Actually, it's been about two months," I said.

"Oh, I feel *much* better," he laughed.

For the first two years at KTAR, I worked directly under Taz. I learned a lot about radio from him and the sales managers. They soon invited me to attend the department head meetings, where each manager would give a report about what was going on. The sales managers would talk about "percent sold out," projections for meeting their objectives for the month, sales training material, and the new sales person they hired. The program director would talk about what talk show topics were planned for the week. Engineering would discuss new equipment, broadcast antenna testing, upgrades to the news vehicles, or sometimes a button on a cart machine that needed to be replaced. I learned so much about operating a radio station from attending these meetings.

All the news wasn't good. Sometimes, people didn't live up to Taz's expectations and he had no hesitancy rolling heads. I saw several people get the ax during the first two years. The firing that most significantly affected my career was when he fired the promotion director. Taz decided that instead of hiring a new promotions director, he would hire a marketing person to handle more responsibilities, which included sales and audience promotion. I naively applied for the job, and Taz, ever the straight shooter, put me in my place. "I'm not hiring you for this job because you're not qualified for this job. The guy I want has years of experience."

Jack Nietzel had been the VP of Marketing for Circle K stores for many years. He also ran his own business called *Store Wars*, which specialized in marketing concepts for the convenience store industry. Well-connected in the Phoenix advertising community, he would be my new boss. They moved my office from the room I had shared with Annette to the former promotions director's corner office. To me, this was great! My own corner office with a window at one of the top news/talk radio stations in the country. I also got a raise and was now knocking down about $38,000 a year in salary, plus the ability to do freelance work.

I liked Jack. He was a workaholic. He would type long memos with concepts we needed to work on and strategies for getting the job done. What I didn't really like was the separation from Taz that I now had to get used to. Taz and Jack would develop the ideas, and I would implement the production and execution. We did some sophisticated stuff, like a high quality, quarterly newsletter called *The K-Lite Letter*. This direct mail piece featured ads that were given to radio sponsors as added value. The production values were very high. It had a large format, roughly 20 inches by 13, and the design of it was outside of my league. That's when Jack introduced me to his longtime friend, Chris Yaranoff who was simply one of the most talented graphic designers in the world.

Yaranoff Advertising was located directly across Park Central Mall on Central Avenue in a second floor office. Chris was a very tall, stout man with a scraggly gray beard. He smoked constantly. He dressed stylishly, always in solid colors. He had a very warm smile for me and there was something about his eyes that was passionate and magical. We quickly became great friends. I learned so much about graphic design from him and spent many hours in his office watching him work. He shared projects with me that he was doing for other clients, and supervised me as I handled the desktop publishing for *The K-Lite Letter*, and all of the other KTAR and K-Lite projects. Suddenly our work took on a much more artistic quality. I would automatically incorporate the lessons I learned from Chris into my work, and then I would learn more. The guy was a genius who communicated his knowledge and his "eye" to me through his rough Bulgarian accent.

I confided in Chris and shared KTAR gossip with him. We made fun of Taz together. We made fun of Jack together. We had lunch often. He came to my son's birthday party. I visited him at his home.

Taz liked Chris as well, but the one thing that irritated him was the time it sometimes took to move a project forward. Art cannot be rushed. The artist must ponder the problem and come up with the solution that works, and that inspiration sometimes takes time. Also, many aspects of graphic design are farmed out to subcontractors, so things don't happen overnight. Sometimes, Taz would force the issue on a project, which irritated Chris. However, Taz was usually right.

"We're not trying to paint the Sistine Chapel here," he would say. "We're tryin' to get a friggin' media kit done." Chris always tried to paint the Sistine Chapel. He was a talented man.

I LEARNED SO MUCH ABOUT MARKETING from Chris Yaranoff, Jack Nietzel and Jim Taszarek as their young apprentice at KTAR.

124

CHAPTER 13

Greg Jr.

ESPITE THE FACT THAT MY FRIENDSHIPS were fading, and regardless of the pleas from my parents to choose another mate, the love Terri and I shared made those sacrifices seem insignificant during the happy days of our decade together. Who needed a bunch of people hanging around when instead, she and I would lie around the house in our underwear, rent movies, and watch games, *Arsenio, In Living Color,* and *Def Comedy Jam,* sharing laughter and making love? We'd go to the movies. We'd go swimming at our subdivision's pool right across the street from our home. We'd go out to dinner. We would entertain company, neighbors or friends from the office, and they all loved her spicy shrimp salad. When they would leave, I would take pleasure in the fact that she had once earned a living in New Orleans as an exotic dancer, stage-named "Butterfly."

One thing I really loved about her companionship was that she was a big sports fan. She would sit and watch a whole ballgame with me, and her enthusiasm about sports made for a good environment. Through my perks at KTAR, we would regularly go to Suns games or ASU games.

When ASU played UCLA, we sat in the wheelchair section, right on the field on the edge of the South end zone. The wheelchair section at ballgames would often be a reunion with old friends we had come to know over the years. Tedde Scharf, the director of disabled student resources at ASU happened to be at the game. I hadn't seen her since graduating from college.

"How are your kids?" she asked.

Terri laughed. "Kids? We don't have any kids!"

"Oh, I thought you had three kids. Maybe I was thinking of someone else." Tedde turned red from embarrassment.

I don't think she was mistaken. I think Tedde has some kind of psychic insight. Maybe if she had said, "I thought you had *one* child," I would chalk it up as a fluke. But *three*? She knew something.

I married Terri because she wasn't feeling well and needed to see a doctor. She didn't have medical insurance, and my job offered great benefits. So on April 20, 1990, after living together for about a year and a half, we went to the justice of the peace in downtown Phoenix and filled out the paperwork. To me, it wasn't a big deal. I was just getting my significant other the health care that she needed. I didn't see it as having any major significance. There was no ceremony. There were no guests. There was no honeymoon. It was just paperwork. I don't even remember my wedding night.

I do remember the night Greg Jr. was conceived. Arizona State played Nebraska and we had end-zone wheelchair seats. We decided to make a weekend of it, so we booked a room at the Tempe Mission Palms hotel. Terri was looking exceptionally good that night as we walked down Mill Avenue, hand in hand. Guys were turning around to get a glance of her as we passed by. All this was a turn on to me.

"Damn baby, you need to get away from that crippled guy and get with me!" one drunk admirer commented loud enough for his intentional message to be effectively communicated. We laughed.

We window-shopped and eventually ended up in a lingerie store, where we made a few purchases before checking into the hotel. After about six hours, Greg Jr. was a living growing thing.

I'm not the kind of person who makes a big deal about milestones in my life. I don't have big birthday parties for myself, even for my milestone birthdays. When I turned 30, I went to a Suns game and chatted with Charles Barkley about how scary turning 30 had been for him. I didn't go to my high school prom. I haven't gone to any high school reunions. My marriage was a non-event. For my wedding anniversaries, I would get roses and wine and do intimate things with Terri, but I've never been big on self-celebrating.

Yet when I learned that I was going to be a father, I went crazy with excitement and celebration. The pregnancy was a magical time of self-discovery. I made sure Terri took her prenatal pills. I enrolled us in

Lamaze classes. We got the book, *What to Expect When You're Expecting* and followed the progress of Greg Jr's development every step of the way. I spoke to Greg Jr. a lot while he was "in the oven." And I was absolutely terrified that something might go wrong.

KTAR gave us a huge baby shower as the due date neared. We turned the guest bedroom into a nursery with a crib. I remember hearing his heartbeat for the first time and learning that it would indeed be a boy... Greg Jr. I was thrilled to have this knowledge. I bought a video camera. My mom flew down to be with us for the birth.

Terri's labor had to be induced because the baby was about two weeks late. I was her Lamaze coach and looking back at the videotape, I was a horrible one. Instead of encouraging her, I was yelling at her as if I was angry with her for being about to screw something up. "Push. Push! The head is out! Push!!!" I yelled with a scowl on my face.

I cut the umbilical cord and listened carefully for his first scream. He was beautiful. He weighed about eight pounds. He had a pinkish, yellowish color. His face was round perfection. When he was all dressed up and ready to go the next day, he looked like a Gerber baby in his blue suit and stocking cap. I remember being so self-conscious about my driving on the way home from the hospital to our house. I had precious cargo for the first time.

When we arrived, I was delighted to see that they had followed my orders. A vendor from KTAR had made good on his promise to install a 16-foot hot-air balloon in our front yard that would illuminate colorfully in the evening sky. The sign on the balloon said, "It's a Boy!" My son's birth was a promotable, celebrate-able, marketable event!

A few weeks later, another vendor, photographer Tom Gerzinzki took the pictures of our naked little baby that I used to create a birth announcement. I was so proud of my son.

HOW CUTE!—Greg Jr. was 20 inches and weighed 8 pounds. (Photo Credit: Tom Gerczynski)

~

CHAPTER 14

"On a Roll!"

IDEAS ARE VERY MUCH LIKE SPERM CELLS. They emerge energetically, eagerly seeking to reach a tangible existence. Like sperm cells, ideas flow, propelling themselves upstream against the odds, through a sea of random thoughts, distractions, fantasies, hopes, fears and dreams. When they reach the dead-ends of passive mindless trances, they reverse themselves undaunted, admirably committed to the realization of their purpose.

In order to survive, ideas seek a connection with the physical world. If that physical connection can be made, which is a very unlikely occurrence, an idea can be born into reality if given the right nourishment. Like individual sperm cells, very few of the ideas that flow through our minds ever reach their cherished goal: to experience the breath of life.

I learned this in the fall of 1991, when we were trying to conceive Greg. Jr. We had begun discussing the possibility of having kids about a year earlier. I figured that a child would give Terri the sense of purpose that seemed to elude her in her pursuit of a career in the medical profession. Furthermore, as my co-workers were having babies and proudly bringing them to the office, I envied the joy on their faces and the profound changes that parenthood brought to their lives. I wanted to be called "Dad."

Terri's doctor gave us a chart to monitor her ovulation. Back at the office, I pulled a manila file out of my desk drawer and grabbed a red Sharpie. On the label, I scribbled the following words:

"Greg Junior."

There it was, facing me every day. A tangible folder with red ink on the tab. That folder was the real fertilization of my baby, the physical connection that began as an idea. It stared at me every day as a constant reminder that "Greg Junior" actually existed. Before he was a fertilized egg, he was a folder. Before he was a folder, he was an idea swimming around in my brain.

Two months later, we were back at the obstetrician's office. It was Halloween. A clown greeted us at the front desk. A witch took Terri's temperature and blood pressure. After a short wait, a cowboy reached for his holster and fired a memorable shot. It was one of the most amazing moments of my life.

"Congratulations," he smiled. "You are going to be parents!"

Ten months later, Greg Jr. screamed for his morning feeding as I was preparing for another day at work, about to enter the shower.

"Terri, can you bring me a towel?" I shouted to my wife as I looked in the bathroom mirror at my naked body seated in my black power wheelchair. Even the slightest chill tenses my muscles and makes mobility painful and slow. The air conditioning in the hallway was uncomfortably high, and I didn't want to leave the warmth of the vent-sealed bathroom, or this part of the motivational tape I was listening to.

As I listened and waited, I looked myself over. Black hair with locks of curls. A well-trimmed beard. Large deep eyes. Golden bronze skin. The muscle on the right side of my neck significantly more developed than the one on the left because it had worked so hard for years to keep my head vertical, compensating for the curvature of my spine toward the left.

My Adam's apple protruded. There was no missing my prominent collarbone. From there, instead of gradual hills leading to the peaks of pectoral muscles, there were valleys, leading to a series of ribs protruding from skin, and then nipples. My thin arms were folded and my left elbow leaned on the armrest of my chair, pushing that shoulder up to a level just below my ear.

The bathroom door opened, banging against the back wheel of my chair. A sleek, golden brown arm extended a towel in my direction, which I grabbed by flipping my arm backward and clasping my skinny fingers. "Thanks, baby."

I cranked up the Tony Robbins tape and rolled the chair over to the shower, where I planted my feet on the floor and stood up, using the chair for stability and balance. I swung my body around, landed my rear on the padded shower bench, flipped my legs one at a time into the shower, and leaned forward with my chest against my knees to turn the water on.

The shower has always been my shrine. It is where the hot water massages my brain and opens up the arteries, allowing for clearer, sharper thinking. I generate my best ideas in the shower. My analysis and decision-making all happen in the shower. That day, my moments of shower solitude were more important than ever. It was time. This was the day I made my stand at work, the moment when my life and my career started heading in the direction I wanted.

Later that day, I found myself pointing the joystick on my power wheelchair and headed down the hall and into the office of Jack Nietzel, director of marketing for KTAR/K-Lite. He had requested a private meeting with me. I knew it was about my work performance and my bad attitude. It was August 1992, and I had been the research director for five years. A day earlier, I had given a sales rep a really hard time after he pressed me to get a sales proposal done much quicker than was possible to do.

KTAR was the station everybody listened to on the way to work. The place where "Arizona's Morning News" was the alarm clock and the passenger on the drive to work for thousands of Phoenicians, followed by the "Pat McMahon Show," with "The Preston Westmoreland Show" in the afternoons. It was the Phoenix home of Paul Harvey, and the Wall Street Journal Report. The "620 Sportsline" show, hosted by Jude LaCava, was at its peak of popularity largely because of his laid back personal style that was heavy on humor, as well as solid sports knowledge. Aside from Jude, the station was the "Sports Giant of the Southwest," the play-by-play home of the Phoenix Cardinals, the Arizona State Sun Devils, the Phoenix Suns. Every major radio advertising buy in the Valley had to include KTAR. We were number two in the ratings, well behind the country station, but always number one in revenue. Our sales reps drove nice cars and took clients to fancy restaurants every day. A necktie was part of an unwritten dress code if you were on our end of the building, where management and sales dwelled. Down the hall and through the heavy doors were the newsroom and the on-air studios, where it was true that the more casual the dress, the harder the work ethic. I spent most of my workday on the quiet, business side of the building. The only consistent sound to break up that boredom was K-Lite, piped into a monitor just outside my office. so that the jocks working on the computers would be able to know when to dart back into the studio to say, "Lite Rock with Less Talk, K-Lite 98.7 FM. We're in the middle of a continuous music set of soft favorites, like this one from Dionne Warwick."

I enjoyed any reason to venture into the KTAR Newsroom to hear the zipping of newswires, the jumble of electronic voices from four television monitors and the on-air feed, the squelch of the police monitor, and the high-pitched gibberish of a reel-to-reel sound bite being reversed and cued up. All these concurrent sounds gave me energy. This was a much faster paced environment than on my side of the building. Often, while getting my afternoon cup of coffee, I'd go across the lobby and hang out in the newsroom for about ten minutes, just observing the show hosts, producers, board ops, and occasionally getting into a sports conversation with Sports Director Tom Dillon or Greg Schulte. Sometimes, I'd be fortunate enough to catch one of Tom's dirty jokes, which always brought uproarious laughter. This was the pinnacle of the radio business in Phoenix. We all knew it, and we were damn proud to be a part of it.

The perks were nice. Going to sporting events was no problem. The station got plenty of tickets to Suns, Cardinals and ASU games. Concert tickets were often available through K-Lite. Publishers would bombard the producers with books in hope of getting their authors a live interview, so there would be continual internal book giveaways for the staff to unload books they simply had no room for. If you were ever out in the community, given poor service, needed special treatment or a good deal, mentioning of your employer would affect how you were treated.

Jim Taszarek, the general manager, would say in his staff speeches, "Ya know, we have a pretty good set-up here. We got good ratings. We're billing well." It really was a good set-up, especially for me. I had my own corner office. My parking space in the underground garage was right in front of the elevator. After a couple of years on the job, I had even worked my way onto the air, doing a show called *Cardinal Talk*, which aired after all the NFL games.

Everybody at KTAR/K-Lite was friendly and professional, but I was unhappy and restless. It had started to show, which probably explained the request for the meeting. I already knew what my problem was. I was bored with the job.

My salary was $38,000 a year after five years, and I managed to augment that by doing some of the typesetting and production on the publications, so I was pulling down about $45,000, not bad for a youngster of 28.

It was an exciting time in my life. Greg Jr. was just a couple of months old. I was so proud to be a father, which I had always known to be a possibility, but never really expected. I wanted the best for my son. It was tough leaving him and my wife every day to drive the 90 minutes into Phoenix and deal with bullshit from sales reps who used the stuff I made to go out and make triple my salary. I wanted more than that for my family.

That morning, my phone had rung with double beep, meaning it was an inside call.

"Greg Smith."

"Greg, it's Jack. Can you come down to my office?" And that's how I found myself wheeling down the hallway.

When I got there, he was seated at his desk with his back to the door typing something into his computer. I respected Jack. He was a nice family man and a veteran in marketing and advertising. I learned a lot from him.

I was so into that job when I first started, zooming down the halls to meet with a sales rep to make sure I really understood the kind of look and feel a specific presentation to a company should have. I felt important, designing the only tangible "thing" that a corporate advertising executive would look at before deciding whether to spend $150,000 on "thin air." But now, after four-and-a-half years on the job, including two years running the fast break down the halls of KTAR working with Jack, I was looking to move to another level in my career.

I felt a lot of pressure to increase my income significantly. I had just become a father. Bills, like my $550 per month car payment and my $700 monthly mortgage, added up, so I was living paycheck to paycheck.

There was one clear way I felt I could significantly increase my salary at KTAR/K-Lite, and it was what I'd always wanted to do anyway—become a sales representative. There were always openings, as this is a volatile position. Either you can sell radio or you can't. Now, into my fifth year at the top-billing combination of stations in the market, I had observed the characteristics of the sales reps who were successful and those who weren't. As the only one in the building capable of putting together presentations, I had inside information on how much money each account executive for both stations brought through the door, and how much they got to keep for themselves. Sales was where I needed to be.

Jack turned around to face me.

"Close the door."

I did.

"How's the baby?"

"Oh, he's crying loud and clear. I think he has a future in radio."

"Greg, I want to talk to you about your meeting yesterday with Jeff Blanchard."

"What's there to talk about Jack? He bops in my office and lays all these logos on my desk and makes drastic changes to the proposal and made unfair demands on me."

"Greg, that's a $300,000 buy. You could have made that the top priority for him since it is worth so much to the station."

"That's just it, Jack. It's a $300,000 buy, but I'm the one breaking my neck, doing the research, designing the pitch, staying here late to produce it, and we'll sell it because it is so well laid out and so thorough and I won't receive an extra dime. Meanwhile, Jeff gets his 20% commission, and frankly Jack, he's an asshole about it."

"But Greg, that's your *job!* It's in your job description. To do specific presentations. I'm just asking you to do your job."

I nodded my head in agreement at first, assuming my "yes-man" position. But then something inside me blurted it out; "Maybe it's time for a new job."

"Well, Greg, your job is very important to this radio station. And if you don't want to do it right, maybe you should get a new job."

"I think that after five years here, I have a lot to offer either of these stations in sales."

"What do you mean, Greg? You're in sales!"

With every reply, our voices grew louder.

"Jack, there's a job open in KTAR sales right now. I know just as much about this station and this market as anybody down there. I would make a great sales rep."

"When you first applied for a job here, you applied for a sales rep job. You didn't *get* that job. You got *this* job."

"Well, Jack, I'm going to apply for it!"

"I don't think you should do that, Greg. It would cause you problems and me problems."

"Why do you say *that*!!??"

"BECAUSE YOU'RE NOT A SALES REP!!!!"

Now we were both yelling at the top of our lungs. I was pissed. I didn't care at this point. Who the hell was he to tell me what I was? I thought it was so pompous and unfair for him to define me like that. I was just starting my career, and he was trying to lay a limiting belief on me. I fired back at the top of my lungs, with my deep, strong voice, the words that I'll never forget: "YOU DON'T KNOW *WHAT* I AM!!"

There was silence. It was done. My life would never be the same. We both looked at each other. I remember thinking how there must be a crowd of people in the hallway listening to this shouting match. It was quite heated. After several seconds of silence, Jack lowered his tone.

"You're right. I don't know what you are. But I do know what the perception across the hall is about what you are, and it's not in sales."

I respected his response. It was very evident to me that there was no way out of this luxurious dead-end job. If I applied for the sales rep job, he wouldn't give me a chance. The facts were pretty clear. I was outgoing, personable and intelligent. I understood the Phoenix radio market and the radio station. I could drive around town and had a lot of ambition and motivation. Still, I knew they'd never give me a chance to prove myself. There was no way they'd award me an opportunity outside the role of research director. I was the one who stays inside and does all the important work, chained to the computer, like a good, productive cripple.

I went back to my office and did the proposal to the best of my ability. We got the sale. Jeff got his commission and I got a new source of energy about finding my place in life.

I went into a kind of hazy period at work after that. Volunteering ideas with enthusiasm is something I had become known for. After that meeting, I just did my job quietly while reaching deep within to find a direction that would nurture all aspects of my identity, including my disability. Sales really appealed to me because increasing my income was a top priority. I had grown tired of spending all my time at work cooped up in a little office. I wanted to get out into the beautiful Arizona sunshine and meet interesting people. I wanted to network, take clients to lunch and dinner, and solve their problems with my product.

I gave a lot of consideration to pharmaceutical sales, because accessibility would not be a problem there. Hospitals and doctor's offices are all wheelchair-friendly. But that wasn't what I knew, it wasn't what I had studied and it wasn't what I loved. I was a communicator. I loved the media, public relations, and getting the word out about things that mattered.

There were about 150 employees at KTAR and K-Lite when I worked there. While everyone was polite and friendly, I never really created strong "hanging out at each others houses"-type friendships with anyone I worked with. In retrospect, I suspect the same awkwardness and hesitancy about disability played a role in how I interacted with my co-workers. Also, I was really into the possibility of moving forward with my career there, and I didn't want to confide in anybody and involve myself in office gossip. So I kept my friendships outside of the office.

After the shouting match, I didn't really care about that anymore, and opened myself up to a few people that I liked around the station. One of them was a guy in engineering named Mike Hagans. He had a great sense of humor and was very kind and thoughtful. We were around the same age, and both had young families. He was a very sharp guy who helped me solve a lot of my little organizational office problems. He fixed my computer regularly and was full of good ideas about making my life easier by using low-tech solutions, like creating a fold away arm for my laptop computer attached to my wheelchair. Like me, he was frustrated with his career growth and had begun his own enterprises, selling equipment that he designed and produced to other radio stations. I had given some thought to starting my own business in the past, but never really developed a solid idea. Mike motivated me to give this more thought.

The 90-minute rush hour commute between KTAR and my home gave me a lot of time to think about making a move in my career. It was somewhere on Interstate-10 that I first developed the idea to combine my disability experience with something media-related. My first thought was to do a magazine. I had published the radio stations' newsletters and magazines for a long time. I understood the printing process. I could write, and I had a great name for it, *On A Roll*.

The name came to me during a football game I had announced in college and stuck with me: "The Sun Devils are really on a roll now!" As an avid sports fan over the years, I'd heard that phrase repeatedly. That was it, a clever play on words, with obvious reference to wheeled mobility. It was also an optimistic and positive title. *On A Roll* would be the name of a new magazine that presented issues impacting the lives of people with disabilities. I was excited about having this concept as a reason to flip out of bed every morning and proceed with life; doing sales material at KTAR/K-Lite wasn't cutting it.

I ran spreadsheets determining the costs of printing and paper at different levels of distribution. I played with various advertising rates. There was a huge panic and fear in corporate America about a new law known as the Americans with Disabilities Act, which President George H.W. Bush had signed into law two years earlier. Now, Title III of the law—the area that dealt with public accommodations—was in force. That meant that if you did business with the general public, you had to be accessible for people with disabilities. I saw it is an opportunity for businesses that *were* accessible to advertise that fact and get a nice return on their investment. I looked at various frequency options. Should this magazine be monthly, every other week or weekly?

The numbers looked pretty good, but the one thing was intimidated me about the magazine was the writing. I could write, but throughout my life, I never considered myself connected to people with disabilities. I didn't associate with people with disabilities and didn't really want to. So I didn't know about a lot of the major issues that impacted them. I really had no expertise on disability issues outside my own experience. In an effort to get material for the magazine prototype, I did some digging about the key elements of life with a disability.

The first person I contacted was Susan Webb, the executive director of the Arizona Bridge to Independent Living (ABIL), one of over 400 centers around the country that give disabled people resources for becoming fully integrated into mainstream society. A couple of years before, Susan contacted me about serving on ABIL's board of directors. What I thought was cool about Independent Living Centers up front was the strictly enforced rule stating that at least 51% of the staff has to be people with disabilities. Also, Susan personified what I wanted to be. Prior to becoming the director at ABIL, she had worked at AT&T for many years in corporate sales. She was a very polished woman with a very professional appearance. She had a manner that exuded confidence. We had lunch one afternoon on Central Avenue.

"I think you should do what you know, and that's radio," she said. I agreed that a radio show about disabilities would be something much more in line with my level of expertise. Doing talk radio was something I had become very comfortable with. For the past three years, I had done *Cardinal Talk* on KTAR after every NFL game. That experience, combined with my college radio airtime and even my high school play-by-play made me comfortable being on the air. Setting up a radio show was much simpler than going through all the production necessary to start a magazine or even a newsletter. The problem, I thought, would be one of financial support. I didn't believe that a program that reached out to people with disabilities would have any interested sponsors. And, I thought, people with disabilities must be such a small segment of the population that it would be difficult to get a station to air it.

I took the radio show idea back to Mike at work.

"Sounds like a pretty stupid idea," he said immediately. "Why would a sponsor want to pay to reach a small, largely unemployed, financially poor segment of society?"

What I didn't realize then was the 54 million people with disabilities represent America's largest minority group, with a combined discretionary income of over $700 billion annually.

The perception of poverty in the disability community and my discussions with Mike led to the option of public radio. I made a phone call to the program director of local public radio station KJZZ. He alerted me to a grant opportunity through the Corporation for Public Broadcasting's Radio Program Fund. I called and requested a packet.

Several days later, the CPB Radio Program Fund envelope arrived. Behind the closed door of my office at KTAR, I pulled out a stiff new manila folder and a red Sharpie. On the label, I scribbled the phrase: "On A Roll."

Now it existed. An idea had become a reality. That's when it all began. That was the start of my passion and excitement; the root of all the energy and heart and soul I've poured into this concept for much of my adulthood.

As I read the request-for-proposals, the words seemed to be speaking directly to my vision and to me personally. It said that they were looking for programming that reached out to underrepresented segments of society; programming from independent producers, and particularly programming produced by minorities. They wanted concepts that would expand public radio's audience.

I concluded that 54 million people with disabilities as a target audience wouldn't be a bad starting point! I dived into the project and within two days, I had a solid written draft ready.

At that point, I went public with my new direction. I shared the CPB package with Taz and Gail Schmeling, KTAR's business manager. I was honest about my lack of desire to do the job there very much longer. They were great about it. Taz spent a lot of time helping me go over the grant and think through the project. Gail analyzed the budget pages and helped me refine the business aspects. I totally immersed myself into the work of producing the best-written response to the grant questions possible.

One Sunday, as the deadline neared, the Cardinals had a home game against the New Orleans Saints. While I worked on the proposal at home, I had the radio on in the background as the pre-game show aired. By now I should have been at the game preparing to host *Cardinal Talk* but I couldn't remove myself from working on the grant in my home office. Before I knew it, the game was in the third quarter!

I needed to ship the grant request overnight on Monday for a Tuesday arrival, and there were some critical elements to the financials page that were not in order. For me, this was a defining moment. A life-long dream of mine had been to be a sportscaster. I had done seven years of high school and college play-by-play, and here I was associated with an NFL broadcast on a weekly basis! And yet, the clarity of my purpose was so evident that the decision I made that day was not difficult at all. I decided that I would not go to the game, nor would I show up for *Cardinal Talk*.

I called the KTAR newsroom and notified them that I would not be going to Sun Devil Stadium that day. On Monday, I was called into Marc McCoy's office to discuss it. I was totally honest with him about the circumstances surrounding my decision. I could overhear the sports guys talking about me behind my back in disbelief that I would do such a thing! I think Marc intended to reprimand me or in some way come down hard on me, but I think after looking him in the eye and sharing how clearly I understood my mission, he sort of envied me, or at least looked upon me with respect. I sent the package the next day, and resumed as host of *Cardinal Talk* for the remainder of that season.

About a month later, in September 1992, I received a letter congratulating me for being a *finalist* in the CPB Radio Program Fund! After sharing this news with people at KJZZ, I learned that this was quite an honor, especially for someone who had never produced a single public radio show. When I got word that out of over 300 proposals, they selected *On A Roll* as one of about 50 finalists, I was certain that my future was set.

The semifinalist presentation called for a demo tape that would give the panelists an idea of what this show would sound like. The process of putting this tape together was the first effort at doing talk radio about life and disability. At KTAR, we had done a montage of our coverage of the impeachment of Governor Evan Mecham, coverage that received the prestigious George Foster Peabody Award. I decided that instead of staging a full-length show, I would put together a similar montage that would give a wider perspective of the kind of issues this public radio show would cover. I interviewed Senator John McCain at the KTAR studios and used some his comments about the disability community's voting power. The tape featured another in-studio interview with a VP from America West Airlines about airplane accessibility. In Milwaukee, a deaf woman had recently sued a concert facility because it didn't provide a sign language interpreter at a Wynona Judd concert. I interviewed her spokesman. The montage featured contemporary music bumpers (segment dividers) and lots of attempts at humor. I wanted to push the envelope. That's my style. That's my personality, and always has been. After sending the package, I felt very strongly that they would fund our show..

Around that same time, I had begun to consider working to help a brother in Phoenix who was starting his own radio station. Art Mobley had been down the same path I had, working at KTAR over a decade prior to my time on Third Avenue & Osborn. He had gathered some investors and was about to launch KMJK—Majik 107 FM for the largely untapped African-American market in the Valley of the Sun. I had never been involved in a station start-up, so when Art called to see if I would be interested in lending my expertise, I was excited about the prospect. We met many times and carved out possibilities for me to do outside sales and on-air work. The first project I did for him was to write the copy for his media kit. I felt a part of the team as we began to socialize with his staff, excited about the launch of the station. It was Art who made a significant suggestion to me that he could not have realized the importance of at the time. We were on the phone talking about one-sheets for Majik when the conversation shifted to *On A Roll*, the pending public radio show.

"Greg, you need to go ahead and just get your show on the air somehow," he said. "Don't just sit and wait for this grant, because what if you don't get it? You've got a good idea. Just go ahead and find a station to get the thing going. Move it from the idea stage to reality."

The next day, I went to Taz with the idea.

"We can't put it on KTAR, Greg," he said. "It's such a small, small segment of the population. But maybe you can find another station in town that would give you a shot."

I only had to make one call. KFNN was a 2500-watt station that broadcast from sun-up to sundown at 1510 on the AM dial. The transmitter was in Mesa, about 30 miles east of downtown Phoenix. Its business offices and studios were uptown. KFNN's format was Financial News Radio. Their strategy was to reach the investment community as well as business people. Its ratings were virtually non-existent, but during the day, the 2500 watts covered the market well. KFNN's facilities were a far cry from the state-of-the-art "set-up" I was accustomed to at KTAR, but I didn't care about that. I was just looking for a "stick"—a radio antenna that could put the show out there. Ron Cohen, the owner and general manager of the station was about my age, maybe a few years older. He was very sharp and professional in that first meeting, and genuinely interested in adding my show to his lineup. He didn't need a demo tape, he said, "because I've heard you do *Cardinal Talk* on KTAR." What Ron wanted was to be paid for the airtime. I left his office with a mission. Find a sponsor that would compensate KFNN to the tune of $250 per week.

I went back to the office, shut my door and started randomly calling some of the big companies in the Valley of the Sun—companies I knew had some interest in their community image. I started off with the big banks I knew spent a lot of money on advertising. I had all the advertising decision-maker contacts from my records at KTAR.

I got lucky on my second call, to Bank of America. The name on my contact list was Steve Carr.

"Bank of America, Corporate Communications, Steve Carr."

"Mr. Carr, my name is Greg Smith. I'm the research director at KTAR and the host of *Cardinal Talk*?" (I said it like a question)

"Yeah Greg! How ya doing?" (I guess he was a football fan)

"I'm fine. The reason I'm calling is I'm also a person who uses a wheelchair. I have muscular dystrophy. And I'm in the process of developing a new radio talk show that deals with disability issues. It's going to air on KFNN, and in order to get the program started, we need to identify some sponsors. And I was wondering if..."

"I didn't know you were in a wheelchair! I thought you were a retired NFL player!"

It just takes one "yes." He invited me to visit his office the next day, and the most difficult part of the sales presentation was finding a place to park. As it turns out, BofA was starting a new loan program for people with disabilities to purchase modified vehicles. They were very much in the spirit of complying with the ADA and making their efforts known to the disability community. We agreed on $250 per week in exchange for banking category exclusivity. Steve and I would record weekly segments in an interview format and talk about different aspects of the bank's efforts to be accessible to people with disabilities. I was jubilant after this meeting.

Now there was no turning back. This idea was starting to develop a life of its own. I had a station. I had a sponsor. Ron and I picked a start date of December 5, 1992 and a time-slot of 3:00 PM. The date was just a month away. Now it was time to get the word out, which is exactly what I had been doing for KTAR for the past five years. My press release netted significant local media coverage: a KPNX TV-12 feature, a lengthy feature article by Bruce Christian in the *Mesa Tribune*, and a clever column in the sports section of the *Arizona Republic* by Bob Cohn.

Despite all this, as the weeks before the debut sped by, I realized that having a show on KFNN did not mean the same thing as having a show on KTAR. The average quarter-hour (AQH) at the time for KTAR on the weekends was well over 17,000 people, which meant that at any given time on the weekend, that's how many people were listening. KFNN's AQH didn't even register in the Arbitron ratings book. Did that mean that nobody was listening? If so, how would I get callers? I knew that the articles and features in the press would create awareness about the show, but that awareness wouldn't automatically equate to listeners. And without listeners, I feared that I would get no callers. The most embarrassing and difficult thing about doing a talk show is to invite callers and get none. I had experienced a little bit of that after pre-season Cardinals games, and as the host of the show, you can only talk for so long about an issue.

Much analysis went into deciding my first move on the air. Initially, the concept was to do an in-depth program about the effect the ADA was having on small businesses. I called several well-known local business owners during the weeks leading up to the debut and listened carefully as they talked about repainting their parking lots and widening their aisles. Frankly, it seemed boring. It just didn't seem like it would have the bang I was looking for. After more introspection, I concluded that I really wanted my show to be about the personal experiences of living with a disability. I didn't want a dry, lecture-style "just the facts" diatribe. I wanted my show to make the point that disability is a natural part of human diversity; that it is not a fate worse that death. And center stage on this show would be the voices of people whose lives prove that point.

Another element that went into my thinking was I knew I'd be nervous for the first show and it made sense to do a topic I felt comfortable with and knowledgeable about. As the host of *Cardinal Talk* and a life-long football fan, a connection between football and disability seemed obvious. Marc Bounicanti, the son of Miami Dolphins Hall of Fame linebacker, Nick Bounicanti, was a quadriplegic, injured in a college football accident. He was the founder of the Miami Project to Cure Spinal Cord Injuries. He accepted my invitation to talk about his injury, adapting to it and the work of the Miami Project.

I didn't feel like that was enough for a full show. On the CPB demo tape, I had interviewed amputee actress Christopher Templeton, who at the time had a regular role on the daytime television hit, *The Young and the Restless*. She was all personality on the radio, very vocal and expressive about the issue of Hollywood's "blackballing" of disabled actors and actresses. She accepted my invitation to join me in the second half-hour. This issue was important to me because I believed so strongly about the media's impact on how society views people with disabilities. For the local connection, I found Christina Paine, who had been a successful television actress in the 60's and 70's. After her paralysis, she continued to model and was featured in a national television spot for America West Airlines. I invited her to come to KFNN and be an in-studio guest.

The Friday before the program, I was paranoid that there would be no listeners and no callers. I started a process some would consider a little extreme. From ABIL's list of about 200 consumers, I dialed every single person, sometimes leaving a message, sometimes talking to people who answered the phone: "Hi, my name is Greg Smith. I'm a wheelchair user with muscular dystrophy. On Sunday, December 5, at 3:00 pm, a new radio talk show on disability issues will air on KFNN 1510 AM. As the host of the show, I wanted to call you personally to invite you to listen, and urge you to call in and participate in the discussion."

The week before the show, I recorded the introduction and other production elements. I chose to use Steve Winwood's *Roll with It* as the theme song.

"*Live from Downtown Phoenix,*" said the announcer...

"*Roll with it Baby!*" sang Winwood.

"*It's On A Roll, the Valley's live radio talk show on disability issues. To join in the conversation, call in right now.... And now, he's a husband, father, writer, drummer, computer whiz, electric wheelchair user, host of this show, and proud of it.... Greg Smith!"*

All of the bumper music—tunes you hear fading up when it's time to take a commercial break, or coming out of a break—was contemporary; music that people would recognize. I wanted the show to be about life and to feature sounds that people could relate to and feel comfortable with, including the music. Everything was set to go. I had recorded Bank of America's interview; the guests were all lined up. All the production was done. I could relax.

On Sunday, I arrived at the KFNN building an hour early. I rolled into the studio and greeted the board operator, Ted Lake, who was handling *Ham Radio & More*, the program in progress. I had printed out a cue sheet, which listed all of the sound elements for the show in order, including commercials, music bumpers and promos. It also had telephone numbers for the guests. I shared it with Ted and we began to discuss what to expect on this maiden voyage. Len Winkler, host of the "Ham" show was background noise to me, talking his amateur radio jargon, which was a foreign language to everybody who wasn't into that hobby. I continued to chat with Ted when all of a sudden a short loud sound interrupted our conversation. SMACK! From behind the microphone, Len had thrown a cart, which is the exact size and shape of an old 8-track tape, against the window between the on-air studio and the engineering studio to get Ted's attention! His facial expression was one of a pissed off man. The light on the phone caller bank had been blinking, which meant that he had a caller, and Ted hadn't been paying attention because he was talking to me. I learned my first lesson about doing an in-studio talk show at KFNN before I even got on the air. Never interfere with the concentration of a "board op" at work. It wouldn't be long before I ended up throwing my own carts and pens at the glass at KFNN!

I left Len and Ted alone and relocated to the lobby to study my cue sheet and go over my notes. Soon, people started to arrive. First Donna Noland, the director of the Arizona Governor's Office for People with Disabilities. She also was the publisher of a national newspaper on disability issues called the *National Focus*. Next, a cameraman from

145

KPNX –TV12, the local NBC television affiliate. And finally, Christina Paine.

The hour zoomed by until finally Len's show was over. My show actually began at 3:05. There was a five-minute network newscast that separated *Ham Radio* from *On A Roll*. This meant we had only five minutes to clear Len's stuff out of the way and get my entourage in place. The studio was so cramped that Len had to hurriedly disconnect a reel-to-reel tape machine and move it to another part of the room to allow me space to enter. Christina Paine followed me in her chair and Ted Lake positioned her microphone. By now, we had two minutes 'til airtime. Ted still had to get Bouniconti on the line and check everyone's levels. Then, all of a sudden, the network newscast stopped! There was "dead air." Ted ran into the control room and frantically grabbed a tape cart and slammed it into the machine. It was my intro… two minutes early!

I wasn't prepared at all to take the air. My headphones weren't even solidly in place when the announcer's voice signified a new era in my life: "… *An electric wheelchair user, host of this show and proud of it… Greg Smith!*"

My heart pounded.

"*Welcome to a new kind of radio talk show ladies and gentlemen, I'm your host Greg Smith. Many of you know this voice as one associated with football here in the Valley of the Sun, but what many of you don't know is the fact that I can barely lift a football. I've had muscular dystrophy all my life, use a wheelchair, and despite all this, I'm a husband and a father, and now I'm starting my own show to give you an introduction to what it's like to have a disability, and just as importantly what it isn't like.*"

I was dancing, for some reason trying to fill time instead of just going ahead with what I had planned to do. I regrouped.

"*Today on this show, I'm going to introduce you to a man who is also associated with football. His name is Marc Bounicanti. You probably know his father, Nick Bounicanti, the famous former Miami Dolphin linebacker. Marc was paralyzed in a college football game and founded the Miami Project to Cure Paralysis. We'll talk about the work being done by the Miami Project and learn a little more about Marc. Also later in the show... Why is it that we never see disabled people as the lead in major motion pictures or at least on television shows? We'll talk to Christopher Templeton, an actress you've seen on the soaps, and Christina Paine, a wheelchair user who was in a national ad for America West a couple years back. Call in and talk to Marc Bounicanti right now at 230-2755. On A Roll continues right after this..."* Music faded up and then a commercial.

"Ted, do we have Bounicanti yet? TED!!!"

He couldn't hear me and was punching buttons in the other room. I knew we didn't have Marc on the phone yet because there were no yellow lights lit on my phone bank. I waved my arms, but Ted didn't look up. Then he suddenly darted from the control room into the on-air studio, climbing over Christina's chair and around the back of mine.

"These damn phone banks. Sometimes they get frozen and I have to re-set them!" He did something, pressing down simultaneously with both hands and then darted back into the control room, picked up the phone and started dialing.

"Now, back to more of On A Roll! Call in right now to partici-pate in the discussion, at 230-2755 or toll free at 1-800-298-8255. Here's your host, Greg Smith."

More tap-dancing. But thankfully, Ted was able to get Marc up on the line in about a minute.

The show was rocky. I was more nervous than on any *Cardinal Talk* shows. There were technical problems, such as dial tones and that irritating phone off the hook sound getting on the air. Still, the guests were interesting. We had plenty of caller participation. And it went by quickly. It seemed like just a few minutes and it was over. I felt relieved. *On A Roll* was a reality. I started thinking of ideas for next week, a process that has continued weekly to this day.

"Special" is a word I have heard all my life from people who care about me. It isn't a word that I particularly accepted or enjoyed hear-ing, but the repetition must have seeped through, because I had always believed there was a major purpose for my life. There had to be some reason that God made a skinny, crippled guy with a deep voice, who also happens to be black, stubborn and aggressive. As I drove home to my family that afternoon, I was someone different. I was a man who knew his purpose in the world.

ON THE AIR—My first moments on the air with my new talk show, "Arizona On A Roll."

CHAPTER 15

On the Air

AS IT TURNED OUT, the Corporation for Public Broadcasting grant was never a real possibility. I had never done public radio and I didn't even listen to much public radio. On paper, the concept of a radio talk show on disability issues was solid enough for my proposal to make the finals. However, in addition to a written detailed proposal, they required a demo tape for the final selection process. My strategy was to create a package that used humor as a bridge between serious issues; shattering the misconception that disability always had to be a heavy subject. The CPB did not find my tape the least bit funny. In fact, one judge called it "hokey."

Now, the commercial show was alive and thriving. I had thrown my hat over the fence as far as my career at KTAR was concerned. They had started recruiting for my replacement. They gave me a fair severance package and continued to allow me to do freelance work for six months.

As a new father, the thought of going without health insurance and the expense of purchasing my own seemed quite daunting. A full-time job as director of marketing was open at the Arizona Bridge to Independent Living (ABIL). I was very passionate about *On A Roll*, but also quite concerned about my financial stability. The job paid $30,000 and offered benefits. I figured I could do this job during the week, which would immerse me into the disability community, and continue to do the radio show on the side.

ABIL was located in central Phoenix just east of the downtown area in a very nice single-story building constructed especially for its use. Executive Director Susan Webb was well known in the Valley as a tireless advocate for people with disabilities and a somewhat controversial figure. Politically, she was a Republican and preached regularly about how people with disabilities should pull themselves up by the bootstraps, not use their disabilities as excuses, and strive for complete participation in the mainstream. Many people in the grassroots disability community felt she was out of touch with the difficulties that uneducated, severely disabled people were facing. I admired her spirit and although I didn't support her Republican views, I believed in the power of the human spirit to overcome whatever obstacles we face.

Moving from the for-profit, commercial world of talk radio to the non-profit, grant-writing world of an independent living center was a difficult transition for me. I wanted to sell everything and find corporate support to fund everything. But I had to learn how to write grants for federal and state monies allocated to help people with disabilities. There were a lot of code words and jargon I had to learn. For the first few months on the job, I was lost. My value to the organization was based on my promotional and marketing skills, writing and producing the newsletter, and managing outreach efforts. Soon I started to learn more about Independent Living, its history and the vision of its philosophy.

The beloved founder of the Independent Living movement was a guy named Ed Roberts. I first learned of him from a *60 Minutes* segment. I learned that Ed was one of the first severely disabled college students to attend the University of California at Berkeley. When he was admitted to school, the headline in the Bay Area newspaper read "Helpless Cripple Goes to School." Other students followed Ed's path. They lived in the campus hospital. They started to befriend each other and developed a sense of brotherhood and pride. In late night conversations with the lights out, after they had been "put to bed," they carved out their philosophy that people with disabilities should be the sole decision makers in all of the areas of their lives. They concluded that independence means *control* of your life, not the ability to do things without help. If you make decisions about who helps you, when you are helped and how you are helped, you are independent. This small group of students created an organization that eventually became the nation's first Independent Living Center. The concept grew and expanded to where there were over 400 such centers across the country; all sparked by the spirit and determination of this one guy.

I called him one day and invited him on my radio show. I remember being so excited and honored that he was to appear. I made specific flyers, promoting the show. I did press releases and distributed them at all of the rehabilitation centers in Phoenix and at all the places where people with disabilities might congregate. I remember studying for this show, reading articles about Ed, and collecting music bumpers from the 60's to play during the interview. In the week leading up to the interview, I talked with Ed at length about my vision. These conversations were so very empowering to me, giving me the fuel that I would need to see my vision remain alive for over a decade.

"I know that my show is only on in one city," I said to Ed, "but I really can see it growing across the country, giving people with disabilities a voice."

"That's so exciting," he said. "If there's anything I can do, please let me know. I wanna help you. You're IT for us in the radio category."

Because of my extensive preparation and knowledge of Ed's story, the show was one of the best *On A Roll* editions of all time. I pre-produced the intro, telling Ed's story over 60's music.

I asked Ed about his feelings on whether he is "proud" of his disability.

"I am totally proud of who I am," he said. "I have worked over the years, coming from a place where I hated myself and tried to kill myself at an early age, to a person who is very empowered and very proud and glad to be a leader in this movement...I think it is critical that we feel proud of who we are. We may have disabilities but we are just as good looking as anybody else. A lot of it has to do with our own pride. When you feel beautiful, you are beautiful. I think we need to help change people. I have been there. I have hated myself. I felt ugly but boy, I like feeling beautiful better."

Being early in our first year on the air, Ed gave me particularly good advice on how we could use the show and the rest of the media to get our story out there. It is advice that I took to heart and continue to use today.

"People (in the media) are still allies. I think if you got a good story, people look for good stories ...Not only (should we) work with press people ...when a crisis comes but to work before, get to know people. Teach them about disability and about the best part ... Because a lot of people take on disability. I became disabled at 14 with polio but a lot of people become disabled for all kinds of things at 50 or 60, or are born with a disability. There are all kinds of stories. Plus some press people who also become disabled because of car crashes or whatever, we are encouraging people to learn that disability is a part of life. We get struck back when they say, 'We don't want to depress our audience. Or there are too many stories about disabilities because people get too depressed and they don't like to hear it.' A good story is a good story."

Finally, being the father of a then-one-year-old, I asked him what parenting had been like for him

"Well, I wondered what (parenting) would be like. How do you discipline a kid when you can't reach out to them? But an important lesson I have learned is that when you are a dad, you are Dad or when you are a mom, you are Mom, no matter if you have a disability. You learn to work with a kid. They communicate. When he was a little baby, he would crawl up in my lap and give me a kiss. He could do that any time he wanted to and I would call him and say 'come over here and give me a kiss.' We learned how to communicate.

"My wife and I agreed we would raise him totally non-violently, we would never spank him. Of course, I couldn't do that anyway. I think we don't realize how spanking and hurting perpetuates the whole idea of violence. I am really proud of this kid. He is 15 and very self-motivated. He decided he would do well in school. You can tell I'm a proud dad."

Ed Roberts passed away less than three years later.

In the Spring of 1993, *On A Roll* was about six months old and living up to its name as a local Phoenix show. Bank of America, Arizona Public Service, the Phoenix Suns and the America West Arena were sponsors who more than paid for the weekly $200 KFNN airtime bill. Major articles had run in the newspapers. The *Phoenix Business Journal's* profile opened the door to sponsorship success. In addition, the local disability community had embraced the show. I was still under contract with KTAR and receiving a large portion of my salary. My job at the Arizona Bridge to Independent Living added to that salary. Times were pretty good.

One afternoon, UPS showed up at the house with a surprise package. It was a free set of Anthony Robbins' "Personal Power" audiocassettes! I had requested an interview with Tony several weeks before and had not received a response. And I never was able to get my interview. But he did me a far greater favor by giving me those tapes. I put them to good use. They helped me get past some limiting beliefs about my new show.

I was struggling to be confident that the show had "legs." Could a show about disability issues be fresh every week with new guests and new topics? I had done shows on disabled skiing, local businesses' perceptions of the Americans with Disabilities Act, guide dogs, computers and assistive technology resources, home modifications, and the public transit system. I was doing the show solo. Calls flowed in some weeks, while other weeks I couldn't get one call. This frustrated and worried me. I had slowly built a database of local area people with disabilities, and every week before the show, I would make about 30 calls, inviting them to listen and asking them to call in and participate. Most people were flattered and appreciated those calls. Only a few left a tone that removed them from the list.

I decided to seek advice from people with disabilities about show content by getting a group together to spark ideas for programming. I called several people I had met who were consumers or staff at ABIL. On the Sunday before my first programming meeting, I got an on-air call from a very articulate guy named Todd. He revealed on-air that he had cerebral palsy. I don't remember exactly what he called about, but I remember staying with him longer that I allow most callers to remain on the air.

After the show, Todd called again.

"Greg Smith."

"Hi, Greg. It's Todd Kimball. I just called in on the show."

"Hey Todd. Thanks for calling in. You really did a great job. You should call in more often."

"Ok. I will. I got a flyer about your show from my dial-a-ride driver and wanted to touch base with you. You know that I have cerebral palsy, but I'm also a radio guy. I did sportscasting for the campus radio station at Fresno State, and I'm studying for my MBA right now at ASU."

"Hey, we're having a meeting tomorrow afternoon at 5:00 over at the disabled apartment complex on Mill Avenue. Do you know where that is?

The next day, Todd arrived at the meeting before I did. About 15 other people with disabilities and some non-disabled folks showed up. I had a pen and paper in hand and asked for ideas for shows.

"You ought to do a show on personal care attendants," one person offered.

"How about doing a show on sex and disability," said another.

"I think doing a show on schools and accessibility would be a good idea," said Todd." And I really think a great way to promote that would be to send flyers to all the schools about that particular show. You could do that every week. Pick a topic associated with disability and promote to that topic's group. It would help you build your audience."

Todd said the words, "I think" a lot that afternoon. He was the only one who ever told me those words. I liked the idea of having someone to help me think and plan the direction of the show, not just in programming, but in sales, promotion and expanding the show to other markets.

Pretty soon, Todd became my co-host, and eventually my partner in *On A Roll*. His cerebral palsy, the result of a premature birth, made his posture awkward. His back was always curved forward and hunched. He often appeared to be staring off into the distance, zoned out, although he wasn't. He was thinking. His legs were stiff. Todd got around slowly with short thrusts of his arms on the wheels of his manual chair.

Todd didn't use a personal care attendant, and you could tell just by looking at him. Sometimes his shirt would be one button off. Sometimes one side of his collar would be up, and the other one down. His face always had a half day's beard growth, sometimes with a hair or two that he had missed protruding from his white skin. His hair was often in disarray. Todd was not a well-groomed guy. But there was nothing in disarray about this young man's mind.

I quickly got past all the other distractions about his presence, and zoned in on the good ideas. We worked on a plan for expanding the show in more markets. The goal, even back then, was clearly defined... to make the show syndicated and available via satellite to radio stations across the country. We investigated the costs of satellite time and found that for about $1,200 per month, we could put it out there "on the bird," as the industry calls Satcom C5. Still, that wouldn't guarantee us any additional affiliates. And even if we did gain more affiliates, that wouldn't bring us any salaries. In the early days, if a sponsor more than paid for the airtime, I would write Todd a check for what I thought I could afford to pay him. We had no formal business structure. We were just two crips who had a vision for how we would change the world. It wasn't long before Todd was footing a large portion of the bill out of his own personal savings.

Getting money out of the fastest growing city in the nation for a program on disability issues became a serious test of dedication to the concept. Every six months, Bank of America would send us a check for $5,200, which, if it had gone directly to the station, would have covered the airtime bill. But we were spending money out of our own pockets for printing and promotion, transportation, and long distance charges, and those expenses came out of the BofA check right away. It always became a struggle to pay Ron Cohen on time, so we hit the streets in search of additional revenue.

We would both work the phones, calling the usual Phoenix suspects for funding—The Dial Corporation, Hinkley & Schmidt Bottling, Salt River Project, Arizona Public Service, all the car dealers, all the grocery stores, Harkin's Theatres. We were able to get face-to-face meetings with most all of them.

I decided that it would be a good idea to take Todd on sales calls. First of all, his disability and my disability are different in appearance, and it would be a good leveraging tool to have someone else there in a wheelchair. Second, the thought did cross my mind that Todd's skin color couldn't hurt in getting a "yes" out of one of these decision makers, all who happened to be white. It worked early, as we landed a sponsorship from Arizona Public Service with Todd present. So we kept it up.

We would have a 10 AM appointment in downtown Phoenix. I lived just off Interstate-10 near Chandler, Arizona. Todd lived 20 minutes away in Tempe, near the ASU campus. My goal would be to leave

TODD KIMBALL—In the early days of On a Roll, Todd Kimball was a key figure in making the show successful.

the house at about 8, but more often than not, I'd get out of there around 8:30 or a quarter 'til 9. I would speed down the Superstition Freeway, passing other traffic, even on the exit, and squeal under the covered parking at Todd's condo.

"Honk, Honk!"

Then I'd sit and wait. After several minutes, I'd see him come out of his patio, feet first, with short little stokes on the wheels of his chair. Only then would I let the door open and the ramp down on my mini-van. I didn't want to release the cool air prematurely. As he neared the van, one of his roommates or a next-door neighbor would come out. Todd would open the front passenger door himself and park his chair as close to the seat as he could. Somehow, he had the arm strength to pull his butt up onto the high seat in the van and get into the chair himself. If we were in a hurry, he'd ask for help.

"Pull me up by the legs, just under my shins," he would say to his neighbor. His roommates already knew the routine. Then whoever was helping him would take the padded seat cushion and hand it to him rather than putting it on the back seat, because if it fell on the joystick of my power chair while we were driving, the chair would engage and there would be damage; a fact we found out the hard way one day. Then the assistant would fold the chair in half, cramming it between the front passenger seat and my wheelchair, effectively imprisoning me in my own vehicle.

We'd either talk strategy or sports on the way to the call. As we became familiar with the routine, it was usually sports. Or women. Wherever the sales call was, we'd pull into the parking lot and wait for someone to approach who looked like they had the time and physical strength to free us from this prison on wheels.

This really bothered me at first. I believed that people with disabilities should be independent and not depend on strangers to help them on a regular basis. But it didn't bother Todd at all to use the common man or woman to help him through the day.

"Excuse me, sir," he would say.

Sometimes, people just ignored him, or pretended like they didn't hear.

"Excuse me," he'd say. "My partner here and I are both in wheelchairs and we need some help getting out of the van. It will only take a couple of minutes. Can you help us?"

It really irritated me that we were begging for help from strangers, helping to perpetuate the myth that the disabled were helpless and dependent on non-crips for everything. I soon became used to it and actually created a way to find fun in it.

We'd pull up to the crip parking slot and kind of sit in wait for the most attractive woman to cross our path.

"How bout this one?"

"Nah. Let's keep lookin'."

"Here we go. Red dress comin' from the left. What do you think Greg?"

I didn't need to answer. I just pressed the button on my door panel letting Todd's window down.

"Excuse me, miss!"

Hey, if you have your choice of having a complete stranger spend five minutes helping you get out of your van, it might as well be a beautiful woman, right? What is also important to mention is that usually, the person who was helping us got more out of helping us than we did. It gave people an opportunity to do their "good deed of the day." We would always mention the radio show and give them flyers. We probably picked up several dozen new regular listeners over the years from strangers who helped Todd get his wheelchair out of my way.

Todd and I also became masters at the airport. We went on a lot of road trips starting in 1994, when we launched the show in Las Vegas. We'd fly to Vegas at least once per month to seek sponsors and promote the show. We flew Southwest Airlines a great deal and they were always great in handling the wheelchairs and not making us wait a half-hour after landing to get our chairs. They were always very quick with delivering our wheels to us without exception. They are the best airline if you want to avoid hassles. The other thing we liked about Southwest is the freedom of selecting our own seats. We'd usually roll our chairs right onto the plane and swing over to the front bulkhead section without assistance. This was much less hassle than dealing with the "straight-back" as they call it. It's also called "the aisle chair," used to get wheelchair passengers from their chairs to their seats on the plane. I hate using those things because the airlines go overboard in their efforts to be safe and avoid litigation. They strap you in at the chest, at the hip, at the knee and at the ankle. Then they fold your hands across your body and strap you so you can't move. It's very much like a straight jacket. My buddy Robby Heisner, from the rock band Van Gogh refers to the aisle chair as the "Hannibal Lechter" chair! The only thing missing is the muzzle!

On many Southwest flights, Todd and I took advantage of people's fear of disability. The airline would pre-board us. Usually, he would take the window seat and would board first. I would take the aisle seat, leaving an empty seat between us and the three seats facing us across the bulkhead. Then, as the rest of the passengers boarded, we'd begin our act. Todd would spaz out, his legs moving as if uncontrollably, bumping into the seat across from him. I'd kind of lean over to the left and let a little drool run down the side of my face. Worked every time! We always had the bulkhead section on Southwest flights to ourselves; our own business class section! Once airborne, we would recline and kick our feet up on the empty seats across from us.

At home, between arguments about me being out of town and in Las Vegas so much, Terri and I continued to share wonderful intimacy. While driving home from work on late afternoon, I was watching the line of fire, and the smoke billowing from a mountain on the horizon when my cell phone rang. It was a short call. As I watched the mountain burn, I had my first realization that my family would be increasing by one.

HAPPY FAMILY—One big happy family in 1995.

Donovan was born on January 20, 1994. He didn't get the fanfare that Greg Jr. received. No hot air balloon. No visit from grandma. But my sister Tonya was there and was a witness to Greg Jr. and Donovan meeting for the first time. Donovan was a much different baby than Greg. He was darker and he had more hair on his head, especially in the back. Terri made the most of the situation by wrapping all that hair in a rubber band and making it a ponytail. He was cute. It was wonderful to have a little baby in the house again.

BABY DON—Here's Donovan at around the age of 1.

CHAPTER 16

Using My Clout

THE JOB AT ABIL WASN'T WORKING OUT. I knew how to do the job. I was capable of doing the job. But On a Roll exclusively dominated my heart and passion. Never before in my life had I been so determined and focused about anything. The energy and enthusiasm I had about my radio show was guided by a calling, a spiritual awakening to a realization of purpose for my life. I was an important figure. People with disabilities were isolated from sharing collective experiences and an understanding that they were not alone. They needed a mass media outreach effort to free them from believing that their problems, stemming from society's handling of their disabilities, were not their fault and they were not alone in their experiences. When I met other disabled people, their encouragement and support was unwavering. It was a mini-movement. We were taking the airwaves and confronting injustices; shedding light on new philosophies that seemed so foreign to the common man.

For example, in 1992, the Phoenix Suns were ready to host the first games at their new palace, the America West Arena. Six months earlier, as a member of the marketing staff at KTAR, I was invited along with about 300 other members of the Phoenix Ad Club to an exclusive tour of the facility. While everyone else in the group sat in the lower seats near courtside, I had to take an elevator up to the concourse level and eat my box lunch in the wheelchair section, 100 feet above everyone else. I could barely hear Suns owner, Jerry Colangelo's presentation. However, this was before my activist awakening. I was just happy to be a member of the Ad Club and delighted to be able to participate in this special tour of this amazing new facility.

Now, six months later, disability activists were outraged by the arena's not offering sufficient wheelchair-accessible seating as required by the Americans with Disabilities Act. Furthermore, the seating they did offer was located directly behind non-disabled spectators. Whenever Charles Barkley approached the hoop to make an accentuated slam dunk, or "Thunder Dan" Majerle squared up for the three pointer, the people in front of the wheelchair section would stand up, completely blocking the view of the paying customers with disabilities. We'd have to seek out one of the many monitors to catch the live action.

ABIL led the charge against the Suns, threatening a lawsuit, picketing and creating bad PR for the Suns. I was well known in the Suns front office, having covered the Suns' home games for KCMO in Kansas City when I was in college, and continuing to attend games regularly as a member of the press after I graduated. I knew Tom Ambrose, the Suns' public relations director quite well. I had met Jerry Colangelo many times. They all liked me and held a great deal of respect for my determination, despite my disability. I knew many of the players. I knew their long-time public address announcer Stan Richards, who had recently passed away, and I had shed tears with the Suns family at his funeral.

ABIL hosted an activist meeting to address the crisis at the arena. I listened carefully to their angry arguments.

"The Suns are pompous," said Susan. "They simply don't care about people with disabilities. They can sell more seats to non-disabled customers and it is all about the bottom line. And they are being arrogant about it."

"What I can't believe is that they spent all this money designing this multimillion-dollar facility, with many accessible features like elevators, and an accessible parking garage, and accessible bathrooms, and the one thing they didn't get right was the concept that people in wheelchairs might actually want to go to basketball games to *watch* basketball," said another advocate.

Finally, I chimed in. "I don't think the Suns are arrogant, and don't think they are slighting people with disabilities," I said. "I think they are victims of poor architectural consulting, and now they're afraid of how much money it is going to cost them to repair the problem."

"I know the Suns front office quite well from my years in the media," I continued. "Perhaps I can talk to them on this group's behalf."

After a couple hours of discussion about strategy, we agreed that I would try to get an "interview" with Jerry Colangelo to get his comments on the situation. We decided that an "interview" would be less threatening, and would build on the already existing relationship. If nothing happened, a lawsuit would soon follow.

Jerry's office was located inside the arena, which in 1992 was truly a cutting-edge facility. As I entered the facility, I received several greetings from familiar faces who worked for the Suns. Everything shined with newness. The Suns front offices were plush, decorated with contemporary art deco furniture, and lots of Phoenix Suns graphics. The carpet on the lobby floor was a giant purple and orange "sunburst" Phoenix Suns logo. After a short wait, Jerry emerged and walked me into his large spacious office.

We chatted before I pulled out the tape recorder.

"Greg, you know, when you build a facility the size and scope of what we have here, there are going to be things you could have done better," he started. "And frankly a lot of noise coming from the disability community angers me. And I understand that when you reach a certain level of success, you become a target to criticism. That Susan Webb is way off base when she talks about this 'universal design' concept. Not everything can be universally designed. But she is an advocate, and I understand that and respect her for that."

I just listened without expression, except perhaps an encouraging nod for him to continue.

"We think we have a solution to the line of sight issue," he said. "Our plan is to insert rafters in the wheelchair sections that would raise the height of the floor another 36 inches. This would create a situation where even if a six-foot tall person stood in front of a person seated, it would not interfere with line of sight."

Installing the rafters would cost the Suns over $100,000, but I knew the Suns would make it right. To make the announcement, Suns officials, including Brian Colangelo, Jerry's son, came down to KFNN to be on my show that weekend. We invited guests from architectural firms who specialized in arena construction and more properly handled the accessibility issues to give input. Brian was concerned that their appearance would be an "ambush," but I assured him this was not my plan. The result was a healthy dialogue about access at sporting events and the concept that people with disabilities were sports fans too.

The controversy soon died down. The line of sight issue was resolved and Phoenicians with disabilities enjoyed very good Suns team during their run to the 1993 NBA Finals.

All the players would remember me today. I interviewed them all. Barkley, KJ, Mark West, Cedric Ceballos, Nigel Knight, Oliver Miller, Tom Chambers, "Thunder Dan" Majerle. What a team! On my 30th birthday, the Suns had just beaten the Lakers and I was in the locker room after the game. A giant screen television was rolled out in front of Charles Barkley's locker so the team could watch the NCAA tournament games while they dressed. The game we were watching was a nail biting, seesaw battle, draining down to the final seconds. All the Suns were crowded around me as I fought for front-row position to watch the end of this game. The team down by one had the ball as the clock ticked down to the final 10 seconds, and they kept passing off! Nobody would take the potential game-winning shot!

"Shoot it!" yelled Barkley. "Do you wanna be a *star*? Shoot the damn ball!"

The kid passed the ball, and they never got a good look. They lost. As Charles dressed, I chatted with him, and at some point, casually pulled out my tape recorder to graduate this conversation into an interview.

"Charles, when we were watching that game, you yelled at the TV, 'Do you wanna be a star? Shoot the ball.' Is that your secret to stardom, the guts to go for it and take a shot."

"No, I'm just a very good basketball player," the Chuckster jested. After we laughed at his humor, he volunteered, "Yes, a person has to be willing to take risks and make something happen. You can't be scared and timid and be successful."

Words to live by.

God, I loved radio. I loved my show. I hungered to make it grow; to become a national figure and give people with disabilities a sense of optimism, and perhaps more importantly, to introduce America to the real personalities and experiences of people with disabilities.

ABIL was a transitional way for me to learn disability issues and if I could help them through the work I was doing with *On A Roll*, it would be best for both organizations. But I wasn't doing my job at ABIL. I was unable to pull my heart and energy away from *On A Roll*.

Susan and I both agreed that if *On A Roll* was going to be my passion, I should devote my time and energy exclusively to it. Now that I learned a little bit more about the disability "system," I learned that it was possible for me to receive Social Security disability benefits and do the show on the side. I had worked for five years earning between $30,000 and $40,000 per year, so as it turned out, my disability payments would total roughly $1,400 per month. Furthermore, I could earn an additional $500 per month and still keep my benefits. This would be an opportunity for me to focus on the show and still have a financial base. So that's what I did. In 1993, I resigned from ABIL and went on Social Security. How ironic was it that I, unlike any other recipient in the nation, was working 70 hours per week! Not only was I working, my job was to build and promote a radio talk show that empowered people with disabilities to free themselves of the very same benefits I was receiving.

I understood the dissonance in that, but felt justified to make this my reality. I also understood the potential controversy and the whiff of hypocrisy that could be associated with this setup, so I didn't tell anyone about it. The ends justified the means. I was reaching out and empowering thousands of people every week. The US government made it possible.

Selling advertising on KFNN did not allow me to earn much additional income through *On A Roll*. We were constantly considering ways to realize our vision of national expansion. We never regarded *On A Roll* as a local Phoenix show. To us, it was a work in progress; a vision that we shared. We realized that we needed to start reaching out to key people on the national disability scene and establish net-working relationships. We needed to attract the attention of people who had power and influence in the disability community. Surely, if leading disability advocates and directors of organizations knew what we were trying to do, they would point us towards possible grants or corporate sponsorships.

One of the national heavyweights I aspired to meet was Lex Frieden from Houston. He was a leader in the independent living movement and was the director of Independent Living Research Utilization (ILRU), an organization affiliated with Baylor University's College of Medicine. ILRU existed as a national center for informa-tion, training, research, and technical assistance in independent living. They were trying to expand the body of knowledge in independent liv-ing and create ways to promote the results of their research and demonstration projects. I was so excited to be meeting Lex because I was certain that expanding the concept of talk radio on life and dis-ability would be a fundable way to promote independent living. In 1994, I learned that he was going to be in Tucson to speak at an event and to meet with one of his best grant writers, Quentin Smith. Lex invited me to meet with the two of them, and from that meeting sprung the idea of applying for another grant.

I had a bad taste in my mouth as far as grants went because of the rollercoaster disappointment with the CPB grant. But Quentin was very upbeat about our chances to get this Small Business Innovation Grant (SBIR) from the National Institutes of Health. We worked tire-lessly on this proposal and drove down to Tucson to spend time at his computer crafting the text, which proved once again to be of no avail.

Despair set in as I read the latest grant rejection letter. There seemed to be no financial home for the concept of a national radio show on disability issues, either in the commercial world or in the non-profit world of foundations and government grants.

I called Ed Roberts. I knew he had close connections with Bank of America, based in his home city of San Francisco. He gave me some names of decision makers there. This led to taking Terri and Greg Jr. on a flight to the Bay Area, where I would meet with two people in

BofA's marketing department. This looked promising. Bank of America's Arizona division had been the first sponsor of *On A Roll* locally in Phoenix, and the relationship was very strong. I brought tape of the two-minute interview segments BofA aired on our Phoenix show to demonstrate the program's effectiveness in targeting banking customers with disabilities. In the Phoenix BofA spots, we talked about Access Loans, which allowed people with disabilities to purchase expensive vehicle modifications by extending payments out over seven or eight years. We talked about their fledgling internet banking system, and having Braille accessibility on their ATM machines. Our weekly interviews with Steve Carr, and then his successor, David Howell intimately connected BofA-Arizona with the Phoenix disability community.

Now in San Francisco, Terri made sure I looked good. My presentation was immaculate and impressive. I brought my family along to introduce them to the bank heavyweights and to demonstrate in living flesh, the potential that people with disabilities had to live wonderful lives. Terri looked great, and I was proud to be able to "wow" business contacts by introducing her as my wife.

I did a great job making the case for expanding *On A Roll* in all of the Bank of America States. We exchanged business cards. With smiles and handshakes, their media department promised to evaluate my presentation and get back to me. I was asking for $50,000 to cover satellite expenses for national distribution. Big money, huh?

Nothing happened. After two weeks, I called to learn that the ad agency had recommended that they not sponsor the show.

"It's ok, Greg. Don't beat yourself up over it. You'll find the money for the satellite. *When one door closes, another one opens!*"

CHAPTER 17

~

Moving Forward

IN MARCH OF 1995, Todd and I decided to attend The President's Committee on Employment of People with Disabilities conference in Portland, Oregon, It would be the first of several national conferences we would attend in our attempt to network and establish connections with the disability power structure. This decision did not please Terri, who felt that my passion for the radio show was far outweighing my passion for the family. My steadfast dedication to my vision was taking its toll on my marriage. The boys were toddlers; Greg Jr. was three, and Donovan was about 18 months old. Terri was becoming increasingly frustrated with On A Roll. I accused her of not wanting to be associated so closely with the disability community. When I was at KTAR, all of my friends were non-disabled people, but now that I was so involved in the disability community, most of the people who came to our house were people with disabilities. I think this bothered her a little bit. She would often make statements to minimize the significance of my work. She often questioned why I would leave a $50,000 per year job to try to do something there was no market for.

"You've been doing your radio show for two years and you ain't makin' no money. You need to let that radio show go and go out and get a job. We got two kids here and we don't have enough money coming in to pay the bills on this Social Security."

From my perspective, it was my love for her and the family that fueled my tireless effort to make the show finally succeed, which would give us the financial rewards we deserved. The weeks leading up the Portland trip were filled with late night work sessions, as I spent time producing sponsorship presentations, collecting e-mail addresses for my on-line newsletter and reading and learning everything I could about disability issues. Terri's constant bickering and complaining was starting to wear on me; it seemed quite possible that my experiment in changing Terri into the woman I wanted her to be was failing. Her attitude was so negative. I was "glass half full" kind of guy. She was a "glass half empty" kind of girl. Perhaps a feeling that this marriage was doomed led me, for the first time, to regard Terri as a temporary solution. I began to think that there might possibly be happiness outside of the dark cloud of negative emotions and arguments, broken dishes and slamming doors that was my home.

In June 1995, we went to the National Council on Independent Living conference at the Renaissance Hotel in Bethesda, Maryland. This was the first time we had ever been around so many people with disabilities who shared information and held the same philosophy on disability equality and rights. It was a paradigm shift for me to see so many diverse manifestations of disabilities. Wheelchair users of all kinds were only a small fraction of the 500 participants. There were people who walked, hobbled and limped in all kinds of creative and unique ways. There were blind people, deaf people, people who stuttered—every disabling condition imaginable and to me, it all seemed so comforting. I felt so at home and among friends at this conference. For the first time in my life, I was not profoundly different from everybody else around me. Can you relate to how empowering that feeling can be for the first time?

Ed Roberts had passed away a few months prior to this conference. He was my main connection, the guy who was going to stamp my ticket as a force to be reckoned with in the disability community. Instead, this NCIL conference became his memorial. His wheelchair was displayed in front of the elevator as a monument.

Now, I was nobody on the national disability scene, but I knew who the "somebodies" were. Todd and I went to the conference with demo tapes of our show, flyers and presentations about our vision to find the funding to pay for satellite distribution, making it available to radio stations nationwide. We met Judy Heumann, one of Ed's most important partners in starting the Independent Living movement. She was a "star" at this conference. Crowds of people followed her everywhere she went. She had hugs and kisses for everyone. We pulled her to the side to explain our vision. On a napkin, I sketched a radio tower, a satellite uplink, a satellite in space, and a downlink dish, along with a miserable attempt at a map of the USA. She quickly "got it," and dictated dozens of contacts that might lead to what we were after.

In terms of money or sponsorship leads, nothing really tangible resulted from attending that first NCIL conference; however, I met dozens of people who would become friends and supporters over the years. This conference was my foundation to connecting with the leaders on the national disability scene. I met Justin Dart, the then-chairman of the President's Committee on Employment of Disabilities. He had been the main leader of the people with disabilities cause for years. He was an amazing orator who rallied the community with words and passion about his vision. He had no idea who I was, but I forced myself to get in front of him and shake his hand after Ed's memorial. I was immediately struck by the wisdom that shined from his eyes. Finally, I was starting to meet people who could help.

When I returned from that trip, Terri greeted me at the airport and she wasn't the same person. I could tell she was keeping something from me. I suspected infidelity. I sought answers, which led to more questions and eventually, a confession. Memories of the demise of my marriage which started a decade before I write these words are very fuzzy, probably the result of a natural human tendency to bury pain. What I do know is that she admitted to a one-night stand while I was away, and that I decided to move to Ohio and live with my parents. Somehow, my two sons ended up living in Ohio shortly thereafter. I remember the pain of my first night sleeping alone on the couch of my parents' den. I would call home just to see if Terri was there. My heart was broken. I was a wreck.

In retrospect, I don't blame her for giving some thought to finding intimacy somewhere else. I was always traveling. In my mind, I never really accepted her as the woman I wanted to be with. I accepted her as the woman I settled for. The only reason I never had affairs was because I didn't have the confidence to approach anyone, or the experience or knowledge to do so. There were many women I knew in Phoenix whom I had lunch "dates" with. I had many opportunities to have affairs, and if I had expressed my feelings, to this day have no doubt that I could have. But I was too naïve. So in my mind, I had cheated. Terri's one-nighter was not much worse.

You never know what you have until you lose it. I was a mess, living in Ohio with my parents, who were glad that I had decided to leave Terri. They never liked her and always figured she was wrong for me.

Slowly, I began to accept that I needed to move on with my life. I contacted the Independent Living Center in Dayton and we soon established an *On A Roll* show on WING AM. The show aired on Friday evenings at 6pm. I had no studio equipment in Ohio so I had to do the show from the station. Every week, my guests and I would meet after the show with the folks from the Independent Living Center at a place called Cold Beer & Cheeseburgers. We'd play pool, talk disability politics, and envision what we could all do together in Dayton. I began to feel immersed in the community. However, after about 10 months, Terri and I decided to try to make our marriage work. I had forgiven her. Our sons needed to be with their mother. Greg Jr. was four and Donovan was not even two. I purchased the plane tickets and called home. She didn't answer the phone. It went to voice mail, and knowing the passwords, I listened to the messages.

"Hey baby, it's me, Michael. Give me a call when you get my message."

She was messing around again, but I had already purchased the tickets and didn't want to endure the embarrassment of telling my parents what I had found out. I went ahead with the decision to return to the Valley of the Sun. I missed Phoenix. When I arrived, I asked her who Michael was and she was shocked that I knew anything about him. I badgered her to find out all I could about this guy, whom it turns out she met while working at a car dealership. I found out where he worked. I called him at his job and asked him if he was messing with my wife. He told me that what my wife and I talked about was none of his business. Then he called back and warned me not to contact him again. I was livid with rage. I got in my van and drove to the dealership to confront him, fueled by sheer anger. I had no weapons, but I guess I planned to charge my chair into his desk and smash him against the wall! Luckily, he wasn't there, or perhaps he was wise enough to tell his receptionist he was out. I went home and began the process of reconstructing my family.

We got involved in a church. My neighbor Al had recently joined the ministry. He and his family embraced mine and helped us develop a closer relationship with God. We went to Fisher Chapel AME on Broadway in South Phoenix every week. I played my electronic drum pads along with the choir. I became a deacon. My spirituality grew and we developed a strong bond with our church family.

We continued to establish momentum with the radio show. I began to get invitations from other communities to come help them establish their own radio shows on disability issues. Soon, there were *On A Roll* programs airing in Dayton, Ohio; Ann Arbor, Michigan; El Paso, Texas; and Topeka, Kansas.

We continued to strategize and labor over how we would take this concept of "Talk Radio on Life & Disability" nationwide. The market-by-market concept of spinning off other shows wasn't lucrative, and it involved a lot of handholding and micromanagement. Syndication was the way to go, but that required a hefty bill for satellite distribution, and a lot of time and effort selling radio stations on adding this show to their programming lineup.

While surfing the net one evening, I found a website for KDWN radio in Las Vegas, which claimed an evening coverage area of eight Southwestern states! We contacted them and learned that we could purchase airtime on this 50,000-watt station for $300 per week. Surely, we'd be able to find sponsorships to support that! We were currently paying KFNN $250 a week for airtime. So Todd and I began calling businesses in Las Vegas in search of sponsors.

We realized soon enough that the only way to sell radio advertising on a new concept like this was face to face. We began our series of trips to Las Vegas soon thereafter. For several months, one of us flew to Vegas at least twice a month, sometimes spending a week or ten days running the business there. We negotiated a cheap living arrangement with a dorm at UNLV. We found the best wheelchair-accessible cab drivers. And we hooked up with the disability community, who again embraced us as heroes.

Soon we had exchanged radio airtime with the local newspaper, and got a nice ad promoting the show in the paper each Sunday. We secured enough sponsors to pay for the airtime, but soon it became obvious that it would be impossible to keep all of these shows spinning.

~

CHAPTER 18

Syndication at Last

When one door closes, another one opens.

W E'VE ALL HEARD THAT CLICHÉ. Words of consolation; "Happy speak" from loved ones who care about us and don't like to see us with our spirits down. They don't want us to mope, and in effect, bring them down either. So everyone says, "It's gonna be OK" or "Don't worry. You'll land on your feet" or "Look on the bright side…"

But we don't. We analyze what we did wrong and ask ourselves all sorts of damaging questions about whether we should even continue pursuing a goal that has been derailed.

"Is this worth it?" we ask ourselves.

"No," we answer.

"Why am I wasting my time on this?

"I have no idea."

"Why was I thinking I could pull this off?"

"Because you're a fool."

Our friends and loved ones remind us of how difficult the goal was in the first place, and we embrace that realization. We feel better knowing that the chances of doing what we aspired to do were very slim and at least we had the drive and the spirit to try. We rationalize that most people wouldn't have even tried.

Then, in a fleeting moment, our great idea ceases to swim. Now it slowly, lifelessly floats with the flow of the stream, away from any possibility of experiencing the breath of life, the tangibility of reality. What does become real is a stain on our brain; a scar of self-doubt about our ability to accomplish, to create, and to innovate. What once energized us and gave us a zest for the day is no longer. We mourn and we move on.

We don't have to do that. We have a choice. But we must make the choice immediately, without hesitation, before the damaging questions emerge.

This is a lesson I have learned gradually over the past 11 years. In 1996, four years into the grind of producing a weekly radio talk show on disabilities and feeling very proud about we were doing on the air, I was determined to see my idea reach a national audience. The radio networks declined.

"Well, I admire your courage and what you're trying to do is quite noble. You are an amazing guy, but a talk show on disabilities seems, well, a bit negative. People turn on the radio to be *entertained*, not educated or enlightened. People don't want to feel bad about the way people with disabilities are treated. If you aren't disabled, why would you want to listen to a show about disabilities, and after all, isn't the percentage of people with disabilities a small, small fraction of the population?"

These objections haunted me in my dreams; non-stop reruns of actual phone conversations and face-to-face meetings with tall, white, physically fit radio network executives, who probably looked at me as that poor little skinny black boy who is trying to make something of his devastating disability. By day, I read statistics from the National Organization on Disability. The results were startling, even to me: fewer than 10% of people with disabilities even knew about the Americans with Disabilities Act and what their rights were under the new law! Some 73% of people with disabilities were unemployed. And 80% of people with disabilities were not satisfied with the quality of their lives.

The market was there. All we had to do was find somebody to say "yes."

One of our most entertaining shows featured Kathy Wolf, an experienced, blind disability journalist from Washington, DC who wrote an article for *The Disability Rag* about biblical characters with disabilities. We got her on the air.

"*Moses was a disabled person,*" she said, "*Because in the Bible it says that he was slow of speech.*"

175

"At the burning bush, he kind of freaked out when God gave him this great assignment and he said 'Lord, are you sure you want ME to do this, cause you know I have this ss-sss sspeaking ppppp pp—problem.'

"And the Lord said, 'Well you got your brother Aaron, and he can go with you and help you if you need to,' so I guess Aaron was the world's first example of a r-r-r-r r reasonable ac—c-c-cc-ommodation!"

On A Roll was making people laugh. It was making people feel empowered. It was making people realize that they were a part of an energetic community of individuals who took action to make the world a better place. If you were an *On A Roll* listener in Phoenix those days, you were on the ground floor of excitement. The relationship between ABIL and *On A Roll* was great. We promoted what they did, and they supported *On A Roll* promotionally and sometimes with staffing.

Just about every week, somebody from ABIL was on the air with us. Either Susan Webb would come down, all the way from her home in Avondale. Or Donna Redford, ABIL's community integration director, a very warm, kind and amazingly intelligent woman whose disability was a form of psoriasis, would drop our jaws with her knowledge and experience. Sometimes, Denise Thompson, with her strong Michigan accent would join us in-studio. Denise was blind and used a guide dog to get all over Phoenix independently. Her personal stories were quite humorous. Morris Anderson, an acquaintance, would come down to watch the show and have fun with me and Todd. His insight and perspective on our weekly topics often got him involved in our discussions and on the air. His sense of humor and contagious laughter added to the shenanigans and helped lighten up the show. He quickly became a regular co-host and added to the diversity we represented to our audience. Morris was energetic and passionate, a paraplegic due to a car accident several years before. He remains one of my closest friends in the Valley. Leslie Brumagin, a cute, redheaded quad who worked at ABIL came on to talk about an accessible ski trip, and because of this, I found myself in a sit-ski in the mountains of Flagstaff, Arizona two weeks later. I was carefully bundled into a kind of toboggan-like contraption, high off the ground on a ski lift, about to slide down a mountain tethered to another skier who guided me from behind.

These were fun times. It seemed like every other Saturday, there was a fun activity in the disability community, which would give us plenty to talk about on the radio the next afternoon. For example, Don Price, a quad from Wisconsin, and another one of my best friends in the Valley, was the president of the local Fishing Has No Boundaries chapter. FHNB is a non-profit organization with chapters in several communities across the country. Their mission is to open up the great outdoors to all disabled persons through fishing. They would have samples of assistive devices to aid disabled anglers on fishing excursions, where owners of pontoon boats would gather and spend a day socializing with fishermen with disabilities. These events were a lot of fun and continue to take place today.

By 1996, it seemed like I would never get sponsorship for syndicating the show. Once again, I went back to the rolodex, talked to Susan and to Lex, and they both had the same suggestion, "Have you ever talked to Evan Kemp?"

Evan Kemp was the Chairman of the EEOC under President George Bush. Like me, he was born with muscular dystrophy. As a child, he loathed watching Jerry Lewis parade disabled kids onto the television set and cry in their hair to raise money for "his kids." He became a disability advocate and learned the ropes of politics in Washington by working for his uncle, political columnist, Drew Pearson. This exposure motivated him to become a lawyer. As an attorney, he was instrumental in crafting the Americans with Disabilities Act, and became a trusted advisor on disability policy for President George H.W. Bush. This soon led to his appointment as Chairman of the EEOC. When Bill Clinton became president, Kemp returned to private business, running a company called Evan Kemp Associates or EKA.

The business had two sides: One, manufacturing durable medical equipment and vehicle modifications and two, marketing to people with disabilities. EKA produced a newspaper called *One Step Ahead*.

It was a high quality publication, featuring excellent journalistic standards, timely news coverage and feature articles about people with disabilities living active, productive lives.

I placed a "cold" telephone call, introducing myself and dropping Lex's name. After several transfers, I landed in the voicemail box of EKA Director of Marketing Carmen Jones. Moments later, she called back. "Hi Greg," we've heard about what you're doing out there in Phoenix. Congratulations for your show's success."

Wow, this was positive. We traded information packages. I sent some sample air-checks of the show and some basic information including a mission statement that clearly stated my ambition to grow the show nationally. They sent me some back issues of their newspaper and a videotape of a television pilot with the same name, *One Step Ahead*. Evan was clearly a guy who knew what he was doing. If he wanted to get behind my show, he could throw it leap years forward.

After arriving at the EKA offices, Carmen, an African-American wheelchair user, led me up an elevator to the conference room where EKA's Chief Operating Officer Bob Funk and Vice President Ann Colgrove were waiting. "Evan would join us shortly after. We spent the remainder of the morning and a good part of the afternoon in deep visionary discussions. Their questions were direct and well constructed: *"How can you be sure that if we invested in the satellite distribution of this show that radio stations would choose to carry it? How can we document the number of listeners? How much advertising can we sell in a one-hour show? Is there a limit to the revenue potential that would make this concept a limiting endeavor? We produced a television show called One Step Ahead and we could not get a distributor for it. How can you get a distribution channel for your radio show?"*

For the next two weeks, Todd and I crafted responses to these questions in the form of a proposal. We flew back to Washington to make our case. After another couple of weeks, Carmen called us with the bad news: they carefully considered our idea but decided that their direction didn't include radio. Another rejection. I couldn't take it.

During the two weeks we waited for a response from EKA, I began to look at other possibilities. One of these was *New Mobility*

Magazine. I had met the founder, Sam Maddox at a recent Abilities Expo and we talked in very general terms about partnering up. When Carmen called, I didn't even hang up the phone. I just pressed the receiver and called Sam!

A week later, I found myself in Malibu, California about to make the same syndication presentation to *New Mobility*, then owned by Miramar Communications. In the contemporary conference room, I met with the owners, Tim and Denise Novoselski; operations manager, Elaine Nesterick; sales manger, Tory Roher; and Sam. This time, I was more relaxed, more confident, and better prepared to handle questions. I proposed that *New Mobility* invest in the satellite time and provide salaries for Todd and me. In addition, I requested a cover article in the magazine and ads promoting the radio show in every issue. In exchange, we would promote *New Mobility* on the air, and give them commercial airtime they could sell to their advertisers in combination with their magazine sales. It was a love fest! They loved the concept, and pretty soon, I was smiling for a national audience from the cover of *New Mobility*!

In 1997, thanks to *New Mobility*, *On A Roll* was syndicated. We started with about 15 stations nationwide, which picked the show up via satellite. We would add another station every few weeks. The content synergy with *New Mobility* was great because we could talk about issues featured in the magazine. Promotionally, I gave them an opportunity to have a face and a name associated with the magazine, so they flew me to all of the consumer Abilities Expos, where we had lots of fun and adventure.

One of the things I learned from this experience was just how little non-disabled people really relate to the disability experience. Traveling with Elaine, Tory and Sam was fun because they were so amazed at all the little hassles that come with traveling in a wheelchair, arranging transportation and getting hotel accessibility; or that transferring on commuter jets during a trip from LAX to New Jersey and then to Washington DC is never easy. Add to that a little rain and some timeline issues, and you have an adventure. Elaine was so fascinated by all of the challenges, she took notes.

On that 1997 trip, we went to a media preview of the new FDR Memorial, which had just opened. There was a great deal of controversy surrounding the memorial because disability advocates were appalled that the sculpture did not depict the President in his wheelchair. We wanted a statue of FDR in his wheelchair so that in the future, young people with disabilities could look at one of the most heroic American figures of all time and be able to say that he was "like me." The main statue of FDR features the President and his dog Fala. FDR is wearing a cape and is seated in an office chair, which quite accurately, had small wheels he would rely on to move about.

There was a steady light drizzle the morning of the press preview. I called for a cab the night before, but in Washington, accessible cabs are not very dependable. I was frustrated and angry as Elaine and I arrived late to the media tour. The tour was just ending as the ramp descended, allowing me to exit the mini-van cab. Officials with the memorial agreed to give me a private tour and I rolled through the press corps to observe the memorial. When we reached the main statue, I suddenly heard the clicking of cameras! I turned my wheelchair around to see literally dozens of photographers all getting a picture of me, one of the first wheelchair users to see the statue of FDR in his office chair with the little wheels. The photo perfectly represented the controversy. The next morning and the next week, that photo was on the front page of *USA Today*, in *Newsweek,* and several other major newspapers and magazines around the world! I was just lucky enough to be at the right place at the right time. The people at *New Mobility* were thrilled with the energy I brought to the team.

We hooked up with Robby Heisner, the lead singer of the rock group Van Gogh. Robby and his brother, Rickey both had muscular dystrophy and had been featured in many disability-related publications and in an ad campaign for Invacare power wheelchairs. They produced the theme song for our new syndicated show! At Abilities Expos, we would do the show in front of live audiences and interview "celebrities" with disabilities live on location. Before long, Invacare was a national sponsor of the show, awarding me me the first of three promotional state-of-the-art power chairs. There was a buzz in 1997.

After a sales meeting in Malibu, I rushed home on an early flight. Terri had admitted herself into the hospital. She was about to give birth to our daughter. When I landed at the airport, I drove directly to the hospital, but I was too late for the C-section. While Terri was sleeping, I had the honor of giving Berkeley Rene Smith her first bottle of formula as I held her soft, tiny hand. She was so beautiful.

COVER BOY—Smiling for the April 1997 *New Mobility Magazine* cover at Lambchops studios in Phoenix.

CHAPTER 19

Spreading My Wings

INEVER REALLY WANTED TO GET A DIVORCE. When I returned from a trip to Miami in December 1997, Terri and I got into a discussion that turned into a violent argument. My father happened to be in town on business. He and I had returned from a rib dinner and he dropped me off at the house. Thirty minutes later, while books, shelves, tapes, and radio studio cords were flying across my home office, I was dialing Dad's number, leaving the phone off the hook for him to hear the screaming. Then I did the same with 911.

Though I had been assaulted in the recent past, I didn't fully know the extent of her violent rage. So out of fear, I reached out for help and this set in motion an irreversible course of events. Dad was enraged. Terri was arrested. The marriage was over.

I returned again to the safety and comfort of my parent's home in Yellow Springs. Their master bedroom suite became my studio/bedroom/office. Mom and Dad moved upstairs and sacrificed their comfort for the safety and comfort of their son and grandchildren. It was a devastating time for me. When you've been married for so many years and you have become familiar with the stability of a warm body next to you when it's time to hit the sack, you're not going to get any sleep for a month.

As I tossed and turned, I regretted making those calls out of panic. We had been in arguments before, and as I found myself in a cold, lonely bed, halfway across the country, I spent many nights wondering what was so different about this fight.

Much of my reflection was stuck in finding blame. I blamed Terri for not taking her medicine consistently and for being so sensitive and resistant to constructive encouragement. I blamed my parents for

ME AND KIDS IN OHIO—Hanging out with the kids in the back yard in Yellow Springs, Ohio back in 1999.

never really accepting her in the first place and their snotty attitude about people not as fortunate as they had been in life. And I blamed myself for modeling the treatment of a wife after what I had witnessed as a child.

Slowly, reflection on the past gave way to realizing that there was a future here in Ohio, and I'd better stop whining and start living. So

HOUSE IN OHIO—The front of our house on Livermore Street in Yellow Springs, Ohio

I did what I do best—radio. I continued to do the syndicated show with *New Mobility Magazine* as the key sponsor, and promoted it locally in Ohio, resulting in newspaper and television features.

My children started to develop strong friendships with their class-mates, and I started to meet some wonderful people. One of Greg Jr.'s best friends was a kid named Max Fleishman. Just about every other day, he and Max would arrange to play together. I'd drive him over there, or his mother and father would bring Max over. They played video games and hit golf balls away from the house in our enormous back yard overlooking what once was a golf course.

One day, unsupervised, Max hit a line drive straight through our plate-glass patio window. When I heard the noise, I rolled my chair down the ramp to the patio just in time to see little Max scurrying in the opposite direction! He was gettin' out of Dodge! My mother had to go after him to get him to come back in tears!

Greg, Max, and Donovan loved playing video games and drawing cartoons. Max's dad, Mike is a graphic artist, and Max definitely inherited those genes. They spent a lot of time together as the three amigos.

Max's mother is Joanne Caputo. In our frequent visits to drop off or pick up our kids, we developed a friendship. Over time, I learned that she was a videographer and had done a film about ballerinas. She broached the idea of doing a documentary film about me and my radio show, and before long, I found myself on my parents' back patio being interviewed on Joanne's little Canon Mini-DV camera.

I must say that I expected very little of this "documentary" idea. Nevertheless, I treated the project with respect and hoped for the best.

My best friend in Yellow Springs was Aileen LeBlanc. She was a broadcaster at the public radio station, WYSO, which housed its studios on the campus of Antioch College. I met Aileen because she had heard about my work and asked to interview me for her show. When she arrived and pulled out her tape recorder, her energy and passion for radio mesmerized me. We hit it off immediately. During the interview, I had her laughing. Suddenly, my dad burst through the door to my bedroom.

"I am so sorry! I backed into your car!"

Dad, who was way too uptight and stressed from a job he didn't like, had let the garage door up, thrown his car into reverse and slammed on the gas pedal, folding Aileen's trunk in half in our driveway. It was the first day I met her.

Over the next couple of years, she was a constant companion.

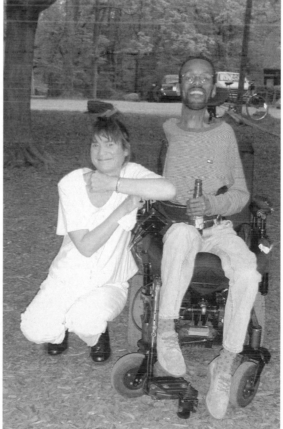

MY BEST FRIEND IN OHIO— Aileen LeBlanc and I were inseperable. Here we are at a WYSO staff party in Yellow Springs.

We developed a very strong bond. She invited me to record commentaries about disability awareness for her radio show, *Sounds Local*, from which I received a lot of positive feedback in the community. My commentaries gave me insight to the potential of sharing the disability viewpoint with the mainstream. One of my commentaries is worthy of re-printing here because it won a national Public Radio award. It was a movie review of the film *Toy Story 2*.

DONOVAN'S favorite toy inspired my commentary about the movie Toy Story 2 which won an award from the Public Radio News Directors Association in 1999.

"With very little doubt, the $80.8 million dollars we all spent Thanksgiving weekend on the movie *Toy Story 2* was well worth it. I really enjoyed the movie. But for me, it required the inconvenience of swallowing a rather large bitter pill in the premise. I won't give away very much that you don't already know, but the plot begins when one of the boy's beloved toys gets its arm nearly ripped off. Suddenly, the boy doesn't want to play with it anymore. In one of the saddest moments in recent Hollywood history, in a split second, the toy goes from being one of his most cherished to the dreaded top shelf. For obvious reasons, this disturbed me early in the movie. In the "Toy Story" world, these aren't just toys. They're living characters. They're people! Were the writers making a statement? That those who are damaged, deformed, broken, disabled are not to be played with? If they were, they've got it all wrong. They could have used more 5-year-old script consultants, like my son Donovan, a kindergartner.

The morning after we saw "Toy Story," I asked my son to go in the playroom and grab his favorite toy. He skipped back in a matter of seconds, holding in his hand the very toy I suspected he would select. You see, my son loved *Toy Story 2*, but he didn't understand the whole premise of a kid abandoning his favorite toy because of a rip in the fabric. His favorite toy is an old X-Man action figure with mammoth pectoral muscles, huge biceps, a rippled abdomen and tree-trunk thighs. His torso can swivel 360 degrees. He has full joint movements at the knees, the hips, the elbows and the shoulders. Oh, and by the way, my son's favorite action figure has one rather obvious disability. His, umm ... head ... is missing. Yes, a hit-and-run power wheelchair decapitated this X-Man over two years ago. But my son quickly embraced the toy after the accident and took advantage of its differences. "His head is invisible," he says. "He can make rescues and the bad guys don't know who he is." Is my son's selection of a headless hero a result of his lifelong connection to physical differences that stems from having a disabled dad? Or is it just a numbers game? Because, much like the real world, in his cluttered playroom, one in five toys has a physical disability! I think the answer is neither. My kindergartner is an average 5-year-old entering the year 2000. His acceptance of differences is a sign of the times. It's unfortunate that the writers of *Toy Story* mistakenly promoted a dying myth: that disability equates to disregarded.

Parents, our children's broken toys offer us unique opportunities to educate our kids about a natural part of the beautiful diversity that is human life. The next time Barbie loses an arm or Ken's foot gets broken off, maybe you can encourage your child to work their action figure's newly acquired disability into their own *Toy Story*—the story line of their imagination. And if the child throws the doll away or puts it on the shelf, that would be a perfect time to have a talk about accepting everyone, even those with physical differences. Disregarding the disabled is a concept that we should leave in this millennium. Universal acceptance of disability as diversity is a concept we should take ... to infinity and beyond!"

~

Aileen's show let me spread my wings, and for the first time, write and produce material aimed at a mainstream, non-disabled audience. I loved it! I had fun and made some points in a creative way.

WYSO's popularity, and the fact that *On A Roll* aired on WHIO, the top news/talk station gave me sub-celebrity status in the Dayton area. Aileen also helped me significantly by producing a five-minute feature about my work for NPR's *All Things Considered*. The piece aired nationwide, making millions of people aware of my work.

Thanks to Aileen, my social life in Ohio was starting to come alive again. Every weekend, a group of us would go out to dinner and have some drinks, usually in Beavercreek or Fairborn because many of the taverns and places in Yellow Springs were not wheelchair accessible. Each week, we would designate it someone's birthday and the restaurant would go through their song and dance, totally embarrassing that week's victim.

My work in Ohio was creating a buzz. The fact that my show aired on the top news/talk station helped. Also, my commentaries were developing a following. Having Senator Bob Dole, Christopher Reeve and others on the show helped to solidify my credibility, and as a result, I received a lot of local media coverage in Dayton and Cincinnati.

One afternoon, the phone rang. It was one of those life-changing calls. The voice on the other end said he was a reporter for the *Wall Street Journal*.

"Yeah right! Who is this really?"

"Greg this really is Joshua Prager, and I am a reporter for the *Wall Street Journal*. I'm thinking about the possibility of doing an article about your radio show."

For the next several weeks, Mr. Prager thoroughly interviewed me. All the while, he made no promises that an article would even run. He had me digging through dusty boxes of old tapes in search of specific interviews, sound bites and interaction with callers. On one Sunday evening, he visited. When he rang the doorbell and limped into the house, it was the first I knew of his own disability. Joshua Prager is paralyzed on one side of his body from an automobile accident.

"I didn't want to tell you because I didn't want you to treat me differently," he said. I respected that.

At 4:00 in the morning, February 25, 1999, I got my first glimpse of the article when it appeared on the *Wall Street Journal* website.

This Radio Host Is 'On a Roll' With a Show for the Disabled

By JOSHUA HARRIS PRAGER
Staff Reporter of The *Wall Street Journal*

"And now, occupying the best parking space in syndicated radio, the wheelchair dude with altitude, the hip crip who gives ya tips: 'On A Roll' radio's host and founder, Greg Smith!"

Radio talk show host Greg Smith

YELLOW SPRINGS, Ohio—The opening rant for his weekly radio show concluded, Greg Smith leans into the microphone, a Velcro harness securing his 65-pound frame into his wheelchair. In a bass voice in sharp contrast to his frail body, he introduces the show's topic: entrepreneurship and disability.

It's a fitting subject for a man who broadcasts from his parents' home here, and yet has sponsors that include such corporate heavyweights as Microsoft Corp., BankAmerica Corp. and CellularOne.

Mr. Smith, 34 years old, hosts *On A Roll: Talk Radio on Life & Disability.* Part Dear Abby for the disabled, part Disability For Dummies, the weekly show is aimed at the disabled and their families and friends. Mr. Smith launched it in 1992, and from the very first broadcast, sponsored by Bank of America as a kick-off to its loan program for the disabled, *On A Roll* has benefited from an expanding line of products and services targeting the disabled as a consumer group.

Like BankAmerica, a growing number of sponsors view the disabled as a promising market, and Mr. Smith's radio show as a unique way to reach them. "Who needs cellular phones more than anybody else?" he asks. "Goodyear's tire that won't go flat—who's a perfect market for that?"

On A Roll

At a time when radio-station managers are being bombarded with program proposals, *On A Roll* is undeniably rolling. In October, the show became syndicated and is now broadcast weekly on 39 stations to an estimated national audience of several hundred thousand. In December, Microsoft signed on as a national sponsor.

The decade since the passage of the Americans with Disabilities Act in 1990 has been an age of opportunity for the disabled, and Mr. Smith's show is fast emerging as its showcase. In his more than 300 broadcasts to date, Mr. Smith has interviewed such disabled notables as Bob Dole, Christopher Reeve and television personality John Hockenberry.

He has fielded calls on the disabled golfer Casey Martin, the wheelchair-bound Barbie doll and the planned monument of FDR in a wheelchair. And he has moderated discussions on disability and employment, disability and medical research, and disability and relationships, all with a mix of sincerity and subtle irreverence.

Marketing to the disabled has become a growth industry in recent years. For example, 15 banks in 18 states have instituted loan-programs for the disabled like the BankAmerica program that helped launch Mr. Smith's show. The default rate on such loans is lower than on others. The proposed federal budget announced just this month, would dedicate $16 million, up from $12 million last year, to guaranteeing micro-loan programs, including those targeting the disabled.

For the companies backing Mr. Smith's program, there's little altruism and a lot of potential revenue involved. "For a lot of people with disabilities, radio is an excellent way of getting the word out. It seems like a very smart investment," says Luanne LaLonde, an accessibility product manager at Microsoft. It advertises how its software can be modified for use by people with varied disabilities, providing them with such features as enlarged icons, audio rather than visual cues and desensitized keys that won't respond to tremors.

Mr. Smith was diagnosed with an undetermined form of muscular dystrophy when he was only three years old. His interest in voice work began shortly after that. In seventh grade, the first year Mr. Smith was confined to a wheelchair, he became the public address announcer for his school's basketball team. In college, he was sports director of the Arizona State University radio station, and later spent five years at KTAR radio in Phoenix, as research director and host of the Arizona Cardinals post-game call-in show.

But a spat soon changed his direction toward advocacy. Mr. Smith asked his boss at KTAR to be moved into sales. "You're not a sales person," he recalls being curtly told. "I yelled at my boss, 'You don't know what I am!' "

Suddenly, being a sportscaster seemed a hollow pursuit. "There will always be hundreds of them. But how many people can do their little part to change the world?"

So, he sought funding to launch On A Roll in the Phoenix area. BankAmerica saw a quick fit with the bank's new program to target disabled borrowers.

Seven years of Sunday nights later, Mr. Smith prepares to take the air at 9 p.m. Eastern time. Using his right foot to operate a joystick rigged to his wheelchair, he moves with ease about the room that doubles as his studio and bedroom. The talk show host takes his place flanked by a scanner, printer and mixer. He leans forward, puts his elbow on his thigh, and rests his chin on his fist.

ADA Protection?

Mr. Smith poses a question to his audience: "Should people who are obese, or people who are otherwise healthy but homely, be protected by the ADA?" Quickly, callers from Maine to Nevada begin to blink on a screen.

"Darryl is calling from Tempe," he tells his audience.

"If somebody just like, over-ate all the time and it's not really a medical condition, then they're not disabled," insists Darryl.

Even though Mr. Smith says he feels healthy now, he needs more and more help to care for himself. "You get to be 35" with the disease, he says, "you're getting up there."

And so he attends to his career with a sense of urgency. He labored over a recent application for a Public Broadcasting grant with such resolve, neglecting to eat and sleep for days, that he ended up in the emergency room. "I get so focused sometimes," he says, "I forget about the basic things." He adds, "Everything in my life is centered on the show. It's my baby."

≈

LIVING IN OHIO—I was feeling good about myself the day the Wall Sreet Journal article hit the streets in February 1999

ME & MISHA—Michelle Hlavek was my girlfriend in 1999 and 2000. She is now Mrs. Peter Carston and we are great friends. Here we are at the premiere of the On A Roll documentary in February 2005.

This was an exciting time for me! In addition to the career momentum, I was falling in love in cyberspace with a lady named Michelle, a quadriplegic fan of the show who had become injured after a head first dive from a pier into a sand bar in 1993.

I had never dated a woman in a wheelchair before. My hunch was that it would be difficult physically. But the more time I spent with her in AOL instant messages and on the phone, the more I realized I was developing strong feelings for her.

We finally agreed to meet after several months of "virtual" dating. What I admired and enjoyed most about her was her nutty sense of humor. When I arrived at the airport in Orlando, it seemed like we had known each other for years. She lived in a two-bedroom condo in Winter Park, Florida, and I really admired the way she had her life organized. She supervised a staff of personal assistants who would get her up and dressed, cook for her, and organize her living space. I learned a lot about how a person with a disability can have her or his own freedom and independence by managing personal assistant services.

We had memorable moments that first visit. At the mall, I took control of her power wheelchair with my right hand and guided us both in unison from shop to shop, insisting that she trust me not to crash her into the wall. We went to see Cirque de Soleil and I returned the trust, not worrying about how she drove her van with hand controls. Our personalities were in sync. However, as I had suspected, physically, we were never able to do what people who love each other do. And trust me. It wasn't due to lack of effort.

Michelle and I are great friends today and will be forever. She is now happily married (to a non-disabled man) and in the process of building a wheelchair-accessible home.

LOVING LIFE IN TAMPA—On the air live from my apartment studio in Temple Terrace, Florida, across the street from AccessLife.com.

CHAPTER 20

The Web Master

FTER THE *WALL STREET JOURNAL* ARTICLE appeared, a new level of opportunity emerged. I secured a new syndicator, Brad Saul, who had developed successful programming in Chicago and was interested in my show because of his multiple sclerosis. He was also starting a non-profit organization called the Radio Center for People with Disabilities, aimed at helping people with disabilities find employment in the radio industry. I got great media coverage and literary agents began to show some interest in me. The article definitely raised my credibility level and led to some significant changes in my life.

Before long, telephone calls started sprinkling in from emerging web entrepreneurs hoping to cash in on the size of the disability market. This was during the Internet "gold rush." They were business people from all over the country, short on connections and knowledge of the disability community and long on truckloads of cash from venture capital investors. I was in a great spot, already having a leg up in the market. A company from San Diego flew me out to tour their facility and requested a proposal for merging *On A Roll* with their web site. While I was still visiting that group, another from New York called, and a third from Tampa. I was in a position of power. Eventually, five major players contacted me.

My favorite was iCan.com, a company formed by entrepreneur Heidi Van Arnem, a savvy marketer who had established a travel agency for people with disabilities in the 90s. That move earned her the title "Entrepreneur of the Year" from the President's Committee on Employment of People with Disabilities. Heidi was very impressive, with an on-air persona that was personable and articulate. I continued to follow her progress as she talked about her vision for iCan. Heidi was a quadriplegic from a gun shot in her early teens. A Detroit native, her charisma and her intellect were complemented by her striking beauty and grace. She had great potential to bring people together and lead the Internet charge. And the disability advocate in my heart made me connect with her because I really wanted to see a person with a disability be successful in this new age of opportunity. Unfortunately, I was not able to convince Heidi and her team that a partnership with *On A Roll* would justify the investment I was seeking.

There were plenty of other opportunities on the table. Just a few weeks later, I had two back-to-back meetings with new dot-coms: New York's Halftheplanet.com and Tampa's AccessLife.com.

I flew to New York to meet with Halftheplanet.com in the Empire State Building. Their offices consumed what seemed like a whole floor of cubicles and computer equipment rooms. The main appeal of this opportunity was the chance to work with John Kemp, one of the most respected leaders in the disability rights movement. He was an attorney who most recently had been the CEO of Very Special Arts, which as VSA Arts today helps five million people with disabilities participate in arts programs each year. John, like everybody who was somebody on the national disability scene, had been a frequent guest on *On A Roll*. The meetings went very well as we talked about the potential for *On A Roll* to move to the next level in the radio industry. If I were to move to New York, the largest media market in the world, I would be able to network with top radio and advertising executives. I left New York with an assignment to create a detailed marketing plan for combining efforts with the new web site.

Three days later, I found myself being wined and dined in Tampa with a young, energetic group of business professionals. Instead of having me take a cab to the hotel, Eric Peterson, the director of marketing at AccessLife.com greeted me with a rented wheelchair-accessible van. We went from the airport to a nice dinner with other members of the team, and then to a hotel near their offices in the Hidden River business district in North Tampa. They explained their business model and how their web site would not rely on consumer e-commerce.

Instead, consumer purchases would be an additional revenue stream for their company, which developed Internet automation of the medical billing process. The radio show would be a promotional tool to drive this business. It all made sense. They showed me my desk and my computer and they treated me with admiration and respect. There was an enthusiasm about the way they held their staff meetings and the way they encouraged each other that I wanted to be a part of. They didn't give me a homework assignment, like my colleagues in New York. They gave me a job offer: $100,000 salary plus 75% of radio revenues.

When I landed the job at Accesslife.com, I gave myself a mental promotion. Finally, the hard work and sacrifices I had made over the past eight years were going to pay off. I was so proud to be able to say that I earned as much as my father and we joked about the rich dad and his rich son. When my parents were in Tampa helping me settle into my apartment, Dad was on the phone talking to one of his buddies, loudly as he often does.

"Yeah, I'm down here in Tampa in this fancy apartment. This little sucker got a job down here making $100,000 a year!"

"Shhhhh!" I whispered. The guy from the office was knocking on the door to install my computer.

I chose a luxury apartment complex less than a mile away from the office. I wanted to get something very close because I had no confidence in my old white van, which was being shipped down from Ohio. Nor did I know with any certainty how much longer it would take for General Motors to deliver my new vehicle.

My job was to write a weekly column, produce segments on the radio show promoting the web site, and assist with marketing strategy to solidify the AccessLife.com brand. Part of this involved public speaking. The timing was perfect. That summer of 2000 marked the ten-year anniversary of the Americans with Disabilities Act, and AccessLife.com was one of the sponsors of the "Spirit of ADA Torch Relay."

Mark Johnson and Paul Timmons cooked up this great idea. The concept was for people with disabilities from across the country to carry a torch symbolizing freedom and independence on an 18 city tour of the United States. Two torches were lit to begin the campaign. Former President George H.W. Bush lit the first in Houston, while Martin Luther King III lit the second in Atlanta. The two torches converged in Houston. I had the honor of being the first person ever to carry the newly lit, *Spirit of ADA* torch (Actually, it was too heavy for me to lift, but they created a special mount that hundreds of torchbearers in wheelchairs used that summer). I didn't really understand the emotional power of carrying a torch until I made that first lap around the track in Houston. At that moment, I got it! The Torch Relay was symbolic of power, potential and shedding light on the truth… that people with disabilities represent an enormous minority group and a beautiful part of the natural diversity that is human life. I felt proud to be a symbol of that message, and as camera crews and newspaper reporters followed me, I realized that America would get that message.

For most of those Torch Relay stops, I hired video crews to follow me around for Joanne's movie. Having somebody follow you around with a camera definitely elevates your presence. I enjoyed what that did to my image.

After our stop in Tallahassee, I was back in the office in Tampa and my phone rang. A strong southern drawl on a cell phone blasted through my headphone so loudly that I had to turn the volume down.

"Greg, this is JR Harding. I met you at the Torch Relay event, and I'm on the way to your office. I need directions."

Out of the clear blue sky, a mammoth of a man in a manual wheelchair, pushed by an even larger personal assistant showed up at my office with a cup full of spit in his lap and chewing tobacco between his cheek and gum. Despite the distraction from his bold mannerisms, his sophistication and intelligence resonated clearly. He worked for the State of Florida Department of Vocational Rehabilitation, and talked about ways that Accesslife.com and *On A Roll* could partner with his department to promote employment of Floridians with disabilities. JR became a close friend. He introduced me to important people in the Florida disability community, arranged for me to speak at events, and hooked me into a chance at a State grant to expand and strengthen my radio show in Florida. JR was a quadriplegic, injured the first time when he was attacked from behind while "walking away from a fight" by someone he had pissed off. JR broke his neck again in a van accident while attempting to turn the radio station on his car stereo while driving. The second injury cost him some significant function. I still find it inspiring that he continues to follow his dreams and aspirations, and embraces life with passion. And he doesn't care what people think about him. What a guy!

The Spirit of ADA Torch Relay took me to Philadelphia where I danced the night away at a 70's bar, being lifted on stage and rolling in the center of attention with several young ladies attracted to the novelty of my presence. The torch lit the way to Montgomery and Selma, Alabama, where I carried it across the Edmond Pettus Bridge, the backdrop of Bloody Sunday during the 1960's civil rights battles. I went from Tallahassee to Jacksonville, to New York and finally to Washington DC, where I watched President Clinton deliver a speech at the FDR memorial on the July 26, 2000 anniversary of the ADA.

My career was on a high as I enjoyed my celebrity status in the disability community, aided by the presence of hired video crews. I loved the handsome salary I was pulling down at AccessLife.com. I dined at the Vice President Al Gore's residence and enjoyed a gala celebration at Union Station. I bragged about the General Motors display that featured a red, fire metallic Chevy Venture with a Ricon lowered floor modification, illuminated with spotlights behind a red rope.

"After this promotional tour, that is going to be my actual van," I said. I was single, on top of my mountain, using all of the energy and panache I could to take full advantage. It was a new millennium in a new city, with a new level of financial freedom. The year 2000 was very good... until Thanksgiving.

I had been making the eight hour drive from Tampa to Ocean Springs, Mississippi, every three weeks or so. My parents had moved into their dream home on Davis Bayou leading out to the Gulf of Mexico. Despite my exciting time in Tampa, I missed my children and took every opportunity to make the drive home. I returned to work after my Thanksgiving visit with them and noticed that there weren't a lot of cars in the parking lot. When I rolled out of the elevator on the third floor, one of my co-workers greeted me with a long face and mumbled, "Chuck wants to see you."

I knew what was happening. The ride was over. Accesslife.com was realizing what thousands of dot-coms were learning the hard way across America. E-commerce wasn't holding up its end of the bargain. People weren't buying wheelchairs online. They weren't buying leg bags and catheters. They weren't buying diapers or any of the other products in our online store. To the corporate principals, my $100,000 salary was severe hemorrhaging.

"You can use the office for a month to get your next move in order," he said. He even offered me the opportunity to take ownership of the site for $1.00 and turn it into a non-profit, but I declined. I was focused on expanding the radio show. I had negotiated a deal with a radio station in Tampa owned by Clear Channel Communications, and had aspirations of expanding *On A Roll* within the Clear Channel family of stations across the country. I decided to remain in Tampa, living off my meager savings and additional radio revenue from GM and other advertisers.

I loved Tampa and didn't want to leave. My friendships with people like Murv Seymour, John Frierson, Alesia Bishop, Deanna Barcelona and dozens of other great people in Florida drew me to think of Tampa as a place where I wanted to live the rest of my life and raise my children. Despite the setback of losing my biweekly $2,600 paycheck, I felt some momentum with Clear Channel and General Motors, and learned that JR's Department of Vocational Rehabilitation had selected my grant proposal as a finalist.

My vision with VR in Florida was to use about $250,000 in State funds to purchase radio airtime on several Florida stations. I would hire local promotional reps with disabilities who would get the word out about the show, sell advertising and coordinate events to build grassroots support. On the air, we were going to motivate and inspire people with disabilities to seek out their career ambitions and utilize Vocational Rehab as a way to reach out and achieve their dreams.

Because of JR's position at VR, he was in the loop to know which grants were funded before the grantees were notified. I called him at his office.

"Well? What can you tell me?" I inquired.

"Show me the money!" he replied.

"Wooo hooo!" I yelled. "I love white people!" I joked, reversing the line from the movie *Jerry McGuire*. JR laughed into the phone.

My celebration was premature. A week later, I received a letter from the State notifying me that they had rescinded all of the grants due to issues with the fairness of the grant process. I would have to wait another six months to reapply. That would not happen. I was out of cash. I had to make a move.

CHAPTER 21

Fighting Through Tough Times

THE DEVASTATING NEWS about my Florida VR Grant was a fatal blow to my dreams of living the remainder of my life in the Sunshine State. I had no real significant revenue streams. Radio revenue added up to enough money to pay for the satellite time and for my producer, Mike Ervin, and that was about it. I wasn't earning any money from network advertising sales. I was getting nowhere in my efforts to get Clear Channel to endorse *On A Roll* for some of their News/Talk stations. General Motors was a satisfied client, but I could not convince them to get their dealers involved and compensate stations on the local level to expand the number of affiliates. I could no longer afford to pay my $1,000 a month rent, plus utilities and a personal assistant. So in August 2001, I embarked on the final road trip from Tampa to Ocean Springs. I appreciated the safety net, but felt like a failure. This was devastating to me.

It had never been in my plans to live in my parents' house in Mississippi. When I was living in Arizona with my wife and children, I was proud of my independence, paying my own bills and creating my own future, or so I thought. Moving back to Ohio after my separations and finally after my divorce took a lot of inner strength because in my mind, a permanent living arrangement with my parents meant that I had failed to make it on my own. I fully expected my time with my folks to be short-term.

When I arrived in Ocean Springs as a new resident, I was greeted warmly by my children, whom I had missed terribly during my year and a half in Tampa. Before I moved to Florida, I had promised I would send for them after I bought a house and we would hire the help we'd needed to have our own place in Florida. That this didn't materialize didn't seem to matter as they greeted me with hugs and kisses. Slowly, I began to settle into the lifestyle of Mr. Mom, taking them to soccer games, to visit their friends and to get a Happy Meal at McDonalds.

All my life, strangers have stared at me, but it seemed that the stares lasted a little longer here in Mississippi. Perhaps it was just my imagination and preconceived notions about this place. I did not like it here. I'd been in Ocean Springs for about a month, living with no real purpose other than going through the motions of producing the syndicated *On A Roll* show. Sadly, maintaining the use of my van from General Motors was my only motivation for continuing the show at this point. I was burned out and depressed, living in my mom and dad's house. I was feeling trapped. How could I do anything great from Mississippi if I couldn't make it happen from places like Phoenix, Dayton and Tampa?

We visited this place every summer as a child, staying at my aunt Georgia's house and going fishing in the Gulf. But this trip to Ocean Springs was permanent. My parents moved from Mississippi in the late '60's in what I always perceived as an escape from something bad. I had a tough time wrapping my mind around a move BACK to exactly what we fled. Dad had a shirt in the shape of a rebel flag with the African colors—red, green and black. In the middle it said "New South." Things have changed, he argued. Buying that required me to stretch my imagination.

One Tuesday morning, after having stayed up late on the computer, my mom woke me up with the telephone in my face.

"Who is it?"

"It's John Frierson."

I scowled at her because we hadn't worked out the protocol for what to do when I get a call and I'm sound asleep.

"Yo," I growled with my morning raspy voice. "What's up John?"

"Man, put your TV on the news. Planes have crashed into the World Trade Center!"

My mother and I watched the crumbling towers from our family room and cried together for the first time I can remember. I was already depressed about my own personal disappointments. This sent me into a much deeper funk, sleeping with the television on while CNN fed my subconscious all the latest updates about the unfolding horror story.

The attacks gave me an appreciation for the real meaning of tragedy and loss of life. It showed me my responsibility as a journalist and trusted communicator for a community of people. It woke me up to my mission and purpose. On the radio, we devoted the next three weeks of programs to discussing how this event had uniquely impacted the disability community. We interviewed a blind guy who escaped from one of the towers with his guide dog. We discussed the fate of the wheelchair users who were told not to use the elevators but to wait for help. These people were among the 22% of Americans with disabilities who were living the American dream. They were at work. They were employed. We talked with disability rights leaders in New York who were on the front lines of a battle to restore vital services to individuals in need.

Susan Scheer, Director of the Center for Independence of the Disabled of New York, (CIDNY) was a guest on our program twice, filling us in on how the attack impacted people with disabilities. She talked about how over 400 home care attendants worked to provide care to clients with disabilities who needed help getting out of bed in the days and weeks after the attack. These heroic workers were among the essential personnel that reported for duty at Mayor Giuliani's request the day after the attack. It was critical that home care services were provided to persons with disabilities during this crisis.

There were so many fascinating angles to this story. One CIDNY volunteer talked about his aunt, a deaf woman and wife of one of the firefighters missing for 36 hours. She was frantic and not able to receive TV news accounts because TV stations cut off closed captioning!

A twenty-one year-old girl with a traumatic brain injury was afraid to leave her apartment near Ground Zero, but had no food or money for two days. CIDNY provided cash and food and called in all of its contacts to expedite benefits and emergency food stamps for this woman.

We learned of a woman who had to rent a hotel room she could not afford after she found out the bed in the Red Cross shelter was too low for her wheelchair-using, disabled daughter. CIDNY provided medical equipment and support to the family.

CIDNY's outcry to the nation itemized their needs: laptops, accessible vans and drivers to deliver food, equipment, and medications to people in wheelchairs trapped in their apartments, medical supplies and administrative staff to provide information and keep track of the people with disabilities flooding their telephones with needs. Mike and I delivered excellent coverage of the 911 tragedy from a disability perspective.

Right after 911, the World Congress for People with Disabilities held their conference in Atlanta. People were afraid to fly. The turnout was miserable. I spent time with Kenny Rudolph, iCan's "Vice President of Inspiration" discussing the possibility of iCan.com taking over my website. In Atlanta, I learned that Heidi Van Arnem, iCan's CEO and founder was gravely ill, and a couple of short months later, she was gone.

Her death hit me very hard, and I think subconsciously made me think about my own mortality. I wondered what would happen to the all the hard work and passion I had put into the last decade if I died.

I was impressed by the iCan team's determination to keep the website running. Kenny agreed to host my website within the iCan infrastructure, freeing me up from the time-consuming task of uploading HTML files every week. I began to work with Bethany Broadwell, a sharp writer/editor who has a form of spinal muscular atrophy and who handled the editorial content for iCan.

Despite the freedom from the web site, I was in an emotional rut. I had none of the passion and energy to do *On A Roll* that I once had. On Sunday afternoons, instead of preparing for the show, I would lie in my bed and sleep. I had to go on the air at 5pm, so I would get up at 4:30, have a cup of coffee and psyche myself to do the show. I would rely exclusively on my natural talent, voice and experience to make the show sound good. I was not passionate about doing this at all. The only reason I kept the show on the air at this point in my life was because I was driving a free Chevy Venture, which General Motors had given me as a promotional vehicle. I regret that in late 2001 and early 2002, the quality of *On A Roll* was poor compared to how it could have been. If I had done any show prep at all, those shows would have been great!

As I began to feel better and the weather started to warm up a bit, things improved. We had top-notch guests in the spring of 2002. Ron Santo, who was a great Chicago Cubs third baseman from 1960 to 1973, joined us for a very intimate conversation. Santo's right leg had recently been amputated due to complications from diabetes, which he has had since age 18. We talked about life with his scooter and his high-tech prosthetic leg. And you *know* we talked about the Cubbies.

In March, we were disgusted to find out that the Academy Awards were being held at the new Kodak Theatre in Los Angeles, and that this beautiful new facility forgot one thing: wheelchair access. Christopher Reeve contacted us to make a statement on the air about it, and was awesome. Reeve had endured a lot of criticism from my audience since his injury and his understandable focus on being cured. But I've always felt that patience would reveal his true character and he would come to see the power he had to change the image of Americans with disabilities through the use of his craft.

On my program in March 2002, Chris Reeve said all right things. He didn't even let me bring up the Kodak Theatre lawsuit. He brought it up first, very angrily.

I remember watching the Oscars and getting pissed. They might as well have hung a sign saying "No Crips Allowed" over the red carpet. I wanted to do something about this in a major way, beyond getting them to renovate the theater. I wanted to use this as ammunition to wake America up about how Hollywood exploits people with disabilities by making disgusting amounts of money off storylines about our lives, yet they starve our actors, giving our roles to pretenders. They don't even want us around on the night they celebrate their triumphs with the world. Ironically on that night, I had mixed feelings watching Halle Berry and Denzel Washington win Oscars, a milestone for "my black people." I also realized that I would not have been able to sit in the audience because of disregard for my "other" people. The disability community is so far behind.

But *On A Roll* wasn't an angry show. We had fun with a monthly segment we subtitled *Physically Incorrect* where we invited two or three characters with disabilities to join us and kick around goofy or strange things in the news from a disability perspective. It was a slam on Bill Maher's *Politically Incorrect*, which sometimes seemed to insult people with disabilities. I loved doing *Physically Incorrect*, with the likes of Dan Wilkens, whose business, The Nth Degree makes t-shirts with disability rights slogans and quotes, many of them humorous. Dan always had a great perspective and approached a topic from a slanty angle. Michelle Hlavek had a very direct style of commentary and was skilled at saying what everybody else was thinking but dared not to say.

In searching for material for *On A Roll*, Mike and I would always check the headlines for disability news. In May 2002, we were shocked to read about Georgia high school graduate Masha Malikina. Here's how I promoted the story in my e-mail newsletter that week:

A Georgia high school graduate, who had been planning for two years to use leg braces and a walker to receive her diploma, was forced to use a wheelchair by her principal in a last minute decision at the graduation ceremony last week. This story has received a great deal of attention in the disability community. The principal says it was a safety issue. The student, Masha Malikina, said she was told that the concern was that she would take too much time. Malikina, who was paralyzed in a 1999 car accident, will join us live at the top of the first hour to tell us how she is planning to respond to what she calls an "incredibly cruel" decision. Have you ever faced discrimination with your own safety being the justification? What do you think the real reason was for the decision to make her roll instead of walk? And does her degree mean any less because she rolled instead of walked to receive it? Plan to call in toll-free at the top of the first hour... 1-800-510-8255. That's 1-800-FIVE-TEN-TALK.

It was a great program. Masha was articulate and passionate about her cause. She promoted her case in Atlanta and a local radio station decided to do something about it. They gave Masha her own graduation at the Phillips Arena! The general public was invited and Atlanta radio stations heavily promoted the event. They chose me to give the commencement address. I was honored to accept, and saw it as an opportunity to take a story that appealed to people's sensitivity and compassion and make it resonate with a message of disability rights and awareness of our core issues. I took my time and crafted a powerful oration that received a standing ovation. Delivering that speech was a proud moment for me. Here's what I said:

You may be a little surprised by the fact that so much noise can come from such a tiny body, and if you feel motivated to holler back at me, don't be ashamed. I get the sense that this is a non-judgmental crowd tonight. It might not come as a shock to you that as a broadcaster, I am intrigued by words and their multiple definitions. And on this festive occasion, I took the liberty of researching a few words of significance to us all today. The first word I want to define in the context of the spirit of the evening is the word WALK. I'm skipping the definitions labeled number one and number two and seeking deeper meaning. It is the third definition on Dictionary.com, which I feel, resonates with the spirit of this event. The third definition of walk is as follows: To conduct oneself or behave in a particular manner; for example to walk in majesty and pride. Masha, you have WALKED, in majesty and pride without taking a single step. And isn't it wonderful to know that you can walk with purpose and confidence for the rest of your life, fueled by energy from the knowledge that your character is not that of a person who would be denied by those who walk in a different manner or with a different purpose. Outside of Atlanta, you may not know this, but the story of Masha Malikina has been talked about from the swamps of South Florida to the snowcaps of Anchorage, and particularly in the disability community everywhere in between. When Masha was a guest on my radio show a few weeks ago, she broke a record for the number of calls received in one hour. They were calls of support. Calls of encouragement. They were calls of shock. Calls of disbelief. Calls of Anger!

And during the broadcast, I'm thinking to myself, "People, what world have you been living in?" Because to be disabled IS to be devalued, disregarded, disrespected, discarded and denied! That's the way it has been for people with disabilities all over the world since the beginning of humanity, but like others who have been denied in the past, we have drawn a line in the sand. We have had enough!

This is a very significant moment in the history of humanity. Please tell me that you'll take the correct meaning home with you tonight. This is not about a single person trying to overcome the "tragedy" of her disability and through the physical act of STANDING UP, using leg braces and a walker, receiving her diploma the way a quote—NORMAL person—end quote is SUPPOSED to receive a diploma. No! No! No! This is so much more significant than that!

This is about thousands of people STANDING UP to the brutality of devaluation, disregard, and discrimination. This is about YOU... look around. You're standing up to the freedom blockers. You're standing up to the dream smashers. You're standing up to the antiquated and outdated boundaries of the old way that people have treated people.

Let's look at the definition of STAND. The seventh definition (we're gettin' REAL deep here...), the SEVENTH definition at Dictionary.com for STAND is "A desperate or decisive effort at defense or resistance, as in a battle." My friends, this is a STAND if I've ever heard of one in my life! You have made a decisive effort in the resistance against denial. To be here tonight is to take a STAND! To sign Masha's petition is to take a STAND! To show up tomorrow night at the Department of Education meeting is to take a STAND! Will you STAND????

Who should determine one's limitations or potentials in life? When I was four years younger than Masha is now, my life was changed profoundly by someone who took a stand for me. You see, I've always had my disability. And having played the drums in elementary school and junior high school, I wanted to be in the marching band in high school despite the fact that I couldn't march, couldn't walk, couldn't even stand up. The year prior, I had three metal rods implanted in my back to correct the curvature of my spine.

When I told my mother about my plan to be in the marching band, she did not say I could not do it. Although she suggested that I might want to try out for the concert band.

When I presented that desire to the band director, a man who was willing to take a stand and demonstrate to ONE YOUNG STUDENT that dreams should be WORKED ON and not denied, he did not tell me that I could not play in the marching band.

Instead, he designed a SYSTEM, which allowed me to drive my power wheelchair with my foot, freeing both of my hands to play drums that he attached to my wheelchair. I played with the band in parades, on the field at halftime of our football games, and in band competitions. And in doing so, he designed a SYSTEM for me to develop wonderful friendships with other drummers and band members that are still strong today.

It was a system that taught me to put no limits on my ambition and my value as a contributing member of society. I share this story because it taught me a valuable lesson about creating my own reality. I joined the marching band and participated fully with the help of Mr. Roseleib and my many band friends at South High School. That experience changed my whole life.

I determined my own limitations. My parents always allowed me to discover what I could or could not do. Masha has taken control of her destiny by setting a goal for which she worked very hard to accomplish. She will walk across the stage to get her diploma. She has taken a stand, one of many she must make in her journey through life.

Unfortunately, our society has just begun to recognize people with disabilities as citizens with equal rights as temporarily able-bodied citizens. Throughout her life, Masha, as well as the other 54 million disabled citizens in America, will have to overcome obstacles in order to accomplish her goals. This first stand lays the foundation for her success.

Had it not been for Mr. Al Roselieb at Downers Grove South High School, would I have a nationally syndicated talk show today? Would I have three wonderful children? Would I have reached so many thousands of people all over the country and the world with a message of empowerment on the radio airwaves?

It will take Masha up to two minutes to walk across this stage and receive her diploma from Dominique Wilkens, (who by the way very rarely "walked" in his playing days with the Hawks!). During the time she's walking, maybe her steps will cause you to find yourself imagining the next time you stand up... or take a stand... so to speak. Doesn't it feel good to take a stand!!?

Maybe you'll imagine yourself at some time in the future when you're building a new home for yourself, telling your builder, "I want my home to have at least one no step entrance and bathroom doors wide enough to fit the wheelchairs of my friends like Masha Malikina!" Can you stand up for that?

Maybe when you're a corporate executive, or some kind of manager in a hiring position, you'll make sure that your company values and embraces the unique problem solving skills that are developed from the experience of living life with a disability, and you'll take a stand against employment discrimination. Can you stand up for that?

Maybe you can consider the possibility that if people were given the choice to spend Medicaid dollars on home care instead of being forced into nursing homes, they may not become so miserable that their own relatives might want to end their lives. Maybe you can stand for the freedom to choose where you live! Can you stand up for that?!!

Maybe while Masha is taking her stand, you'll decide to take a stand for public education in the least restrictive environment for ALL students, including students with disabilities, and maybe those who feel that special ed is an albatross around the school system's neck deserve something else around the figurative necks of their careers! Had to get that in there.

Maybe while Masha is walking, you'll think about your own issue and your own stand that will make the world a better place, no matter what it is. I'm not just talking about disability issues. There is a multitude of opportunities all around us to improve the world we live in. If you can inspire one person and help make that person's dream more possible, maybe that person's dream can affect thousands, millions! Seek your own dreams. And at the same time do everything you can to empower the people around you to achieve their dreams as well. If everyone would just do that, wouldn't the world be a better place?

Jeff Dauler and the people at Q100 did that by organizing this event today! I want you to holler for Jeff "Dollar." (pause) What the world needs is a million dollars.

The third and final word that deserves definition is the word graduate. Again, looking beyond the obvious first and second definitions and seeking deeper meaning, to graduate means to prepare gradually; to arrange, temper, or modify by degrees or to a certain degree.

To Masha: We don't care if you walk, crawl, roll or fall! Just keep taking a stand.

To the Berkmar High School Class of 2002, congratulations for being a part of something that has moved our society closer to that specific temperature, that certain degree of comfort for all, with all. Your final lesson in high school may be your most valuable one. Never forget it. Never forget the real meaning of this occasion. Take a STAND. Walk with majesty and pride. And do your part to follow your dreams and help the dreams of others so that our society can graduate to the degree of full human potential. God Bless you all!

Not bad, huh? I was interrupted by applause several times.

That speech made me see the true power in public speaking as a primary career. For the first time, I started to think that maybe, instead of being a radio host who does speaking, I was becoming a speaker who does radio. It was interesting food for thought.

In June 2002, Justin Dart, the father figure in the disability community, had been suffering from congestive heart failure for quite some time, and with Father's Day approaching, I thought it might be good for our audience to hear his voice. I was concerned about his strength and his ability to do the interview, but he wanted to do it. He was determined to do it. He was on his deathbed, but he wanted to reach out to his people. Imagine the raspy voice of a tired warrior on the other end of a telephone, probably held to his ear by his beloved wife Yoshiko and turn up the radio in your mind:

Me: *It's been a while since we have heard from you Justin, and on Father's Day do you have a message you would like to say to the disability community? I know you have got a neat perspective having seen things develop over 40 years. What would you like to tell us now?*

Justin Dart: Well I would like to say that we are so proud to have passed the ADA built on the 504. And that attitudes of all Americans have changed about people with disabilities. We are real human beings in the human race. That's different than it used to be. However, now we have to get out and get our rights enforced. While no minority has all their rights enforced, we have to do it, because nobody ever gave rights away. We have to get out of life as usual and become fully 24 hour a day, 365 days a year passionate single-minded advocates for disability rights.

Me: *Absolutely. Justin, what would you say on Father's Day about the institution of fatherhood? You are a father in the literal sense in addition to the figurative sense in being the father of the disability rights movement. Do you have any specific messages about fatherhood for us?*

Justin Dart: Being a father, whether it's a symbolic father like I am or if it's a blood father entails lots of responsibilities. And those responsibilities include having to give your sons and symbolic sons the hard advice that the time has come for them to be soldiers of justice. They have to give up life as usual, give up politics as usual and fight for the coming elections to elect people who support disability rights. And they got to fight every day as citizen advocates to create a society where no politicians or no media person would dare attack disability rights because they would risk getting re-elected.

Me: *How do you feel about what the Supreme Court has been doing recently in terms of whittling away at the Americans with Disabilities Act case by case?*

Justin Dart: The recent court decisions on ADA and others have shown that states' rights controls the course and they are trying to take us back to the days of states' rights and power and privilege and the fact the states can do anything they want to people with disabilities and the federal government has no general authority to protect people with disabilities and other citizens on a federal basis. This is truly distressing.

Me: *Yes it truly is. Listen, Justin, I wanted to take a few moments to kind of summarize my feelings about you and what you have done. We are so privileged to have you as a*

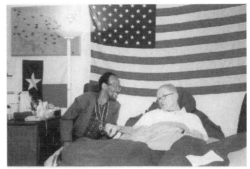

WITH JUSTIN DART—It was a great honor when Justin allowed me to wear his Presidential Medal of Freedom, America's highest civilian honor, in 1999.

leader in our community. There is so much love that is expressed whenever your name is brought up. It's just tremendous. And I have never ever seen that about anybody personally. I have heard about that kind of reverence with others in the past that I've admired. But to see it first hand and to feel the power and the influence you have had in your life and your career is just amazing. So, Justin, Happy Father's Day to you. We love you.

That interview was June 16, 2002. Justin left us on June 22.

∾

In July 2002, I received a call from General Motors, notifying me that there had been changes in their risk management procedure. They were now requiring a $5 million umbrella insurance policy on all promotional vehicles. I made a few calls and got nowhere. I notified GM of my failure to get this kind of insurance and went on with my life.

∾

In October, the disability movement's master networker in Atlanta, Mark Johnson connected me to representatives from the Disabled People's International 6th World Assembly in Sapporo, Japan. They needed a speaker from the United States to talk about personal assistant services. There would be no speaker's fee, but they would pay all travel expenses for me and an attendant. I decided to hire Joanne Caputo, the filmmaker of the *On A Roll* documentary as my assistant so she could also get videotape for the film. We flew for 20 hours so that I could give a 20-minute presentation!

It was amazing to meet people with disabilities from totally different worlds. Over the past ten years, I had been to many disability events and had become very good at "diagnosing" people from looking at them! I can tell whether someone has Cerebral Palsy, Muscular Dystrophy, MS, is a stroke survivor or has a spinal cord injury, with about 90% accuracy, just by looking at him or her. In Japan, the same held true. These people from different worlds were physically just like us. The biggest differences I noticed were in the quality of their durable medical equipment.

After I made my presentation on recruiting, hiring and employing a personal care assistant, they opened the floor for questions and discussion. Mahmood, from Kabul, Afghanistan, rose to his feet and spoke passionately through interpreters. I pressed my wireless headset close to my ear and watched Mahmood wave his arms.

"You speak of money to hire a person to come to your house and help you get dressed so you can go out and go to work," he said. "In my country we have no money for this. Many of our disabled people have been reduced to begging in the streets. We have no support for our disabled people. We need wheelchairs, artificial limbs, braces, crutches and primary and higher education.

"I have plans to take people abroad for higher education," he continued, "but presently we are giving the priority to direct accessibility for our disabled. We have many disabled, but they have nothing in our country. They are very poor. There is no job in our country. Their life is very simple. There is no accessibility in our hometowns and in our streets. Many people with disabilities are staying 24 hours in home because they have no support to take them out for anything."

I could hear the anger growing in his voice as clearly as I could feel the compassion building inside myself. It took a trip around the world to bring into focus not only the reality that we take so much for granted here in America, but also a question we?ve been neglecting. If the disability community is indeed a community of brothers and sisters, don?t we have a responsibility to advocate for all of them, not just the ones fortunate enough to be born on American soil? Of the 3,000 attendees at DPI, only about 20 were Americans.

I returned from Japan humbled by the experience. Mahmood told me privately that if I lived in his country, I would not have a fancy power wheelchair that tilts and reclines. I would be placed on a rug and dragged through the streets on the rare instances when I had the opportunity to venture outside my home. The whole Japan experience made me really appreciate how well we have it in the United States.

I needed the perspective I gained in Japan because shortly after my return, General Motors called me with devastating news about my van.

"Greg, we're going to have to park the vehicle on General Motors property until we get this insurance situation resolved."

On the day before Thanksgiving 2002, a tow truck came and hauled my freedom away. I was now a prisoner in my parents' home. I went from "world traveler" to "house arrest" in two weeks.

If you use a power wheelchair for mobility, you can only go places using a wheelchair-accessible van with a ramp or a lift. Power chairs are too heavy and bulky to lift into people's trunks. The other option for transportation is to be lifted into the passenger seat of a car or truck and loading the manual wheelchair in the trunk. It also means that when you get to your destination, you're helpless, unable to turn around to see a different view. For all practical purposes, you're stuck wherever you are.

Surely, Christmas would bring some joy. As the yuletide season drew near, for the second straight year I started to notice the accumulation of mucus in my lungs. One afternoon, while watching my beloved Sun Devil football team play valiantly in a loss to Kansas State in the Holiday Bowl, I thought my life was over in one terrifying moment: I started to cough, and mucus got stuck in my throat, clogging me so that I couldn't breathe!! I struggled to make the air go either way but wasn't successful! I was choking on my own phlegm!

I frantically darted to the kitchen in search of somebody to do the Heimlich maneuver. Just before I began an all-out panic, I managed to expel some of the thick white junk and immediately asked to go to the hospital. I had pneumonia and spent eight days in a hospital bed.

Eight days of stagnation when you have a neuromuscular condition is not good. When I felt well enough to get out of bed, my body was so weak that I could hardly sit upright.

After my discharge, I began a three month, at home physical therapy program that was very effective in helping me gain my strength back. My therapist, Lori, was even able to get me on my feet and to take a couple of steps! She was a miracle worker. Walking was something I hadn't been able to do in years! I was so isolated at home that I really enjoyed her company and looked forward to her showing up. She inspired me.

During that time, I did get out occasionally. I was the assistant coach of my son Donovan's youth league basketball team. Mom had to lift me into her SUV, load my manual wheelchair in the back and cart me to every game, where I propelled myself with my feet like I did my freshman year of high school.

All the while, I was wrestling with the big corporate giant to try to get my wheels back. Can you imagine how frustrating it would be to have your only mode of transportation towed away and stored at a dealership a mile away from your house?

On one hand, I had a valuable sponsor with whom I have had a long relationship and a bright future. Yet it seemed like nothing was happening to bring resolve the situation. Finally, I got a call saying that they would sell the vehicle to me directly and the price would be absorbed into the advertising sponsorship renewal figure. But even after this decision, I painfully learned how slow the big corporate wheels turn.

In my desperation, I wrote a very clear e-mail to the head honchos.

I'm begging you. Please do more than leave a voice mail or send an email to somebody in an effort to resolve this. Can you TAKE ACTION and move this ball forward? I'm out of time.

My mother is 59 years old. My three children are in elementary school. We all live here in my parents' home. My father works in New Jersey and commutes home once per month. My children are active and involved in extracurricular activities including sports and they have games every night. My mom has to lift me up into her new Chevy Yukon, lift my manual wheelchair into the back and drive us to all the games. It is a strain on her but she does it out of love. She has had back problems in the past. It is so difficult for us, and what makes it so frustrating is that the van sits at a dealership less than a mile away! Let's negotiate a deal and get this thing done.

I would live like this for six months. Trapped in my parents' house, I decided to make the most of a negative situation. During those months of imprisonment, I made great strides toward writing my book. I rededicated myself to *On A Roll* and decided to get some help with the on-air stuff, too.

So I called Judy Heumann, the "mother of the independent living movement," who had done some disability radio in the past. We announced this legendary disability rights leader would be my co-host. Judy did an amazing job.

Momentum continued. In March, I landed a local station on the Mississippi gulf coast to carry the show. The programming improved because I became more passionate about it.

In May, I had my wheels back. I vowed never again to sit around the house and not enjoy the freedom of independent transportation! This time, I promised myself that I would use all eight of my wheels to go places!

CHAPTER 22

A Dream Realized at Wrigley

WHEN I GOT MY WHEELS BACK, I was determined to use them to take me to a destination of success and happiness! But OnStar could not give me directions to that location. How could I finally find a comfort zone where I was financially independent and productive for mankind? I knew I wasn't far from the course, but I also felt some basic adjustments were necessary.

I'd been doing *On A Roll* for over ten years and where had it taken me? I was living with my parents at age 39, unable to support my own family financially. I had no love life. I wasn't diminishing the significance of my accomplishments; rather I was once again being introspective. Great things happen when you tell the truth to yourself and act accordingly. It was time for searching my soul.

I was also inspired at that time by Anthony Robbins' *Get the Edge* CDs and modified his processes to fit my own life. I started asking myself questions, using my radio studio to record them onto my hard drive as MP3 files. They were deep, thought provoking inquiries. To complete the production, I then mixed them into some ambient music. Between each question, I would leave perhaps 30 seconds of music to give my subconscious mind some time to process effective and empowering answers.

At night, I would set the files to play continuously. I would turn the speakers down very low to the point where the sound was barely audible, and then go to bed. I was programming my subconscious mind. I carefully crafted the questions with wording that would only return very encouraging, very positive, inspiring answers.

Here, I'll share the questions I actually recorded and mixed with very peaceful, relaxing music, and played to myself as I slept:

220

- How does the knowledge that you have love and warmth in your life change the way you embrace this very moment?

- Does it do any harm to express appreciation and gratitude openly to the people who help you or have helped you in the past? How do you think being in touch with your appreciation and gratitude serve you?

- How can you become even more curious? If you continue to ask "I wonder" questions and actually seek out the answers, how much more intelligent will you become? Maybe you shouldn't just wonder. Maybe you should act on your curiosity immediately by ASKING, "How will you become a better person as a result of this? Is there really anything you can't learn if you put your mind to it? What do you really want to learn? What are you waiting for?"

- What about your life gives you a tremendous feeling of excitement and passion? What are you so enthusiastic about that you jump out of bed and get moving with excitement and energy? Is it obvious that you are a person who lives with passion?

- If you don't change your behavior and continue to do the things you have been doing, where will you be in one year? In five years?

- What if you make changes that empower you in your daily habits? Will that change the course of your destiny?

- How does the "you" in five years who made the changes compare to the "you" in five years who didn't? How much happier will you be if you make these changes?

- Do you believe you can live your dreams? Do you need to believe it in order for it to happen? What is the difference between a dream and a fantasy? If you believe you can realize your dreams, would you give in to settling for fantasy instead of creating the reality?

- If you realize that the way you have been doing things isn't working, are you ok with changing the course? What would be the benefit of not attaching too much meaning to any one particular outcome or goal?

- What characteristics do you possess that give you the confidence to know that you are worthy of your dreams, and of surprises that the universe will present to you? Why do you expect to be successful?

- What would happen if you smiled more often? Laughed more often? Does a smile or laugh release chemicals in your brain communicating a state of happiness? Isn't that good for your health? Isn't cheerfulness an attractive quality? Isn't laughing fun? How can you create an environment that facilitates laughter?

I think listening to these messages every night as I slept brought me closer to the truth than I've ever felt in my life. It was a breakthrough.

I began to use the concept to develop answers to specific questions to move my career forward as well. For these questions, I would use high-energy "trance" music. I would burn CDs and play them in my car as I drove around, or in the shower as I started my day.

For example, here are some questions I recorded and played over and over again, mixed with a driving techno beat:

- What other ways are there to get more speaking engagements?

- How can you change your speaking presentations from fact telling to story telling; from presentation to PERFORMANCE?

- What other groups can you contact in numbers to pitch yourself as a speaker?

- How can you tap into the diversity speaking market?

- How can you take advantage of local opportunities to speak at casinos/resorts conferences?

- Whom do you need to associate with to get casino/resort business?

- What do you want to stress in your next speaking engagement? How will you begin? How will you end?

- What can you do to get your book published?

- Who do you need to talk to in order to make your own house a reality?

- What can you do every day that will lead to a relationship?

- Why are you capable of attracting the woman of your dreams?

- Can you get 10 packages out in the mail this week?

- Why don't you mail things out immediately?

- Who are some powerful people you have the potential to bring into your circle of influence and what strategies will you implement to reach each one of them?

- What contacts or opportunities are you allowing to fall through the cracks?

- What are some universal empowering questions you can include in this technology that will program everybody who listens to it for success?

What happened was simple. The universe started to open up to me. It was around the time of this subconscious awakening that I was beginning to establish wonderful relationships with people in the Mississippi State government. In October 2002, I gave the keynote address at a national developmental disabilities council meeting in Point Clear, Alabama. Like always, I prepared a personal, uplifting presentation, showing pictures of my accomplishments, my family and highlighting all the good that my radio show had accomplished. Among the crowd of people I met while shaking hands on the platform was Ed Butler, the director of the Mississippi Developmental Disabilities Council.

Ed's first words revealed his strong, articulate Mississippi accent. "Greg, I must admit that I'm embarrassed that you're from Mississippi and I've never met you," he said.

I explained to him that I was born in Mississippi, lived here for the first three years of my life, and just moved back two years ago. He asked many questions about my vision for using radio to help the lives of people with disabilities. When I returned to Ocean Springs, we continued to talk by phone and he introduced me to several people and a barrage of ideas.

Kim Dillon, a director at the Mississippi Department of Vocational Rehabilitation soon called, seeking a dynamic speaker for grand scale event: "A Celebration of Achievement." Heather Mills McCartney, the wife of the legendary Paul McCartney (and a person with a disability) would be the main attraction. I would be her warm-up speaker. When we signed the deal, a large-scale promotional campaign landed me on television, in newspapers and on the radio statewide.

A conference with an audience of movers and shakers in the disability community, the media and government was the perfect place for me to shine and receive my standing ovation. Yet I was unaware of the impact that speech would have on my life.

Weeks later, Ed invited me to submit a grant proposal for funding to promote what Mississippi was doing to better the lives of people with developmental disabilities. In August 2003, I submitted a grant request for $77,000 and in September, they selected my application. Now I was in business in my home state, developing a weekly disabilities show airing statewide on SuperTalk Mississippi.

SUPERTALK—After our meeting sealing the deal to broadcast statewide in Mississippi, we posed in the on-air studio. (Left to right: Kim Dillon, Ed Butler, me, Beth Ballard, Butch McMillian, Stephanie Tucker)

This grant gave me a comfort level from where I could start to do more effective long-term planning. With all the traveling and speaking I was doing, I depended heavily on Mike to set up the topics and guests for *On A Roll*. He was doing a great job.

He landed former US Attorney General Janet Reno who was honored by Chicago's independent living center, Access Living for vigorously enforcing the Americans with Disabilities Act.

He set up an interview with a young Philadelphia music producer named "Simon Illa." Brad Gilbert, AKA "Simon" is a hip-hop music producer who has osteogenesis imperfecta. His music was used in an Emmy award-winning television production about 911, and his list of artists is growing due to his unique ear for sound. We talked about his shattering stereotypes; being a rising force in hip-hop despite being disabled and white.

We chatted with Kate Adamson, a brain stem stroke survivor who emerged from "locked-in" syndrome, a condition where she could feel and hear everything around her and was fully capable of perception and feeling, but whom physicians regarded as comatose. Kate used our air to speak out in support of Terri Schaivo, the Florida woman who was in a legal battle to keep her feeding tube and not starve to death. That interview led to a wonderful friendship.

Another interesting guest was Candia Dye, a person with a disability and a certified life coach. That interview intrigued me because I often wondered about how a coach might impact my business. As a result of that interview, I eventually signed a contract with her to be my coach. Candia's guidance has been a primary reason why my speaking career, radio show and writing have been successful. She started to make it clear to me that I was running my business in reactive mode, rather than putting together a plan and sticking to that plan. I learned that all kinds of opportunities are going to come along, but that I needed to ask if and how these new possibilities fit into my plan. A great resource that helped me was The *One Page Business Plan* by Jim Horan.

I was finally starting to put all the pieces together. Once again, *On A Roll* was rolling! I was energetic. Instead of viewing the show as something I had to do, I looked forward to Sunday nights and began to take pride in what we were doing.

I was embracing life; determined to make it a well-rounded effort. As a father, I wanted to do something very special for my boys and saw an opportunity to live a dream come true that July.

From now on, I'll celebrate my own personal Father's Day on July 10. That will forever be the anniversary of one of those rare realizations of a dream; a life-long fantasy finally manifesting itself into sights, sounds, tastes and smells. This accomplishment was the result of a conscious decision to put practicality aside and create a lasting moment. Our lives last for decades, but the lasting moments are precious.

The moments I write about needed over 30 years of development to have significance. As a child with muscular dystrophy, I could not swing a baseball bat. I could never use a baseball glove because my fingers were not strong enough to squeeze the leather around the ball. I could throw a baseball accurately, but not far enough to reach from the mound to the plate or from second base to first base. But I loved the game. Growing up in suburban Chicago, on days where my school friends were actually playing baseball, I was watching. I would go to their little league games and always watched the Chicago Cubs on WGN.

The summers were boring for a child who could not go swimming, ride a bike or keep up with the neighborhood kids in all of their physicality. Yet at 1:00 pm, most weekdays, there was always *The Leadoff Man*.

I would sing along, "*Let's go.... Batter up.... We're takin' the afternoon off! It's a beautiful game for a ballgame... For a ballgame today....*"

I'd listen and learn from Jack Brickhouse and Lou Boudreau as they set the stage for the Cubs' challenges. When school was out for the summer, the Cubs would be in first place, seemingly destined for a pennant that had eluded them since 1945. That feeling was exhilarating. But by the All-Star Break, hopes would fade in the wake of the Pirates or the Phillies and perennial Cub Killers like Dave Parker or Mike Schmidt.

On May 17, 1979, in my freshman year of high school, the disabled students' class went on a field trip to Wrigley to watch the Cubs play the Phillies. We arrived at the park early to allow time for positioning the 20 or so wheelchairs in our group in the wheelchair section behind the plate. Four hours later we had seen 44 runs scored, eleven home runs blown out of the park, and the score was tied 22-22! In the top of the 10th, a Mike Schmidt home run ended the game, sending us home dejected, but appreciating having witnessed a lasting moment in baseball history.

If I'm "the man," Mike Ervin is the "Co-Man." As the producer of "On A Roll," and now "The Strength Coach" radio shows, he is a major reason why we have been successful. He is also a reknowned activist, writer, playwright and one of my best friends.

The Cubs never did win the pennant. Now, 24 years later, I still couldn't lift a baseball bat, but my two sons could. They played their first year of Little League ball in the Ocean Springs, Mississippi, Park Commission league that year. I was at every game, camcorder loaded.

For most of the first half of the 2003 season, the Cubs were in first place. Because of my boys and the Cubs early season success, I found myself checking the box scores every day, watching all the games on WGN again, and actually paying the $14 per month to have access to the non-televised games live on the Major League Baseball website! My boys were equally hooked.

It suddenly became clear what I had to do. I called the Cubs box office and bought tickets for games against Atlanta on July 10-11. I shopped for a good deal on airline tickets, and arranged to stay at my producer, Mike Ervin's condo in downtown Chicago. He is another lifelong Cubs enthusiast. In my dream, it was all very clear: We would take the subway to the games. We would immerse ourselves in the city atmosphere and create a life-long memory, and the Cubs would win two against the powerful Atlanta Braves! I also made contact with my old high school buddies who were drummers in the marching band, Kevin Toye, Keith Wiegold and Doug Roselieb.

In the gift shop at the New Orleans airport, we were delighted and surprised to see the current issue of *Sports Illustrated* with Cubs pitchers Kerry Wood and Mark Prior gracing the cover. "Maybe we'll get them to autograph it," said a smiling Donovan.

After arriving in Chicago and taking a cab from Midway airport to the city, Mike took us to a local restaurant, where the boys and I ordered slabs of barbequed ribs, which were tender and delicious. After dinner, Mike rolled with us to the subway elevator that we would use the next day for our trip to Wrigley Field.

Back at Mike's place, we unfolded the sofa bed, unrolled the egg crate mattress and slept soundly. Actually, Greg Jr. sat up and watched TV until 2 AM, but Donovan and I slept well. The next morning, I was excited about the game, yet cautious and concerned about safely navigating my two little boys across busy downtown Chicago streets and the subway system. Once we got on the train, I could relax until we neared the Addison Street stop and saw for the first time, the towering lights of Wrigley Field.

In Chicago's subway system, there is a gap between the platform and the train, which requires that a ramp be set down to allow wheelchair access. My "crip sense" started telling me that perhaps the operator that let us onto the train had not notified the conductor which stop we planned to exit. I called Mike on my cell phone several stops in advance.

"Block the door and have one of the boys run up and tell the conductor," was his advice.

Great. Send one of my sons off a train in a strange and dangerous city and just hope the train would not leave my boy stranded and terrified. Greg Jr. got the assignment of being the runner. Donovan got the duty of holding the door. As we neared the Addison Street stop, I barked out the instructions like a military commander about to send his troops on a mission.

"Donovan, whatever you do, do NOT let that door close. If it does, your brother will be left behind. Greg, if you DO get left behind, here's my cell phone number. Wait in a safe place at the Addison Street stop, and we'll be back."

When the train stopped, Greg darted off and Donovan braced his back against the door. I eyed the gap between the train and the sidewalk. Too much time was going by! "Doors closing," the automated voice announced. Donovan and I panicked at the same time, and I gunned the joystick forward, bouncing off the train without the ramp!

No damage done. No abandoned kids. No time or mood to file complaints or be the advocate. We were here for baseball!

Our seats were in the darkness of the Terrace section in left field, under the upper deck and protected from the light drizzle that threatened all morning. Whatever the kids wanted, I bought. Greg Jr. ate a roast beef sandwich, nachos, cotton candy and Cracker Jacks, not to mention drinks. Donovan had a hot dog and fries. I bought three fitted Cubs caps and spent nearly $200. While the boys were devouring snacks, and the Braves were devouring the Cubs, my high school friends and I joked about the memories of our youth. During the Seventh Inning Stretch, while we sang the traditional *Take Me Out to the Ballgame,* I thought I was videotaping the moment, but had pressed the wrong button on my camcorder.

"You idiot!" yelled Kevin. "No more beer for you."

After the game, we paid a cab driver $50 to take us to Oak Park to visit Kevin's family for a barbeque. We took the scenic route. The boys were wide-eyed as we saw the newly constructed renovation of Soldier Field and made a stop at the United Center to see the Michael Jordan statue. When we arrived in Oak Park Kevin's son Conner played catch with Greg Jr. and Donovan in the front yard, a great moment to witness. Kevin's large Victorian home was not wheelchair accessible, but his back porch was. We enjoyed barbeque and a nice visit, but when I called for a cab ride, it looked for a time as if Kevin would be carrying me up stairs again as he had many times in high school. Soon, however, we were able to find a wheelchair-accessible cab for returning to Mike's place.

The next day, we sat behind the plate in the same wheelchair section our high school class enjoyed 24 years before. The Cubs strictly followed a policy allowing only one person to accompany each wheelchair user in that section, which is why with only one wheelchair; we had to sit in the Terrace Section the day before. But this time, Mike Ervin joined us with his power chair, so the four of us parked ten rows up, directly behind home plate.

The threatening dark clouds proved to be much more merciful than the bats of the Atlanta Braves, who for the second straight day pounded the Cubbies. We witnessed a scary moment when Cubs pitcher, Mark Prior collided with Braves second baseman, Marcus Giles. Both players lay on the field in pain. The crowd was hushed and concerned about Prior, one of the main reasons the Cubs had such a successful first half of the season. We applauded when he walked off the field and again when he went back to the mound in the next inning.

Donovan had his glove ready for foul balls that never came. But we did see Sammy Sosa connect for an immediately obvious home run. With the crack of the bat, people in front of us jumped to their feet, blocking our view of Sammy doing his little hop in front of the plate. It was still great to be there! We just looked at each other and high-fived. A few innings later Sammy did it again! But the Cubs could not generate enough additional offense. In the 8th inning, Mike and I did a little play-by-play recording of the game on my camcorder, throwing out one-liners about the Cubs until one of the many attractive young women at Wrigley that day passed in front of my camcorder, which immediately panned and zoomed with precision.

"Forget about the game, ladies and gentlemen," said Mike. "Outstanding work by our cameraman, Greg Smith on the babe-cam!"

After the game, it was time to seek autographs. The boys got the *Sports Illustrated* out of the bag behind my chair and we fought for position outside the Cubs clubhouse under the left field bleachers. Cubs pitcher, Joe Borowski was the first to emerge, surrounded by dozens of kids hoping for an autograph, including Donovan, who was not in the right space and wasn't forceful enough. Borowski passed him by. I gave Don some advice about speaking louder and being more aggressive.

Then Kerry Wood walked out. The crowd was thicker and Donovan tried harder, but he was not successful. Several minutes went by while we waited and hoped for Sammy Sosa or Moises Alou, our two favorite Cubs to exit. Then Wood stepped out again. I took matters into my own hands using a combination of my deep loud voice to attract his attention, and my presence in the wheelchair, which probably appealed to his sense of compassion.

"Kerry... One more?" I yelled clearly and forcefully.

He was about 30 feet away, but when I yelled, he looked up and immediately walked directly to me, signed our *Sports Illustrated*, left the pens of other autograph seekers waving, and walked away. Donovan and Greg beamed smiles that would have made the highlight reel of our memorable father and son's baseball vacation.

Before we left Chicago, we presented Mike Ervin with a game ball autographed by Greg Jr., Donovan and me... "To Mike. Thanks for everything. Cubs vs. Braves. July 10-11, 2003."

BOYS AT WRIGLEY—We will never forget our magical time in the "Friendly Confines."

CHAPTER 23

Our 11-Year Roll

W ITH *ON A ROLL'S* 11TH ANNIVERSARY coming up in December, Mike and I gave some thought to how we'd commemorate that event on the air. I decided that after 11 years, I ought to be able to tell non-disabled America 11 things they should know about people with disabilities. We posted them on our website and blasted them across the Internet, which led to some interesting conversations and analysis. Here are my 11 things:

1. **Lifestyle not medical.** Instead of looking at disability as a medical condition, look at it as a social movement, a lifestyle, a diversity element.

2. **Anyone can join.** Remember that you can become a member of the disability community in the very next moment, and that if you do, your life will change, not necessarily for the worse.

3. **Don't Fear.** The fact that you could become disabled makes you fear disability. Face up to your fears and realize that the most horrifying part of being disabled is the way society will treat you when you do because of its fear. Dealing with the physical loss is much easier than the social stigma.

4. **If you're in, you're in.** Realize that the term disability covers a wide range of conditions and that if a person has a "minor" disability, he or she is still a part of a larger community.

5. **Still human.** Disability does not change basic human needs and desires.

6. **Disabled rights are YOUR rights.** Think of disability in terms of the whole of society, not from the standpoint of disabled people being "them" and non-disabled people being "us," because the civil rights protections for people with disabilities take into account the newly disabled among YOU.

7. **Life equal to cure.** Our society places too much emphasis on curing disabilities and not enough emphasis on living with a disability.

8. **Invisible in the mirror.** The mainstream media fears disability and is only slowly coming around to representing our community in frequency and appropriateness of coverage and depiction. That "ain't" us in the media mirror.

9. **Coming over to your house.** Not being able to visit people in their homes is one of the most damaging aspects of living life from a wheelchair. If you have a friend in a wheelchair and don't have a way for him or her to enter your home, such as a $5.00 piece of plywood from Home Depot, I question your level of commitment to the friendship. If you are building a new home and aren't planning to have a no-step entrance, you're perpetuating the problem.

10. **Our homes, not nursing homes!** Why does our government pay three times as much for putting a person with a disability in a nursing home (off the streets, out of sight, out of mind) instead of affording them the opportunity of living in the community with personal assistant services at home?

11. New friends often say, **"You aren't like most disabled people,"** or "I don't think of you as disabled," or "The wheelchair seems to vanish when I'm around you." The truth is most people have a false perception of what a disabled person is supposed to be like.

While I was at it, I decided to write, publish and broadcast my *Top 11 things I would like to convey to Americans with disabilities.*

1. Get to know and socialize with other people with disabilities.

2. Get a job, or act as if you have one.

3. Don't give away your expertise.

4. Keep your pride. Look good; value yourself, your time, your activities, and your reputation.

5. Become politically active and aware.

6. Find a way to be involved in the things you enjoy, even if you can't do them like everybody else or with everyone else. Modify. Don't hate. Participate!

7. Be Persistent. Don't let speed bumps become roadblocks.

8. Raise your expectations of yourself and create a plan to achieve those expectations.

9. Know your legal rights and exercise them when necessary.

10. Find a way to make your disability work as an asset instead of a liability.

11. Be proactive. The subject of your complaint has room for you to become a part of the solution.

It was not very difficult to find material for *On A Roll* programming. A steady flow of e-mail and postal packaging arrived daily from people who wanted to be guests on the show. The difficult part was choosing material that worked well. It was a challenging prospect when you consider the complexity of our audience and our desire to provide programming that would connect.

At least 90% of the unsolicited stuff didn't interest me. I was looking for topics and guests that helped make the case that disability was not a fate worse than, equal to, or just slightly better than death. I wanted every show to offer a sense of possibility and enthusiasm, so that disabled people in the listening audience could realize they were not alone and they were part of a massive community that was now, for the first time in history, becoming sentient and recognizing it had a heartbeat and a soul.

There were three distinct sub-categories of listeners I had to consider when choosing what to do with two hours of weekly airtime. More than 10 years into this venture, I continued to be unsure which set of ears was the most important to appeal to.

One category of listener was the non-disabled, largely unaware, mainstream news/talk radio listener. He or she might have tuned in and heard a newscast while driving back from a Sunday picnic, when all of a sudden, "The Hip Crip who Gives You Tips" came on the radio! That was a good thing. I had to remember that *On A Roll* was a commercial radio talk show and in order to exist and survive, the program had to attract as many listeners as possible, and furthermore, could not offend or otherwise "turn off" the affiliate station's existing listeners. To that end, I had to present programming that covered disability issues in such a way that the mainstream talk radio listener would find it interesting. I would like to think that when people just happened upon *On A Roll*, they were intrigued by a line of thought they had never heard before. We had to approach each week's program remembering there were going to be people who were hearing our show for the first time. We couldn't assume they had been listening all along and had a clear understanding of progressive new concepts like independent living and disability rights. So when we did present topics rooted in the disability rights model, we did it from a fundamental perspective, allowing those who had never heard these concepts before to become enlightened.

Let's go to Frank in Jacksonville, Florida. Frank welcome to On A Roll, how are you doing today? We're talking about disability pride.

"Greg, I've never heard this show before, but this is quite interesting. I have a nephew who has muscular dystrophy, and I find it a little farfetched for you to say that you feel proud of your disability. How can you feel proud of something that is a negative?"

"Well that's just it, Frank. I don't see it as a negative. I see it as a characteristic. Just like the fact that I'm black. If I can be proud of the fact that I'm black, why can't I be proud of the fact that I'm an American with a disability?"

"But it's not the disability that you're proud of. You might be proud of the fact that you have the patience and the mental fortitude to go on with your life and be successful, despite your disability, but I don't get how you can be proud of a disability."

"Well, yes, I am proud of what I've accomplished in life in the face of obstacles that have been placed in my way. And by the way, most of those obstacles were not due to the disability itself, but instead the way society responded to my disability in the form of placing undeserved limitations on my opportunities. So yes, I am proud of my accomplishments. But I am also proud to be a part of this community. This community has so much of what makes the human spirit so powerful. There's so much character and purity among us that I'm very proud to be among my brothers and sisters with disabilities. And you know what, if I didn't have my disability, I wouldn't have all of these insights, so yes, Frank. I am proud of the disability itself; just like I am proud of the color of my skin."

I loved those kinds of exchanges. Frank might never have understood; but maybe he could start to think of disability in a different way. Maybe he would be more prepared for the disability that would eventually enter his life or the life of someone close to him in the future. On the radio, we were expediting a revolution of thought. We were pushing the clock forward to a time when people truly view disability as a beautiful part of the natural diversity that is human life. And we were not doing it one mind at a time. We were doing it thousands of minds at a time. I would say that the non-disabled, non-aware, mainstream news/talk radio listener was the largest slice of the *On A Roll* audience pie. It was also the most important to appeal to.

The smallest part of the *On A Roll* pie was the "core disability community." There is a distinction between the phrases "core disability community," and "people with disabilities." People in the disability "core community" were people who sought out *On A Roll* because they were already passionate members of the disability rights movement. They were advocates. They volunteered for disability rights, or worked for disability organizations. They were parents of kids with disabilities, or in some other way closely related to a disabled person. They understood disability rights, disability pride and independent living. They were the choir with whom I sang. They subscribed to my newsletter, bookmarked iCan.com on their Web browser, read *New Mobility Magazine*. They read *The Mouth*, and the *Ragged Edge and other*, disability rights publications. They attended the conferences. They worked for government agencies. They subscribed to disability empowerment newsgroups online.

While the core community members represented a small portion of the overall audience, they were the most active participants. They were the ones who called the show. I really viewed them as *part* of the show. A large percentage of my guests came from the core community. They had the best stories to tell. They were living examples of what was possible for people with even the most severe disabilities. They were the heartbeat of *On A Roll*. I loved them.

Finally, there were people with disabilities who were not members of the community. It was very important for me to reach this group. These were people who happened to find *On A Roll,* just as the non-disabled, non-aware mainstream talk radio listeners did. They stumbled onto the show and hopefully heard new ideas. While they used a wheelchair or leg braces or a crutch; while they had a "handicapped" parking placard due to a heart condition that precluded them from walking long distances; while they had cancer or lived with the effects of a stroke, they weren't "handicapped" in their own self-perception. They wouldn't associate themselves with a group of disabled people. Many of them were blissfully unaware that disabled people were part of the community, doing quite well, were self-sufficient, employed, married, and parenting. Heck, that was me in 1991! But I would suspect the majority of them had a different mindset that was not so empowering. They were separated and isolated, both from other people with disabilities and from a feeling of equality and oneness with the souls and surroundings of their non-disabled environment.

What divided "core community members" from the disconnected majority of "people with disabilities?" Let me give you an example. On March 5, 2003, I was weeding through the "spam" in my e-mail when I found a message about disability in the media posted on a listserv called *Mediatalk*, subscribed to by writers and journalists with disabilities as well as leaders who understood the importance of the media in pushing the disability movement forward. The message was from Dan Wilkins, a community member who owns a company called The Nth Degree. Dan is a leader in the core community who designs t-shirts, hats and other novelty items with clever disability rights slogans on them.

In the subject line: "Here's a real stomach turner."

I opened the e-mail to find a link that contained the phrase "Sports Illustrated" and immediately clicked on it, which led to legendary columnist Rick Reilly's essay, *Extra Credit*.

"The best college tradition is not dotting the *i* at Ohio State. It's not stealing the goat from Navy. Or waving the wheat at Kansas." Reilly wrote. "It's Picking Up Butch at Middlebury (Vt.) College."

"For 42 years Middlebury freshman athletes have been Picking Up Butch for football and basketball games. It's a sign-up sheet thing. Carry the ball bags. Gather all the towels. Pick Up Butch.

The article went on to paint a picture of heroic student athletes rescuing Butch from the misery of his disability. It also suggested they abandoned him during the off-season.

"They put him in his wheelchair and push him out of the house, or one guy hauls him in a fireman's carry. They pile him into the car, cram the wheelchair into the trunk, take him to the game and roll him to his spot in the mezzanine for football games or at the end of the bench for basketball.

Butch always smiles and says the same thing from the bottom of his heart: "CP just sucks." Cerebral palsy. While his fondest dream has always been to play basketball, it'll never happen. There is little that he can physically do for himself.

As is often the case when non-disabled, non-aware journalists write about disability, this column suddenly took an offensive tone. The overall message: Butch's life was tragic, save one thing—college students who gave him the only thing he enjoyed in life; a ride to a game. If it wasn't for them, he'd be miserable. Reilly's column nailed this sentiment in its dismount:

"Now comes the worst time of the year—the months between the end of the basketball season, last week, and the start of football in August. " It stinks," Butch says. He sits at home lonely day after day, watching nothing but Boston Red Sox games on TV, waiting for the calendar pages to turn to the days when he can be one, two, three, together again with the students he loves. On that day, the door will swing open, and standing there, young and strong, will be two fresh-men. And, really, just seeing them is what Picking Up Butch is all about."

After reading the article, I posted the question, "What can we do about 'ol Butch?" The e-mail firestorm began. Steve Brown, co-founder of the Institute on Disability Culture wrote an angry letter to *Sports Illustrated*, stating that the question should be, "What can we do about Rick Reilly and SI running this pitiful story instead of a great one that could have been written about why someone with CP who wants to attend games only believes he's capable of doing it this way."

"Where's the community's Personal Assistance Services so he does not have to stay in bed all day if he doesn't want to? Where's the accessible transportation so he can get to the games any way he wants to. Where's the accessible housing so he might not have to live with his mother if he doesn't want to? Where's the wheelchair seating in the venues? Where's the Center for Independent Living or other advocacy organization that might be able to provide Butch peer support and inform him why even if he always believes "CP sucks," there might be others out there who believe in their CP with pride?

"Why is the pity story still the one that runs, when the belief in pride is what gets all of us—disabled and not—through each day believing in the dream of living, not the despair of life?"

Wilkins wrote, "Let's take him out and show him the difference between the pity and paternalism of being a school project and the power and pride of true equity, respect and friendship. This would probably involve beer or margaritas."

Two weeks later, a guest cancelled at the last minute and I was left scrambling to replace about a half hour of programming. One feature we could always do was *Physically Incorrect*.

We only had two stories in the PI file, but I thought they were both good ones. The first one was Butch, and the second was about a guy charged with DUI and assault whose accident victim needed to use a wheelchair through her rehabilitation. The judge sentenced the guy to spend six months in a wheelchair as a part of his punishment. I called two of my closest allies to be the panel: Todd Kimball, my ex partner, and Michelle Hlavek, my ex-girlfriend.

After reading excerpts from the column, the barrage began. Michelle led off:

Michelle: I think it's a wonderful story and I think every town should have a Butch.

Me: What about the party after the game? Do they take Butch there or do they just bring him home?

Michelle: Yeah, right! What about setting Butch up on a date?

Me: There ya go! It sounds to me like they just come in and grab this guy, take him to the game, let him enjoy the game and his hot dog and then drop him home.

Todd: It's almost set up like a fraternity hazing or something. Or some sort of ritual. And you would think after all the years that they've spent with him just taking him to games that somebody would say, "Hey, let's see if we can get his everyday life more accessible and see if he can do some more things on his own."

Me: Some of you may be listening, thinking 'My God, how can this guy be criticizing such a wonderful humanitarian thing; taking a disabled person to a game.' If you feel that way, I want to hear from you. I think we need to reach out to Butch, and we need to explain to him that there's a bigger potential for his life than just sitting around waiting for these college boys to come pick him up so they can look good to their girlfriends! We've got JJ on the line from the Florida Keys. JJ welcome to *On A Roll*.

JJ: Listen, I think Butch is a sports fan! And I think they take him to the game. They sit him right up front. They sit with him between plays and afterwards they take him out for pizza with the team. I think he's having a *hell* of good time. I think he misses it, and I think he should miss it. Hell, I would miss it if I had that chance.

Me: What about during the off-season?

JJ: During the off-season, hey, I miss football and basketball too!

Me: Yeah, but you're not sitting at home lonely!

JJ: Who says? (Laughter)

More callers flooded the lines with comments about Butch and the tradition at Middlebury College, to the point where we had no time to talk about the story of the judge sentencing a criminal to a wheelchair. We agreed on the air that a must-do item would be to get Butch on the show. Two weeks later, it happened.

I started the show by airing a reading of excerpts from Riley's column, followed by the above clips from the previous week's show. I instructed my studio engineer, Peter Trahan, to make certain that Butch could hear what was being said on the air. After the comments aired, I introduced Butch. He wasn't pleased.

"Can we cut out the bullshit?" he said. He defended his role as an inspiration to the team and said he didn't feel like an object of pity. I asked him about some of the words used in the article and particularly about the "CP Sucks" quote.

He said, "CP does suck and it robbed me of all kinds of things in my life, like being a doctor or a lawyer or playing sports."

When asked if he had any friends with disabilities, he responded, "I don't want any disabled friends because I have enough of my own problems. I don't need anybody else's problems."

He said, "There are no services for transportation in my town and there's nothing to do here. It's a small town, OK?"

He was understandably surprised and angered that we questioned his core beliefs about his life and his disability. After the show and throughout the evening, I felt somewhat amiss about ruining poor Butch's day, when he probably had thought we were going to profile his tradition at Middlebury. His statements, tone and attitude, truly made me wonder how many people with disabilities out there feel this way.

I didn't know much about Butch, but I do know that as I write this, I intend to seek out advocates in Vermont and hopefully make a difference in his life. Butch was 54 years old when we spoke; I was 39. We're both quite severely disabled. How is it I have been able to live a wonderful, enjoyable life while there are people like Butch out there who may be quite content settling for a lifestyle I would find tragic for myself? How many people with disabilities feel shame, despair, hopelessness and self-loathing? What can we do to empower and enlighten them? Until the day I die, I will continue to do my best to be a part of the solution to this tragic problem.

On A Roll was only a partial solution. It was effective to its limited audience. We had great content and interesting guests. But sponsorships were not coming in. Revenue was not what I needed it to be. I was still living with my parents, unable to contribute and feeling like a failure amidst all the outward success I was experiencing. Something was missing.

IN 2004, BEARS RUNNING BACK GREG SMITH JR—advertised his dad's business every time he broke off a long run from scrimmage in practice! My dad, right, was the head coach. I was the assistant.

244

CHAPTER 24

The Strength Coach

ON THE PLATFORM—When I'm in front of an audience, I'm never nervous because I put it all in the hands of God.

M Y PROFESSIONAL SPEAKING CAREER officially began in the early morning hours of July 25, 2003. I arrived in my hotel at 1:18 AM because I had stopped at a club in Pensacola, en route to Tallahassee. I was to speak at the Florida Youth Leadership Forum, a gathering of over 200 youths with disabilities between the ages of 16 and 21. I was exhausted as I entered my room but feigning to check my voice mail.

"You have six new messages. Message one, marked urgent, at 4:01 PM."

"Greg, this is Abby Cruz from the Able Trust. Just wanted to check to make sure you're okay. It's 4 o'clock and we called the front desk and they say you haven't checked in yet. We're very concerned.

We know this isn't like you. We still have an hour and we look forward to getting everything set up. Call me."

My heart skipped a beat as the hair on my back seemed to poke out of the cloth in my shirt! Had I arrived a day late?

"Message two, marked urgent, at 5:15 PM."

"Greg, this is Abby. It's after five and we're serving dinner. You're our keynote speaker and you're not here. I hope you're okay. Call me."

"Message three, marked urgent, at 7:36 PM."

"Greg, we're sorry we missed you. We are very concerned about you. We have not been able to get an answer on your home phone or your cell phone. Please call us to let us know you're alive."

OH MY GOD!!! I had marked the wrong date for the speech on my Palm Pilot. I cried in my pillow. I beat up my pillow. I beat up myself. How could I do this? How could I have been so stupid to have not looked at the contract, or confirmed the date of the speech? What a bonehead!

This wasn't the first speech I had ever given! I was a professional. This was a nightmare but I wasn't sleeping. I didn't get any sleep that night. At 7 AM. I called Kristen Knapp, the Director of Marketing for the ABLE Trust.

"Kristen, I must have had the wrong date in my calendar. I AM SOOOOO SORRY!"

"Greg, we were sooooo worried about you. We thought you had an accident on the freeway or something. I'm happy to hear you're okay."

"I'm not ok. I feel terrible about this. Is there any possible way I can address this group today?"

"We may be able to work something out, but maybe you can come down on the speaker's fee a bit."

"It's free!"

"Alright! How about speaking at lunch today?"

Before I was introduced at the luncheon, I was overcome with embarrassment, and actually wondered if everyone in the room knew I was a flake. When I got on the platform, I gave my standard motivational speech, showing PowerPoint slides with photos from various milestones in my life.

My message to the youth was to get involved in activities in school —to integrate themselves into the academic and social mainstream. The reception was warm and the applause was lengthy.

I did a fair job touching this group. I did not get a standing ovation but then again, there were a lot of people in the room who didn't have that physical ability.

In the after-talk lineup of well-wishers, one young man in particular related closely to the story of my playing drums in high school marching band. He was in high school and played trumpet in his band from the sidelines. Meeting that kid really energized me to where I felt I had redeemed myself.

I was also feeling good because I had plans to meet a young lady who had driven from Georgia to visit me. Julie Prough was sitting on a bench just across the elevator when I descended after my speech. I had totally forgotten the fiasco of the night before as the two of us embraced.

The rest of my weekend in Tallahassee with Julie gave me time to reflect and to realize that my professionalism as a speaker needed desperate attention. There's no way in hell that a professional speaker can put the wrong date down in his calendar and expect to remain a professional speaker for very long. This was a wake up call.

A few months earlier, I had submitted the paperwork to become a member of the National Speakers Association. My certificate arrived in March and I had continually received materials in the mail and via e-mail about the organization's annual conference. This year, it was to be in New Orleans, just a few days after my no-show keynote address in Tallahassee.

I decided that I would drive to New Orleans, register for one day of the conference and learn as much as I could about how to make it as a professional speaker. When I arrived at the Sheraton Hotel, I felt a little intimidated as a first-timer at a new industry conference. The meeting had events scheduled for four days, but I arrived on the last day and paid the $200 one-day fee with reluctance. I received a badge that had a "VIP" tag, which meant that this was my very first NSA Conference.

After leaving the registration booth, I was greeted by warm hellos and friendly smiles. I rolled through the exhibit hall and was approached by Mike Frank, president of a speaker's bureau and a former NSA President. He sat down with a pen and paper and talked to me about my fee strategy. We didn't use real numbers but he told me about how to structure my fees and the importance of not negotiating with clients as if I was selling used cars. "You're selling your knowledge and expertise," He said.

I'd been at the conference for five minutes and had already received my money's worth. I attended workshops about effective storytelling, using technology to create products, and structuring your business to generate continued revenue from the work put into one speech. This was amazing knowledge, and the speakers were tremendous. My mind was dizzy as new ideas flowed from every session! This was the best $200 I had ever spent. I decided immediately that I would never miss another NSA event.

In the hallway, the chatter was very loud as the professional speakers networked. I noticed that there were more people with disabilities at this conference than at the National Association of Broadcasters, National Association of Black Journalists, or any other non-disability related industry meeting I'd attended. I met Sean Stephenson, W. Mitchell, Rosemarie Rosetti, and saw many other people with disabilities that I didn't get a chance to meet.

Between sessions in the crowded hallway, I rolled up on a conversation between NSA speakers Don Cooper and Peggy O'Neil. Don has established a niche as one of America's leading experts on networking. Peggy, a little person, labels herself "The little speaker with the big message."

Peggy was direct and insightful, aggressively helping this VIP newbie.

"What are you an expert on, Greg? What message can you communicate to your audience better than anyone else in the world can? What is your unique value to your audience?"

I thought about it while I bumbled through a rushed, abbreviated, yet lengthy telling of the *On A Roll* story. In the previous session, we had discussed "Elevator Introductions," having a short, concise answer to the question, "What do you speak about?"

First, I thought about the fact that after hosting America's syndicated radio show on disability issues, I was an expert on disability. But I dug deeper in those few, short critical moments. I was looking for my speaking to appeal to a larger, broader audience. Disability was a part of my message. But how could I take the lessons from my disability experience and make them apply to a mainstream audience?

"I think I'm an expert on strength," I concluded. "I don't have physical strength, but I think living my life, pushing aside all of the obstacles that I have faced makes me an expert on inner strength."

"So you teach organizations and individuals how to increase their personal power and strength?" said Peggy.

"You coach people on how to overcome challenges through inner strength," said Don.

That coach word triggered an "Aha!"

"Strength Coach!"

I just blurted out the phrase and knew immediately that this would be my hook. *On A Roll* officially died at that moment. It was perfect. My imagination raced into the future. I could immediately imagine myself, this little, skinny 65-pound guy in a wheelchair, calling himself "The Strength Coach," speaking to professional football players and calling them wimps. I imagined telling stories of true struggle and motivating them to go out on the football field and fight with the same drive that I used to face every day. I imagined how effective it would be, and I thought about how I could use that name to reach corporations, schools, and industry meetings. I also thought of the media applications and how I could change my radio show to become more mass-appeal.

My smile of gratitude to Peggy and Don for stimulating that level of thinking was enormous. Did they create "The Strength Coach"? Possibly. I don't know if I would have stumbled upon that name without that particular hallway conversation. That's the beauty of NSA. No matter what industry you're in, no matter what your passion is, it is a lesson about encouragement and teamwork. If you can help someone, do it. If you can surround yourself with teammates who want to see you succeed, do it. In doing so, you'll be helped in return.

Weeks later, Murv Seymour, my buddy from Tampa mumbled through his crackly cell phone.

"Yeah, man, I'm broke. I might just disappear into the woods and start living on berries."

Murv is one of my best friends. He'll probably be pissed to see the phrase "one of" in that description. He's among my top few when I pause and reflect on what a true friend is supposed to be.

Murv is a creative genius. He has a great voice. He is intelligent, articulate, and well trained in television journalism. He's won awards for his reporting including four Emmy nominations. Murv is a big fella, standing about 6'5" and weighing close to 300 pounds. And he is absolutely freakin' crazy! I have had many laugh-induced stomachaches from just hanging around the guy. He has that standup comic gift; the wit to find the uniquely hilarious in situations that are a part of everyday life.

In 2000, Murv made a courageous decision. He walked away from a successful career as a television reporter to follow his dream of being a professional standup comic. The next few years landed him in all 50 states in all varieties of clubs, sometimes bringing the house down, and on a few occasions, talking to the wrong crowd on the wrong night. His voyage in comedy lasted for three years but by this point, he was broke and thinking about getting back into television.

"Yeah, man, I gonna grow a long beard and live in the woods."

"They're gonna think you're the Sasquatch!" I joked.

"I'm sorry, was that supposed to be funny?"

Murv had always been a good friend to dream with and share my abundance of optimism. While he was at a point in his career when financial realities caused him to seek a more stable setup, I was at an enthusiastic point. My direction as a speaker was set. I was about to receive the grant from the State of Mississippi's Developmental Disabilities Council to do a statewide disabilities show. Things were more promising than ever before.

After several conversations, we decided that Murv would move to

Ocean Springs, live upstairs in our guest room, and serve as my personal assistant while he conducted his television job search. While here, he would assemble the videotape from my best *Strength Coach* speeches and put together my speaking demo video that I'd need to get speaking engagements.

"Only one thing, man," demanded Murv. "I ain't wipin' your ass!" I wouldn't want him to. Thank God I can still manage that skill.

There's nothing like having your own live-in comedian. The next four months gave us plenty of ideas for sitcom material. Murv would imitate the raspy-voiced movie promo announcer.

"One frustrated grandma... One helpless father... three bad ass children.... And one washed up comedian... "Dysfunctional Black Family." Starts Friday at a theater near you!"

My mother was delighted to have someone help me with daily living, because she had been doing it all for nearly two years. Every day, Murv would turn on the light at 6:00 AM and lift me into my chair, whether I was awake or not.

The first morning, he alarmed me. "What the hell is going on here?" I screamed. Over time, he learned how to do it correctly. For example, when he would lift me into the chair, he would grab under my arms and hoist me way up into the air before setting me in the seat of the chair. Maybe it was easier for him this way, being so tall, but for me it was an unnecessary elevator ride when he could have just as easily shifted me over into the chair with my feet planted securely on the ground. I learned to communicate what I needed and he was very coachable.

He made fun of my toes and the way the big toe crosses the second toe. "Your toes are throwin' up gang signs!" he remarked.

He made fun of the hair under my arms. "You look like you got Gary Coleman in a headlock!" Murv was a load of laughs.

Between the goofing around, we had some good strategic marketing discussions. It was great to have someone I could bounce ideas off. One day, before a speech at the Ocean Springs Rotary Club, Murv came up with a great concept: If I'm going to be speaking as a coach, I ought to look like one. So he went to a sporting goods store and purchased a red hat and a coach's whistle. Murv again videotaped and did a great job taking photos. He would continue to accompany me on speaking engagements, promotional appearances and interviews. I was aggressively promoting the new concept and because of my new grant, made trips to Jackson, Mississippi in September and October, with Murv in the passenger seat, handing me sodas and potato chips along the way.

Murv's skills were adequate as a personal assistant, helping me get in and out of the shower and dressed. But his real value came in giving me feedback on my presentations and suggestions for radio content, website design, business cards and letterhead. He has a graphic designer's eye.

MURV AND THE KIDS—"Daddy, when is Murv coming back?" I get that question a lot. My kids love my best friend, funnyman Murv Seymour.

In early October, I spoke at the Career Opportunities for Students with Disabilities (COSD) conference on the Microsoft Campus in Redmond, Washington. COSD, located on the campus of the University of Tennessee in Knoxville, is an organization that helps connect career services departments on college campuses with disabled student services. A few days later, Alan Muir, executive director of COSD was on the phone.

"I really, really enjoyed your speech."

"You know Alan, I'd love to speak at the University of Tennessee at some point. Any chance of that?"

A day later, I found myself on the phone with Dan Carlson, former director of the disabled students program, a quadriplegic who had recently taken a job as the academic advisor for UT's football players. Here was the possibility of a dream come true; the opportunity to give an inspirational message to a major college football team!

When we landed in Knoxville, they took us directly from the airport to the practice field. It was a hot, sunny afternoon as the Volunteers were wrapping up a grueling practice and dripping with sweat. As we observed the workout and chatted with Dan and other staff from UT, Coach Phillip Fulmer approached and introduced himself with a wide smile.

After the pleasantries, he got specific. "What do you want to talk about?"

Tennessee had just lost two conference games in a row, and they were on the verge of suffering a hopeless season, despite pre-season predictions saying they would contend for the conference title. Their next opponent was the Alabama Crimson Tide, their bitter rival, so today's practice had been especially hard.

Alabama. Crimson Tide. What was I thinking, showing up to give a motivational speech to the orange Volunteers of Tennessee, wearing my generic RED hat? While I was giving Fulmer my elevator speech about inner strength, he reached on top of my head and snatched the hat away, replacing it with the Tennessee hat from his own head!

"Ok, I'll give you 10 minutes."

He blew his whistle. Suddenly, on this hot sunny day, I found

myself in the shade, surrounded by towering linemen who had just finished a long workout in the hot sun. The last thing they wanted right
now was a *speaker*! I was nervous as hell, but wanted to do a great job
and capture some great video for the demo tape.

"Gentlemen, I'm here to challenge you today," I began. "I call
myself *The Strength Coach*. I know you're thinking, 'How can this little guy in a wheelchair call himself a strength coach?'

"Well, I'm talking about inner strength, not physical strength. You
get stronger by lifting the weights of life's challenges." I gave my background and ended by asking them the question, "How do you feel?"
They'd learned earlier in my presentation that the proper response was
"Strong!" I made them yell it in unison, while considering the points I
had made about inner strength.

That Saturday, the Tennessee vs. Alabama game was televised here
in Mississippi. Our whole family, including Murv was glued to the TV,
rooting for Tennessee as if they were the Chicago Bears, our favorite
team of all sports! Tennessee simply MUST win this game, or it would
have put a huge dent in my credibility as an inspirational speaker.

AT TENNESSEE FOOTBALL PRACTICE—A different point of view: Dan Carlson (right) set up
an opportunity for me to speak to the Tennessee Volunteers football team in October 2003.
They won 5 straight after that.

WITH COACH FULMER—After Coach Phillip Fulmer removed my red hat and replaced it with his Tennessee hat, and after I delivered my 10 minute speech, we posed for this shot. Photo by Murv Seymour.

The game started out as a defensive struggle with fumbles and a lot of mistakes by both teams. It was 6-3 at halftime with Alabama out front. In the second half, I watched James Banks sprint in from 25 yards out and remembered his face from my audience as Tennessee took a 10-6 lead. A few minutes later, I was relaxing as Tennessee kicked a field goal and took a 13-6 lead. But with 4:42 left in the third quarter, Alabama scored on a 36-yard touchdown pass to tie the score.

In the fourth quarter, Alabama scored a touchdown to go up 20-13, but Tennessee stepped up to the challenge as quarterback Casey Clausen marched the Volunteers down the field to score on a 1-yard touchdown pass to Troy Fleming with 25 seconds left on the game clock!

We were all going nuts! I couldn't be still and kept rolling around the living room yelling at the TV.

Each overtime period was agonizing to watch as the teams traded touchdowns and field goals. My whole family, wearing the orange Volunteers t-shirts I'd purchased for them, knew the importance of a win for my career! All the guys in the house, my father, Murv, my sons Greg and Donovan, and I were screaming at the television!

Finally and mercifully, it ended. In the fifth overtime, Tennessee's defense shut down the Crimson Tide to preserve a 51-43 victory in what then had been the longest game in college football history! The Volunteers had called on their inner strength and defeated Alabama in a grueling struggle.

Boy, did I take full credit for the victory! Honestly, I know that had I not spoken to the Tennessee Volunteers the Wednesday before that game, it may not have had any impact on the outcome. But in a game so closely contested, perhaps one word or one sentence I said was absorbed into the mental makeup of a Casey Clausen, a Cedrick Houston, or a James Banks.

Whatever it was, it worked. The next week, Tennessee beat #2 ranked Miami 10-6 and went on to win the remainder of their games! Every time they won, my confidence and credibility grew! After their final regular season victory, I called Dan Carlson.

"Dan. You know, Tennessee is 6 and 0 since I delivered my speech. You oughta' consider having me come down and speak to the team during Peach Bowl week."

"That's a good idea. Let me get back to you."

A few days later, he called and told me that it wasn't going to work with the schedule. No Strength Coach.

Peach Bowl, January 2, 2004, final score: Clemson 27, Tennessee 14!

It wasn't long before I changed the name of the show. *The Strength Coach* concept energized me. Many of the problems I had with *On A Roll* found solutions with this new concept.

First, although I had become burned out doing the same disability show for over a decade, my heart still desired to be a part of the solution for making life better for people with disabilities. I was actually ashamed and disappointed that *On A Roll* never really became a truly nationwide program that carried the clout and power of the mass media. The show did a great job of connecting the disability movement and giving those close to its core a forum to share ideas and commonality, but it really had no influence on the general public. If you didn't have a disability, you probably never even heard of *On A Roll*. If you had a disability and were remotely connected to the movement, perhaps you've heard of the show but probably couldn't hear it on a radio station in your area.

With *The Strength Coach*, I felt that the concept of "Inner Strength" had a universal charm. Each of us wants to build our inner strength. With *On A Roll*, instead of reaching the mainstream with a message of disability awareness, I felt like I was cramming tablespoons of good medicine down America's throat. Understanding disability rights and disability pride was a good thing for America, but Americans do not like when others tell them what to think or how to behave. *On A Roll*, as good as it was, involved a lot of not-so-subtle finger pointing at non-disabled America and tried to correct what was wrong with the way people with disabilities were treated.

With *The Strength Coach*, I felt like I would be the "ice cream man," welcomed into neighborhoods, delivering treats that everyone wanted. All my life, I have been called "courageous, inspirational, motivational, and heroic." I don't know if it's true or not, but I realized that the perception makes the reality. I knew that when I rolled into a room, 99% of the people who saw me felt a combination of pity and admiration for the fact that despite my severe physical challenges, I smile, crack jokes, flirt with women and try to succeed in business. I started to realize the power I had to be an example of a person with inner strength. And I saw the potential popularity of that message.

I started to realize that everybody wanted to know how a guy who weighs 65 pounds and has metal rods in his back could be so happy. How can I sit strapped into a wheelchair and be so optimistic? That's what people wanted to know. That's what they wanted to learn from me. They could care less about employment discrimination against people with disabilities. They felt guilty when I would tell them about the millions of people with disabilities who are stuck in nursing homes against their will. They would look at their shoes when I'd ask them whether they could even invite a person like me into their homes because most people's homes are not wheelchair accessible.

While the issues that impact the lives of people with disabilities are valid and critical to a future that gives equal opportunities for the

American dream to all, I began to realize that telling people what to do and think so overtly would never work. With *The Strength Coach*, I could offer resources instead of making demands. I could serve positive mental nourishment as the main course and spice it with a flavor of disability awareness. I could wrap the important disability messages inside something much more appealing to the general public.

With *On A Roll*, I was never able to get the guys in the suits at the radio conventions to give me a serious listen. It became more and more depressing to do great radio shows and know that my audience was small. *The Strength Coach* offered the promise of mass appeal.

Regarding the bottom line, selling advertising to support *On A Roll* was always a challenge. Over the years, I was able to sell sponsorships to Microsoft, Invacare, General Motors and several companies that targeted the disability community, but it was always a tough sell. "How many listeners do you have? Are you on in New York? Are you on in the top 20 markets?" These questions all received less than desirable answers and the rejection made me even more frustrated with my position in the world. With *The Strength Coach*, I realized that the revenue would come, not from selling advertising, but from promoting my speaking business and being hired as a professional speaker. And it worked! In the first year, I did over 40 paid speaking engagements and earned a considerable amount more than I ever earned selling advertising for *On A Roll*!

I also believe that the radio show has tremendous potential to be widely accepted in the radio industry. It is a "feel-good" Sunday evening program, offering uplift, positive mental nourishment that people need to develop the energy to face the challenges of the coming week. I have not even tried to push the show and do aggressive affiliate relations to expand my market base, but I will.

When I started *The Strength Coach*, people told me not to change the name of the show. "You've built up 11 years of brand identity with *On A Roll*! Don't throw all of that away," they said.

My gut was telling me differently. It was time for a major face-lift. I assembled a team of winners as independent contractors. I think it is very interesting that most of the folks on my team are people with disabilities. It speaks to my belief that inner strength is a quality that my people add to the melting pot that is America.

Bethany Broadwell, who handled iCan.com's web site, became my web master. Terri O'Hare, a fan of *On A Roll* created our logo. Simon Illa, the young hip-hop music producer from Philadelphia who has Osteogenisis Imperfecta, created the music you hear on the show, and contracted with rapper Brian Desind AKA "BD" to develop *Strength*, the show's theme song.

The composition of the Strength Coach theme song led to a sound that people at Warner Music liked so much that a new band, "The Answer" was born. If you think I'm exaggerating about being the reason for the creation of a rock band, check out their web site: http://www.theanswernyc.com, which says:

"The Answer is BD, Mitch, Brian and Paul. The Answer came to be when New York based Rap artist, BD, was asked by Philadelphia producer, Simon Illa, to write and record a Rap song for a national radio show." (THAT WOULD BE MY SHOW!)

Now armed with a new theme song, logo, web site and a lot of passion for what I was doing, it was time to structure the new show on the air. My fear was that I'd lose my base. I had nightmares about disability rights advocates calling me a "sellout," saying I had used the disability community's struggles as a stepping-stone from which I was trying to climb to stardom.

Despite those fears, I moved forward with my mission. Having Mike Ervin to help keep the effort pure, we developed some interesting shows. My programming formula was to offer my own insights about inner strength, combine my views with other motivational speakers and authors and make the show have a slight sports swagger with an occasional coach or athlete. Sometimes I'd blow my coach's whistle into the microphone on-air as I gave my tips for success and happiness.

We started with Bill Treasurer, a fellow National Speakers Association member who is the author of the book *Right Risk*. Since I was taking a major risk in starting a new radio show, he was the perfect kickoff guest.

During the first year, we had outstanding guests and interesting conversations. I have a few favorites.

My dad and I recorded an interview for Father's Day, which revealed a lot about the strength a good family bond can create. That interview, aided by a glass of wine or two, captures the essence of what I want this show to be. I'm into emotions. I'm a very sensitive man, and I see that as a great part of my strength. I was able to get my dad to relax and speak from the heart. It was one of my best interviews.

Another of my favorite shows was an interview I did with legendary UCLA basketball coach, John Wooden. Prior to interviewing him, I read his book, *My Personal Best*, aloud to my children. Coach Wooden was impressed with my preparedness and rewarded me with a warm and personable conversation. After the show, I received an email from Steve Jamison, the co-author of the book *My Personal Best*.

"Greg. Got your CD of the interview with Coach Wooden. One of the best I've heard."

I'm very proud of the *Strength Coach* show and I'm looking forward to pushing it forward, gaining hundreds of affiliates and major corporate sponsors.

In March, I was feeling good about having interviewed Boomer Esiason, one of the National Football League's leaders in all-time passing yards, career completions and career attempts. Now Boomer and his wife, Cheryl, were using their inner strength to fight against cystic fibrosis. Their son, Gunnar, was diagnosed with the disability in 1993. In the interview, Boomer described the "quarterbacks' crusade." It is strange that Boomer, Jim Kelly, Doug Flutie—all top quarterbacks— have children with disabilities. That commonality exists in my family too. My father was a quarterback.

Also in March, I received a call from Joanne Caputo, my filmmaker. Just weeks before, we had a conversation in which I urged her to aggressively push the film and get it out there. She told me that she was at peace with the movie and that the universe would see it and move it forward at the right time. When the phone rang, she was calm, but I could hear the smile in her voice. PBS had selected it for the series *Independent Lens,* to air nationwide in February 2005!

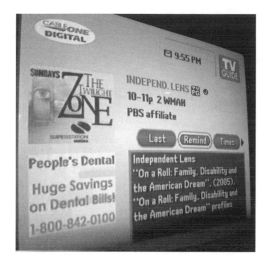

JOANNE CAPUTO at the National Liberty Museum's '33 Exceptional Americans' exhibit. Photo by Michael Ivey.

Wow! A nationwide movie about my life on millions of television sets across America. With PBS's selection of her film, Joanne received funding to come down to Mississippi and shoot some more video of me and my family. She and producer Michael Ivy were once again tagging along with me here in Mississippi. But this time, they were bossier, telling me I couldn't wear my beloved Chicago Cubs Sammy Sosa jersey because it would be difficult to get permission from Major League Baseball and ignoring my wisdom about how I'm much more photogenic from the right side than from the left! They got on my nerves! Joanne completed the film in 2004. It received several awards before the nationwide broadcast.

If you've seen *On A Roll: Family, Disability and the American Dream*, you know that it is a very frank telling of my story from a variety of perspectives. It does a great job of introducing the mainstream to one example of the disability experience in a personable and inviting way. I'm glad the movie happened and I'm appreciative to Joanne.

As the subject of the documentary, I was given absolutely no control over the content, and that is how a documentary should be.

"This is not a promotional movie about 'The Strength Coach,' or Greg Smith," Joanne would say every time I made a suggestion. This is a documentary."

Some say the film is brutal on me, but I don't see it that way. I do think that it is too hard on Terri and focuses on the things that split us up, while failing to communicate the joy we shared when we were married.

I also feel it presents my experience at KTAR as a negative. The people who are presented in the film as discriminatory were the same people that gave me a break in the first place. I learned so much from Jim Taszarek, Jack Nietzel and Chris Yaranoff. I couldn't have done any of this without them.

In all, it was a very enjoyable experience to work with a creative talent like Joanne Caputo. She deserves a lot of credit for sticking with her vision for the movie and not getting frustrated along the way. She overcame many challenges—including breast cancer, and has emerged victorious. Her film started out from a wholesome place, the fact that our children played together. It wasn't an idea cooked up in a corporate boardroom, with thousands of dollars pumped into it. It was started by two parents, one camcorder and no budget. It is a story of perserverence. I am so glad she is my friend.

In August 2004, as a member of the National Association of Black Journalists, I went to Washington DC to attend "Unity 2004," a conference of 10,000 minority journalists. While there, I attended a session entitled "A Conversation with Dick Parsons." I entered the large meeting room as Mr. Parsons, COO and Chairman of the Board for Time Warner was being introduced. This was the man in charge of Time Inc., Time Warner Book Group, Warner Bros. Entertainment, New Line Cinema, Turner Broadcasting System Inc., Home Box Office (HBO), Time Warner Cable and America Online Inc. (AOL). Parsons, a man of color, is one of the most powerful men in the media industry!

After his presentation, there were opportunities for questions, so I rolled up to the mic. There was an awkward delay as the microphones had to be pulled down and adjusted for me.

"Mr. Parsons," I began. "This is a wonderful gathering of diversity, but one element of diversity that is not represented here is America's largest minority group, people with disabilities. Early on, I was told to forget about television and so I went into radio and have

GOOD LOOKING ENOUGH FOR TV? I asked Time Warner COO Dick Parsons his opinioin at the Unity Journalists of Color conference in 2004.

been very successful as an entrepreneur. My question is how can Time Warner lead the way to including a message of strength from America's disability community into the media, because I refuse to believe those who say that I'm not good looking enough for television!"

The room, packed with journalists, erupted in applause and laughter, which lasted for about thirty seconds! I didn't know this until afterwards, but the entire thing was airing live nationwide on C-Span!

Parsons went straight to his sense of humor. "It's an interesting question," he began. "A questionable observation," he joked referring to my good looks. "But an excellent question."

"As you were asking the question, I was thinking to myself, 'We've spent a fair amount of time over the past two years trying to figure out what the right complexion of the company ought to be and who are the groups we need to reach out to.' And I have to be honest with you. It didn't even occur to me until you just asked the question that we haven't spent enough time thinking about persons with disabilities."

He went on for a few more minutes, thinking aloud about my question. He alluded to some personal reasons why he was upset with himself for never having thought about it and said, "Shame on me," before concluding his answer:

"I'm rambling a bit because I don't have an answer but I'll say this, you've given me something to think about."

Hopefully in twelve years of hosting *On A Roll*, I've given many people something to think about. When I started the show, I dedicated my career to helping push the disability rights message in the mainstream media. I've worked to promote issues like home- and community-based attendant care, housing, transportation, employment, visit-able homes and many others. I've talked about that stuff for years, but now I'm realizing that the best thing I can do for the disability community is to become a star!

CHAPTER 25

The Ramp to Stardom

LARRY THOMPSON, A NATIVE MISSISSIPPIAN, is a Hollywood agent and executive producer who has managed the careers of over 200 stars and produced 17 movies for television. He's the author of *SHINE: A Powerful 4-Step Plan for Becoming a Star in Anything You Do*. I was so inspired by his book that I invited him on the show, and while I was talking to him on the air, realized I have an obligation to become a star.

Think about it. How many "stars" with disabilities can you name? Perhaps the biggest was Christopher Reeve. There's Michael J. Fox, Richard Pryor, Marlee Matlin. Can you name any others? There are several more, but the point is, the list isn't long enough. The timing of the loss of Christopher Reeve was very unfortunate for many reasons, but from my perspective, he was well on his way to focusing the bright mass media spotlight on the humanity of disability, and the celebration of its existence as a natural part of life. Two months before his death, he completed directing *The Brooke Ellison Story*, an A&E cable television movie based on a quadriplegic who rose above her disability and went on to graduate from Harvard University. The film was accurate regarding her disability, strengthened by the knowledge and experience of the director.

Inspired by the lives of Reeve, Justin Dart, Ed Roberts and others, I look to the future with a sense of responsibility that drives a passionate pursuit of my goals. My goal is greater than to be on Oprah or on Larry King. My goal is to *BE* Oprah. My goal is to *BE* Larry King. Only from a platform so lofty can I truly make a difference for people with disabilities while offering a message of inner strength to everyone.

My mission is clear. I'm supposed to communicate to the world about the power of inner strength. I'm supposed to live my life, with all of the physical limitations binding me, as a breathing, rolling example of the power inner strength has to overcome any situation or setback, and emerge stronger and more capable of experiencing life to the maximum. I'm supposed to be a reminder to everyone about the need for accepting and integrating people who are different. I'm supposed to write, broadcast and speak about the balance between personal drive, ambition and power on one hand, and compassion, sensitivity and acceptance of everyone on the other.

I can clearly see my goals. I have folders, the tangible existence of my ideas, seeds that will soon emerge into the light of reality.

There will one day be a Greg Smith Disability Media Institute, perhaps at my Alma Mater, Arizona State University. There, students with disabilities who want to make it big in the media are going to be recruited and accommodated to receive the same excellent broadcasting education at the Walter Cronkite School of Journalism I received 20 years ago. They will also have the wonderful support system of an accessible campus, warm weather and the help of ASU's Disabled Student Resources. It worked for me. Let it work for many.

I can see the establishment of 50 independent statewide *On A Roll* radio programs, hosted by people across the nation and funded by developmental disabilities councils, departments of vocational rehabilitation and local and national corporations. This will continue to give America's disability community a radio voice of empowerment, encouragement and on-air peer support. That this no longer exists nationally serves as motivation for me to see these statewide shows develop soon. In addition to being important outreach vehicles, these shows will be the breeding grounds for the next mega-media talents who happen to have disabilities.

I can see grant initiatives that help disabled youths get involved in sports activities as public address announcers, statisticians and most excitedly, play-by-play radio announcers on low power radio stations, with an audience of parents at the games. Just because kids with disabilities can't play sports doesn't mean they can't be involved and receive all of the lessons and values that participating in youth sports teaches. These kids are going to be socially integrated into all of the excitement and team connection. That's what happened to me. If I had not been a manager of my junior high basketball team, would I have gone into radio? Any initiatives that can get kids with disabilities socially integrated into the mainstream will make a powerful, positive impression on not only that kid, but everybody else—the team, band, organization, parents, community and the world at large. Let's get our disabled kids involved in sports!

I can see myself serving as a media consultant, advising CEOs of media entities how to tap into the power of appealing to America's largest minority group and their friends and families. The round of applause I received on CSpan when I asked Dick Parsons that question indicates that the old stereotypes and fears have passed. People with disabilities are no longer hidden in back rooms and basements. But if that is the case, why don't we ever see them as television reporters, actors in sitcoms, or in motion picture releases?

And another thing: I've watched baseball on television for 30 years and have never seen ONE fan shot of the wheelchair section! Not one. Why is that? Who will be the first?

I can see myself as one of the most dynamic, most powerful, most sought after motivational speakers in the world. Everybody wants to build his or her inner strength and I am the man to teach it.

I can see myself with a multi-media empire built around the concept of inner strength. I can see a wonderful life-long love affair with a woman I trust and embrace with all my heart. I can see us working together, traveling together and reclining in the bliss of knowledge that we are making the world a better place with every activity we do. Maybe she is reading this book.

Every morning, I can't wait to get out of bed and get on with the work of the day. Yet I realize that so many people have to drag themselves out of bed, go to a job they hate, live with a person they would rather not be with, and never appreciate all the beauty in this world.

They're stuck in their own self-imposed limitations. And most of these same people feel sorry for *me* when I pass them at Wal-Mart.

The only thing that can stop me from achieving any of the above is my own death. The truth is, I feel my body downshifting. How long will the metal rods attached to my back hold on? How long will my heart, with its irregular rhythm, keep its cadence? Yet the passion and optimism keep me going strong.

Dammit. I'm going to make it to see those things become real! But if I don't, I can rest in peace knowing that YOU will take what you've read and put your own personal spin on inner strength, drive, ambition, aspiration and compassion. One person can influence millions. You have that potential. You have the inner strength. You are on a roll!

Dive Into Your Dreams

I LOVE IT WHEN THE PHONE RINGS. More often than not, it is a positive experience; an opportunity for me to move my mission forward, reach out to more people and slowly change the world. My phone rang the afternoon of September 27, 2004. On the other end was a man with a strong Caribbean accent.

"Hello, Strength Coach? This is Wilbert Francis calling from the University of the Virgin Islands. We would like to see if you can come to St. Croix and St. Thomas to speak for the Virgin Islands Center for Excellence in Developmental Disabilities!"

Three weeks later, I found myself on a plane, headed for a paid gig in paradise. I remember thinking and laughing aloud about how most of the people I encounter feel sorry for me, and here I was getting paid thousands of dollars to fly to the Virgin Islands!

I decided to take Lori Juneau as my personal assistant for this trip. Lori was a marketing student at the University of New Orleans whom I had met about two years before at a nightclub. We had remained in touch via e-mail and I had happened to see her online while pondering my options for this trip.

I spoke at an event called "Voices that Count," two forums that featured the disability community and candidates for public office. The day after my motivational speech to the disabled citizens, each candidate would answer audience questions about transportation, education, employment, health care and mental health issues. My job on the second day was to moderate the panel discussion. I was invited to do this twice, in St. Croix and St. Thomas.

I connected with my audience in St. Croix as I had never done before. We were all black. We were all people with disabilities. They

WITH LORI IN ST. THOMAS—Lori Juneau and I had a free day in St. Thomas to shop for jewelry. Here we are with a donkey who was being walked down the sidewalk.

hung on my every word with undivided attention, nodding their heads, laughing and crying at all the right times.

After the panel discussion the second day, I asked Wilbert to allow me to address the audience before we took a seaplane from St. Croix to St. Thomas. I told them that of all the speeches I have given, this audience opened their hearts to me more than any I could remember. This had been the most enjoyable speaking event in my career. I didn't know that the best was yet to come.

St. Thomas was more of a tourist destination than St. Croix. On the seaplane, we flew over cruise ships and hotels. We stayed at the Holiday Inn Winward Passage, checking in on Tuesday evening. My next speaking engagement was Thursday morning so we had an entire day of leisure.

Lori and I went shopping the first day, buying t-shirts and inexpensive jewelry. After returning to the hotel, I saw a salon and decided to get a haircut. The door was too heavy for me to open. Usually when people see me struggling, they rush to my aide, but this time, none of the women in the salon made an effort to assist me. Unimpressed with their customer service, I knocked on the glass and finally got the young girl behind the counter to put down her magazine.

When I entered, one of the stylists spoke in my direction while looking at my wheelchair. "May I help you?"

"I need a haircut."

"There's gonna be a wait."

"How long?"

"It might be a while."

I sat for five minutes and received no encouragement from anyone. I like to shoot the breeze with people but after a few failed attempts at conversation, I realized that a haircut was not worth an hour of my precious time in St. Thomas. Now I thank God that I didn't get that haircut. God decided to move me in a new direction.

I left and wandered into the lobby to look at brochures of things to do. One brochure struck me as interesting. It was a brochure for a submarine! I had always dreamed of going underwater. While on a cruise in Cozumel a couple of years before, my father was told by a submarine captain, "He no walk? He no go!" In Mexico, there is no Americans with Disabilities Act. Here, in the U.S. Virgin Islands, I stood a chance.

I asked the concierge for more information and he pointed me to the dive shop, located by the pool.

Marty Martinez was on the phone when I sped my chair into the Admiralty Dive Center. While I waited, I browsed around the shop and looked at the spear fishing guns, regulators, masks and tanks. Suddenly a huge dog approached me and started sniffing me up and down. I interrupted Marty's phone conversation to ask if the dog was ok. He nodded.

When he got off the phone, we shook hands. Marty is probably in his 50's with olive skin and dark, graying hair. I could tell he had personality and attitude the moment I met him. I confirmed my hunch with our first conversation.

"Do you know how I can find out more information about this?" I said, holding up the submarine brochure. "I tried to go on a submarine in Mexico a couple of years ago and they refused me because I couldn't walk."

271

"Well my question to you is why would you want to do that?" he asked with his raspy voice.

"I've always dreamed of going underwater."

"Well have you ever thought about diving?"

"Thought about it? I've *dreamed* about it. I've *fantasized* about it. But I can't do that. I can't swim. I don't have a lot of lung capacity. I don't have the strength to carry a tank on my back."

Then Marty hooked me. "One of my customers took his wife on the submarine. When he came back, I asked him how it went and how it compared to diving. He said 'Going in the submarine is like watching a movie about sex. Going diving is like actually having sex!'"

I laughed both at the analogy its effectiveness. He actually had me considering doing this!

He told of his experience with taking people with disabilities diving. But when people tell me about things that other people with disabilities can do, I get cautious because nobody's disability is quite like mine. When I sit strapped into my chair, I look a lot more powerful and capable than I actually am. The fact is I can't raise my hands over my head.

We agreed to meet at the swimming pool the next day at noon. We'd try it in the pool and see how well I could handle it. If successful, we would go out on his boat. I left the dive shop excited and a little skeptical.

As I was leaving, Marty comforted me by saying, "I don't want you to have the attitude that you're going to do this come hell or high water. The last thing I wanna do is take you out there and kill you. If you try it in the pool and decide it is something you don't want to do, you can back out of this with no problem."

Lori invited her friend Mark Hunter, who lived in Miami to meet us in St. Thomas the next day. Mark arrived just before my speech on Thursday and I immediately put him to work, snapping photos of my presentation. In my speech, during the part where I talk about lifting the weights of life's challenges, I varied from my memorized script.

"Sometimes, the challenges we face in life come in the form of fear. All my life, I've been fascinated with the ocean, having been a boater and a fisherman. I've always dreamed of going underwater. But that fascination has come with a respect for the ocean and a fear of drowning. Today, I'm stepping into that fear. At noon, I'm going to get in the pool and attempt to scuba dive. If I'm successful in the pool, tomorrow, I'm going out in the ocean and will breathe underwater! I am pushing fear aside and bringing into my life something I've always wanted!"

The audience smiled, nodded and applauded.

Around noon, I rolled nervously to the poolside, wearing my orange swim trunks and a t-shirt. I find it interesting that I had no hesitation about taking off my shirt in front of people. Most of my life, I have been so ashamed of my body that water sports were off limits. Maybe after a year of being the Strength Coach, some of my own material started to seep in. Lori took off my shirt. Marty and John Rubbitino, my dive instructor worked hard to stretch the child-size wet suit over my unbendable arms. Then they lifted me into the pool.

Fear dominated. I wanted my feet planted on the floor and I wanted to be vertical. John wanted me to put my head underwater and breathe! The regulator in my mouth required tight lip pressure and at that point, I didn't think I could do it. Did I have the lip muscle strength necessary to hold it in place? We tried another regulator, which seemed to fit better, and I slowly gained the confidence and trust necessary to go under and take a few breaths.

Then I decided to test John. Although nothing was wrong, I made the hand signal, waving my hand from side to side and pointing up with my thumb. He immediately brought my head above water.

"What was wrong?"

"Nothing. Just testing you!"

John and Marty laughed. We were bonding. After about 30 minutes in the pool, I started to get tired and it was time to get out. Since it was an overcast day, the water temperature in the pool made me uncomfortable. When my body gets cold, my muscles don't work at all. I was completely paralyzed when they pulled me out, and completely exhausted.

The next day, as Marty's boat pulled out of the harbor, I was praying for sunshine. It was overcast again and the forecast called for "boomers"—thunderstorms—approaching from Puerto Rico. Soon, we reached our first dive destination. Everyone got their gear and dove in the water. Mark and Lori assisted me with my body sleeve and wetsuit. I was excited but very nervous. They lifted me onto the platform on the stern and John got in the water as my feet dangled below the surface.

We decided not to use flippers on my feet. I went barefoot because John was my means of locomotion. The tank was so heavy on my back that I couldn't sit upright. Then, Mark lowered me into the salty water. I was terrified, but eager to see what I could do as we hovered at the surface

"OK, ready? I'm going to lean you forward!" said John.

He made he hand gesture for OK. I responded, making a circle with my right hand. I bit down hard on the regulator. Suddenly, all sounds ceased except a Darth Vadar-esque inhale, and then a bubbling sound as I exhaled into the regulator.

I panicked. I wasn't comfortable with the position of my body. I wanted to be vertical and he had me leaning forward, totally out of control. I feared that he wouldn't know if something was wrong, so again, I tested him. We surfaced again.

Lori, Mark and Marty were cheering, "Yeah!!! Go Greg!"

The encouragement helped slightly. I gripped the regulator with my left hand and held it in my mouth. I nodded my head. This time, I trusted John a little more. We went underwater. I inhaled. It was not difficult. I exhaled. No problem. I took a deeper breath. I let it out. I was breathing underwater!

I started to look around. John pointed at a school of yellow fins. I nodded my head. This was so beautiful. I was seeing colors I had never seen before. It was amazing! Then water started to accumulate in my mask. I signaled to John that I wanted to surface and he obliged immediately.

When we cleared the mask, a little water got in my nose and I started to cough. After a few minutes on the surface, I wanted to go down again. This time, I had the courage to signal John to take me deeper than one or two feet!

He clamped my nose shut so that I could blow to equalize my ears. We swam down about six feet! I looked up at the bottom of the boat! It was so incredible to see a boat from below. I had been on boats all my life and never thought I would ever witness this. The water was crystal clear with a deep blue background. But soon, the ladder leading to the deck was right in front of my mask. John decided that about 20 minutes underwater was long enough.

They lifted me into the borrowed sports chair and covered me with towels. I felt an incredible sense of accomplishment. It was a remarkable feeling. It seemed to me that everyone aboard was inspired by our accomplishment.

Before long, we had reached our second dive site and I was back in the water again. This time I would make the most of it. When we submerged for the second dive, we didn't surface much. We went a little deeper and stayed underwater a lot longer. I saw other divers from other boats. I saw the underwater BOBS, little motorcycle-like vehicles that people used to motor beneath the sea. And the life beneath the surface was breathtaking.

When I saw the boat ladder again, I was highly disappointed. I was not ready for this to end. That evening, we all went to Marty's dive shop, where I held a secret, private screening of the *On A Roll* documentary on Marty's VCR. The women cried during the film.

Afterwards, we all went out to dinner. I made a toast:

"Aside from the three birthdays of my children, today was the greatest day of my life! I enjoyed it so much that I've decided I wanna do it again, tomorrow!"

We were supposed to fly back the next day, but I decided to extend the trip a day to experience this wonderful environment once again. The next day, the weather was much nicer. I had no fear and a lot of swagger. I was cracking jokes and everyone was having a great time. This experience, shared with a group of strangers, had created amazing bonds. When we anchored at our dive site, Marty smiled as he turned the volume up on his boat's stereo.

A deep familiar melody blared out of the speakers. It was the theme from *Jaws*!

That excited me. In our dinner conversation the night before, we talked about sharks, manta ray, and barracuda. I was comforted that even if we saw any of those creatures, the chances of them doing us any harm were very remote. Very few divers in these waters have ever been attacked by sharks but thousands of divers have seen sharks. I wanted to see one.

The second day was a beautiful experience. The sunshine lit up the water so the visibility was even better. We dove at Flat Cay Chrysler and submerged about 15 feet to the opening of a cave. There was an actual shipwreck there and we were able to see the amazing life below. Schools of blue tang slowly maneuvered by, so close that I could almost reach out and touch them. We saw an eel caressing the bottom. We saw beautiful coral reef and sea urchins.

Amy, John's girlfriend picked up an urchin and put it in the palm of my hand. She did the same with a starfish. All the while, Tori Collins was snapping underwater photos. I had learned the first day that when she took my picture, my eyes were wider than the goggles. I had a "deer-in-the-headlights" look in too many of the shots. On the second day, I made sure that my eyes were normal-sized. I actually found myself posing to look cool for the camera!

Suddenly, John twisted my body to the right and there was Tamiesha Britton, a newscaster at the local radio station who had reported about my presentation the day before. She waved at me and we smiled with our eyes. He turned me to the left and there was Mark, deep diving down from his surface snorkeling position, giving me a thumbs up! It was incredible the way we all interacted with each other in this otherworldly environment.

Having read this book, you know that I am very goal-oriented. On the second day, I had a goal in mind. I wanted to touch the bottom of the ocean with my hands. I signaled to John with a thumbs down. He pinched my nose and we dove down. I equalized fine and gave him the OK signal.

It seemed quieter as the sand on the bottom of the sea started to

DREAM DIVE—Touching the sandy bottom in St. Thomas was one of the greatest thrills of my life. Photo by Victoria Collins.

become detailed and focused. There was a strong current as little white particles flowed by. I could see the sand move toward shore an inch or two and then move back, like waves along a beach in reverse.

John touched the bottom, grabbed a handful of sand and put it in my hand. That wasn't good enough for me. I signaled with thumbs down. I reached out toward the sand myself, but my arms couldn't reach. John realized what I was doing and tilted me forward. In one amazing moment, I grabbed a handful of sand with my own hands! I was touching the bottom of the ocean!

I thought about my parents. I had not told them what I was doing because I didn't want them to worry or try to talk me out of it. But while I was touching that sand, I thought of how exciting it would be to share this with them. I remember wishing they were there to join me in this triumph. I thought of my children and imagined a day when we could all go scuba diving together. I thought of sharing this experience with other people with disabilities who never imagined they could do this. And I thought of my new friends here in St. Thomas. It was a very emotional moment.

On the flight back to Miami, the movie was *Notebook*, a love story about a woman with Alzheimer's and her devoted husband. It was a touching story about human connection. Both Lori and I cried while watching it, and later agreed that a good cry was what we needed. It wasn't the movie that inspired our tears. It was the amazing experience we'd had. If you can live a dream come true, don't let fear stand in the way. If you can help someone live a dream, you may find that dream making becomes a dream of your own. I came back from St. Thomas with a new personal manifesto: "Dive into Your Dreams!"

AT HOME IN OCEAN SPRINGS—My beautiful family is the source of my inner strength.

NOTES

P. 67—"Who Can It Be Now," lyrics copyright 1983, Colin James Hay; Blackwood Music, Inc.

P. 69—"Once In a Lifetime," lyrics copyright 1980, David Byrne, Brian Eno, Peter George, Christopher Frantz, Jerry Harrison, Martina Weymouth; Bleu Disque Music Co., Inc.

DA BEARS—Dad and I coached Greg Jr's youth football team in 2004. Greg was "Offensive Player of the Year" and "Scholar Baller," earning the highest grades on the team.

www.TheStrengthCoach.com

- See all the photos from this book in color.

- Browse through dozens of photos Greg wanted in this book but didn't have space for.

- Hear streaming radio shows online.

- Contact Greg about speaking engagements.

- Order products that will build your inner strength.

- Learn about other books published by *On A Roll Communications.*

On A Roll Communications
P.O. Box 1077
Ocean Springs, MS 39566
Phone: 877-331-7563